# ESSAYS IN MUSICAL ANALYSIS

*By*

DONALD FRANCIS TOVEY

IN FIVE VOLUMES

*With an additional volume containing
a Glossary and Index*

## CONTENTS

I. SYMPHONIES

II. SYMPHONIES (II), VARIATIONS, AND
ORCHESTRAL POLYPHONY

III. CONCERTOS

IV. ILLUSTRATIVE MUSIC

V. VOCAL MUSIC

GLOSSARY AND INDEX

# ESSAYS IN
# MUSICAL ANALYSIS

*By*

DONALD FRANCIS TOVEY

REID PROFESSOR OF MUSIC IN THE
UNIVERSITY OF EDINBURGH

*Volume III*

CONCERTOS

LONDON
OXFORD UNIVERSITY PRESS
HUMPHREY MILFORD
1936

OXFORD UNIVERSITY PRESS
AMEN HOUSE, E.C. 4
London Edinburgh Glasgow New York
Toronto Melbourne Capetown Bombay
Calcutta Madras
HUMPHREY MILFORD
PUBLISHER TO THE UNIVERSITY

PRINTED IN GREAT BRITAIN

# CONTENTS

LXXXIV. INTRODUCTION TO VOLUME III . . 1

LXXXV. THE CLASSICAL CONCERTO (1903) . . 3

LXXXVI-CXIV. CONCERTOS IN CLASSICAL FORM 27-158

## MOZART

LXXXVI. PIANOFORTE CONCERTO IN A MAJOR (Köchel's Catalogue, No. 414) . . . . 27

LXXXVII. PIANOFORTE CONCERTO No. 15, IN B FLAT MAJOR (Köchel's Catalogue, No. 450) . . 30

LXXXVIII. PIANOFORTE CONCERTO IN G MAJOR (Köchel's Catalogue, No. 453) . . . 33

LXXXIX. PIANOFORTE CONCERTO IN A MAJOR (Köchel's Catalogue, No. 488) . . . . 37

XC. PIANOFORTE CONCERTO IN C MINOR (Köchel's Catalogue, No. 491) . . . . 42

XCI. FLUTE CONCERTO IN G MAJOR (Köchel's Catalogue, No. 313) . . . . 47

XCII. FLUTE CONCERTO IN D MAJOR (Köchel's Catalogue, No. 314) . . . . 48

XCIII. ANDANTE FOR FLUTE WITH ORCHESTRA (Köchel's Catalogue, No. 315) . . . 51

XCIV. CLARINET CONCERTO IN A MAJOR (Köchel's Catalogue, No. 622) . . . . 52

XCV. VIOLIN CONCERTO IN D MAJOR (Köchel's Catalogue, No. 218) . . . . 54

XCVI. VIOLIN CONCERTO IN A MAJOR (Köchel's Catalogue, No. 219) . . . . 56

XCVII. ADAGIO IN E, FOR VIOLIN WITH ORCHESTRA (Köchel's Catalogue, No. 261) . . . 59

XCVIII. CONCERTO FOR FLUTE AND HARP (Köchel's Catalogue, No. 299) . . . . 60

## HAYDN

XCIX. VIOLONCELLO CONCERTO IN D MAJOR . 62

## BEETHOVEN

C. PIANOFORTE CONCERTO IN C MAJOR, Op. 15, WITH BEETHOVEN'S CADENZA . . 64

CI. PIANOFORTE CONCERTO IN C MINOR, Op. 37 . 69

CII. PIANOFORTE CONCERTO IN G MAJOR, Op. 58 . 75

CIII. PIANOFORTE CONCERTO IN E FLAT, Op. 73 . 84

CIV. VIOLIN CONCERTO IN D MAJOR, Op. 61 . 87

CV. TRIPLE CONCERTO FOR PIANOFORTE, VIOLIN, AND VIOLONCELLO, Op. 56 . . . 96

## CHOPIN

CVI. PIANOFORTE CONCERTO IN F MINOR, Op. 21 . 103

## JOACHIM

CVII. HUNGARIAN CONCERTO FOR VIOLIN WITH ORCHESTRA . . . . 106

## BRAHMS

CVIII. PIANOFORTE CONCERTO IN D MINOR, Op. 15 . 114

CIX. PIANOFORTE CONCERTO IN B FLAT MAJOR, Op. 83 . . . . . 120

CX. VIOLIN CONCERTO IN D MAJOR, Op. 77 . 126

CXI. CONCERTO FOR VIOLIN AND VIOLONCELLO, Op. 102 . . . . . 139

## DVOŘÁK

CXII. VIOLONCELLO CONCERTO IN B MINOR, Op. 104 . 148

## ELGAR

CXIII. VIOLIN CONCERTO IN B MINOR, Op. 61 . 152

## ARTHUR SOMERVELL

CXIV. VIOLIN CONCERTO IN G MINOR . . 158

CXV–CXXXV. VARIATIONS AND CONCERTOS WITHOUT RITORNELLO . . . 164–220

## JOACHIM

CXV. VARIATIONS FOR VIOLIN WITH ORCHESTRA . 164

## CÉSAR FRANCK

CXVI. VARIATIONS SYMPHONIQUES FOR PIANOFORTE WITH ORCHESTRA . . . . 166

## ARTHUR SOMERVELL

CXVII. 'NORMANDY': SYMPHONIC VARIATIONS FOR PIANOFORTE WITH ORCHESTRA . . 169

# DOHNANYI

CXVIII. VARIATIONS ON A NURSERY SONG, FOR ORCHESTRA WITH PIANOFORTE, Op. 23 . 173

# SPOHR

CXIX. SCENA CANTANTE FOR VIOLIN WITH ORCHESTRA . . . . . 176

# MENDELSSOHN

CXX. VIOLIN CONCERTO IN E MINOR, Op. 64 . 178

# SCHUMANN

CXXI. PIANOFORTE CONCERTO IN A MINOR, Op. 54 . 182

CXXII. VIOLONCELLO CONCERTO IN A MINOR, Op. 129 184

CXXIII. INTRODUCTION AND ALLEGRO APPASSIONATO FOR PIANOFORTE WITH ORCHESTRA, Op. 92 . 188

# SAINT-SAËNS

CXXIV. FOURTH PIANOFORTE CONCERTO IN C MINOR, Op. 44 . . . . . 189

CXXV. VIOLONCELLO CONCERTO IN A MINOR, Op. 33 192

# MAX BRUCH

CXXVI. VIOLIN CONCERTO IN G MINOR, Op. 26 . 194

# C. V. STANFORD

CXXVII. CLARINET CONCERTO, IN ONE MOVEMENT, Op. 80 . . . . . 197

# ELGAR

CXXVIII. VIOLONCELLO CONCERTO IN E MINOR, Op. 85 . 200

# DELIUS

CXXIX. VIOLIN CONCERTO . . . . 203

# RICHARD STRAUSS

CXXX. PARERGON TO THE 'SINFONIA DOMESTICA', FOR PIANOFORTE WITH ORCHESTRA, Op. 73 . 206

# GLAZOUNOV

CXXXI. PIANOFORTE CONCERTO IN F MINOR, Op. 92 . 209

## SIBELIUS
CXXXII. VIOLIN CONCERTO, Op. 47 . . . 211

## FRANZ SCHMIDT
CXXXIII. VARIATIONS ON A THEME OF BEETHOVEN FOR
PIANOFORTE WITH ORCHESTRA . . 216

## RESPIGHI
CXXXIV. CONCERTO GREGORIANO FOR VIOLIN . 217

## WILLIAM WALTON
CXXXV. VIOLA CONCERTO IN A MINOR . . 220

# ADDENDUM

SINCE my analysis of the work known as Haydn's Violoncello Concerto Op. 101 was written, a miniature score has been published giving the work in its original form, with a preface explaining that Dr. Hans Volkmann has proved that this concerto is not by Haydn but by Haydn's pupil, Anton Kraft (1752–1820). The demonstration is admittedly not complete, but I find no difficulty in giving Kraft the credit for a very pretty piece of work in a form in which Haydn never put forward his full powers, and which, if genuine, would have belonged to a period at which his style and forms were imitable enough to tempt many publishers to secure a market for other composers by ascribing their works to a master whose early popularity was so remarkable. My analysis will not, I think, be found to contain anything committing me to uphold this charming concerto as a great work. The average quality of Haydn's output at Esterhaz is such that the greatest scholars have been compelled, when selecting the unquestionably authentic symphonies, to make a longer list of doubtful than of spurious works. A stroke of genius will settle the question, and so will any high power of composition: that is why I see red when musical philologists cast doubts on Bach's tremendous D minor Concerto. But the absence of these qualities will not settle the question with early works ascribable to Haydn. The only thing that puzzled me in the present instance was the prominence of a definitely Mozartean cliché in the opening themes of the first movement and slow movement. The slow movement begins with two bars of pure Mozart followed by two of pure Haydn. In an analytical programme it was no part of my business to disturb the listener by questions which are vexing as long as they raise doubts. Now that I have no doubt, I shall in future give Anton Kraft the credit of his very pretty work; and I shall expect my audience not to be snobbish about it.

# LXXXIV. INTRODUCTION TO VOLUME III

THIS volume deals mainly with the classical concerto as described in the first essay: secondly, it deals with a few *concertante* works in variation form. These ought by rights to have included Beethoven's Choral Fantasia, but it is so obviously an unconscious study for the finale of the Ninth Symphony that the temptation to put it after that work was irresistible. The rest of the volume is devoted to concertos and *Conzertstücke* that are not based on the classical notion of the ritornello.

The origin and character of the earlier polyphonic type of concerto is fully discussed in the first essay (LXXXV); but works of that kind (including some modern examples) have already been dealt with in Vol. II as arising from the general problem of applying polyphonic forms to orchestral music.

Although this volume thus presents a greater coherence of subject than the other volumes of these essays, it is by no means better calculated for continuous reading. On the contrary, the difficult and complex theory of concerto form, though elaborated systematically in the first essay, is repeatedly summarized in several others; and the reader will be well advised to treat this volume, like the others, in the way in which all my essays were treated by readers who saw them in their original form of programme-notes. They are separate accounts of individual works of art. Two individual works of art do not quote one another when they use the same forms; and the same illustration may serve for more than one analysis if it is the best illustration for more than one case.

# LXXXV. THE CLASSICAL CONCERTO
## (1903)

### INTRODUCTION

Without a sound appreciation of those peculiarities of form which distinguish the classical concerto from the classical symphony the concerto can only be very imperfectly understood, whether by performers or by listeners; for the rational enthusiasm for great classics is the outcome not only of natural taste, but also of long familiarity with all that is purest in art; and so far as the opportunity for such familiarity is wanting, so far will current ideas and current criticism be vague, Philistine, and untrue. Now the number of great works in the true concerto form is surprisingly small; far smaller than the number of true symphonies. And of this small collection a good two-thirds has been contributed by Mozart, whose work has for the last fifty years been treated with neglect and lack of intelligent observation, for which we at the present time are paying dearly with a notable loss both of ear for fine detail and of grasp of musical works as definite wholes.[1] On the other hand, every virtuoso whose imagination is fired with the splendid spectacular effect of a full orchestra as a background for a display of instrumental technique has written concertos that express little else than that effect. Thus the name of concerto is assumed by literally hundreds of works that have not even an academic connexion with the classical idea of concerto form and style; while of the very small collection of true concertos the majority, those of Mozart, are ignored, and the remainder not nearly so well understood as any classical symphony. No composer attempts a symphony without a strong sense of responsibility, and some appreciation of the greatness of the classics of symphonic art, and so neither the number of spurious symphonies nor their tendency is such as to set an entirely false standard of criticism for the art. But that current criteria of the concerto are false, no one who seriously studies that form can doubt. The idea that the professed purpose of the form is technical display has been actually maintained by musicians who yield to none in their reverence and love for the great concertos of Beethoven and Mozart. Yet that idea is in flat violation of almost every fact in the early history of the form; and those who hold it seem to let it

[1] I do not know how many people in 1903 foresaw the vindication of Mozart, of which on the Continent the main impulse was given by Richard Strauss, and which dates in England from the memorable performance of the *Zauberflöte* at Cambridge some eight years after this essay appeared. That performance marked the first stages of Professor E. J. Dent's work upon Mozart's operas.

remain comfortably in their minds side by side with the opposite, and scarcely less untrue notion, that in the works of Bach and his contemporaries the solo part of a concerto is no more than *primus inter pares*. The first idea springs from the assumption (difficult to avoid, where bad works so overcrowd good ones) that art-forms are invented by bad artists to be disgustedly improved off the face of the earth by the great men; and the second springs from the difficulty of recognizing in ancient art anything that does not happen to take much the same shape in modern art.

The only way to avoid these pitfalls is to seek out the typical artistic idea that is to be found in the concertos of the greatest composers. To avoid repeating what I have written elsewhere, I propose to follow out this train of thought in an historical, or at all events chronological, sketch, instead of applying it merely to any particular concerto. Opinions differ so much as to the way in which musical history should be written that I hesitate to call this sketch historical. Its object is to trace the successive forms in which what I shall call the concerto-idea has been realized. Those forms in which it has been falsified by vanity, or obscured by imperfect skill or vague thought, will not come under discussion at all, though to many historians that which is transitional and immature is often more interesting, and always more easy to discuss than that which is permanent and self-consistent.

To avoid a frequent source of misunderstanding, I must point out that neither here nor in any other of my analytical essays is the basis of analysis technical. It is frequently urged as an objection to all musical analysis that to investigate 'how it is done' distracts the mind from the poetic enjoyment of a work of art. So it does; you cannot, for instance, enjoy the first move-ment of Beethoven's Eroica Symphony if you insist on thinking the while of Beethoven's seven or eight different sketches of its exposition. They are among the most wonderful documents record-ing the profound workings of a creative mind; but the only way in which they can help you to enjoy the symphony is by directing your attention to what it is. Follow up the sketches, then, as they approach the final version from something now more monotonous, now more violent, now smaller, now dangerously large, always changing with the surprising purpose and power of a creator who ruthlessly rejects all that will not remain as an inspiring force for all time, when what common admirers of genius call 'the inspira-tion of the moment' has gone the way of dreams and moods. Follow this up until it leads you to the ideal, the realized Eroica Symphony; and you will no longer think that there is anything prosaic in investigating 'how it was done'. But you will see this only if, as you listen to the symphony, you forget the sketches utterly, as Beethoven himself forgot them. They have helped you, not because they showed you 'how it was done', but because they drew your attention to *what* was done; and on that, and that alone, your attention must remain fixed, or the whole object of all that loving and laborious sketching is lost.

Musical analysis then is concerned with *what* is done. Unless the composer has left sketches, any attempt to speak of '*how* it is done' is downright charlatanry, a pretence of solving a problem that is beyond the human intellect. Beethoven himself must have found his old sketch-books a series of perpetual surprises if he ever looked at them a year or two after finishing a work.

An analysis that gives a faithful account of what is done in a work of art cannot but be a help, so long as it is not one-sided and is used in a practical way. [Hence in my early essays I have aimed at quoting or at least mentioning] every theme in the works analysed, so that the material may lie conveniently before the eye. On the other hand, I have from the outset abandoned any attempt to confine the letterpress to what can be read in the concert-room. Quotations in musical type can be seen while they are heard; but the kind of prose explanation that can be read while the music is going on is as useless in the concert-room as it is at home.

Lastly, as this is an essay on a musical subject I have tried to treat it from a musical point of view. This again is not a limitation to technical matters; music is music, and does not become technical as soon as it is not discussed as if it were a nondescript mixture of intellect and emotion and poetry. As a plain musician I believe music to be music; poetry, a form of literature; painting, one of the plastic arts; and *all* to be poetry. But when I discuss music I shall speak of things musical, as beautiful harmony, breadth, firmness and depth of modulation, nobility of form, variety and contrast of tone, clear and well-motived contrast and harmonious fullness in those simultaneous combinations of melodies which we call counterpoint, for it is these things and others equally musical that make a concerto or a symphony what it is. And if it is objected that these things, as they occur in classical music, are non-poetical, or mere technical means of expressing some poetic idea that lies behind them, I can only reply that, so long as music remains music, this poetic idea will only be attainable through these musical phenomena. Certainly a criticism or an admiration that scorns the musical phenomena does not thereby become poetical; on the contrary, the man who expects music to give him poetical ideas while he refuses to listen to it as music, will infallibly, if he looks at other things as he looks at music, value poetry for the information it conveys when paraphrased in prose, architecture for the problems it solves in engineering, science for its practical use, and in short, everything for its lower and more accidental qualities, and this is the very type and essence of the prosaic mind.

To sum up: I believe the classical concerto to be a highly dramatic and poetic art-form, having nothing in common with the popular and pseudo-academic idea of the form except a few misleading superficial resemblances. I therefore propose to illustrate the poetic and dramatic expression of this form by an analysis that has nothing to do with technique, though it will use any good technical term that may substitute a word for a paragraph; nor anything to do with *a priori* theories of absolute music which will apply equally well to absolute nonsense, though it declines to talk of poetry when its business is to describe musical facts. I merely attempt to describe what may be *observed* by any one really fond of music, who takes pains to study the works of great composers in a spirit that endeavours to understand the ways of minds other than one's own.

### THE CONCERTO PRINCIPLE

The primary fact that distinguishes all works that have in them the character of the concerto style, is that their form is adapted to make the best effect expressible by opposed and unequal masses of instruments or voices. Whenever in classical or indeed in any really artistic music, you find that an art-form is to be expressed by a mass of instruments (under which head we may for present purposes include voices), and that this mass inevitably divides itself into two parts that cannot without some embarrassing limitation or *tour de force* be made to balance each other: then you will assuredly find that the form has been modified so as not merely to fit these conditions but to make them a special means of expression.

Hence arises at least half of the prejudice which many fairly experienced lovers of music, and nearly all inexperienced students of composition, feel against the concerto forms. When our experience is no more than enough to give us a keen pleasure in following the normal outlines of an art-form, and in seeing how they give reality and inevitableness to the contrasts and crises of the music, then we are prone to resent any influence that modifies the form, and we do not stop to see whether the new form may not be as grand as the old.

That the conditions of concerto form are in themselves unnatural or inartistic can certainly not be maintained in face of the facts. Nothing in human life and history is much more thrilling or of more ancient and universal experience than the antithesis of the individual and the crowd; an antithesis which is familiar in every degree, from flat opposition to harmonious reconciliation, and with every contrast and blending of emotion, and which has been of no less universal prominence in works of art than in life. Now the concerto forms express this antithesis with all possible force and delicacy. If there are devotees of 'absolute music' who believe that this is the very reason why these forms are objectionable, as appealing to something outside music, we may first answer that, if this were so, then neither Brahms, Beethoven, Bach, Mozart, Haydn, nor any person of so much calibre as Clementi, ever was an 'absolute musician', or had anything to do with such a mysterious abstraction. And secondly we may reply that this dramatic or human element is *not* outside the music, but most obviously inherent in the instruments that play the concerto; and that, so far as such a feebly metaphysical term as 'absolute music' has a meaning, it can only mean 'music that owes its form, contrasts, and details solely to its own musical resources'. As long as musical instruments or voices exist, there will always be the obvious possibility of setting one instrument or voice against many; and the fact that this opposition exists also in human affairs is no reason why music should cease to be 'absolute' or self-supporting —unless we are likewise to reason that man ceases to be human in so far as his five senses are shared by lower animals.

We must now see how the classical composers, to whom music was music no matter how profoundly it reflected humanity, adapted their art-forms to this condition of the antithesis between one and many, or between greater and less. I hope to show that the distinctive mark of the classical work is that it delights in this opposition and makes it expressive, while the pseudo-classics and the easy-going, thoughtless innovators, though they continually try to use it, miss the point with a curious uniformity amid diversity of error, and find every special condition of a concerto embarrassing and uninteresting.

Let us take these conditions in their earliest and, in some ways, simplest form. It is no use going farther back than the aria of Alessandro Scarlatti, or, to keep to familiar examples, Handel, in whom the conditions are not appreciably more developed. The Handelian aria is a clear and mature, yet an early and simple art-form. It owes almost its whole vitality to the opposition and relation between the voice and the accompaniment. When Handel was at work it was already dying of conventionality. And on this point I must beg leave to digress.

Conventionality is generally understood to mean something vaguely to the following effect: that a device may occur a very large number of times, say five hundred, in as many different works of art, and yet be in every instance the right thing in the right place, and therefore good and not conventional; but that the moment it occurs a five-hundred-and-first time, it becomes conventional and bad for all future occasions; so that we are entirely at the mercy of custom and history in the matter, and must know whether we are listening to No. 500 or to No. 501 before we can tell if either is beautiful or conventional. Now, though this is the real basis of more than half the current uses of the term, no one will believe it to be true when it is put before them in this form. The real meaning of 'conventionality' is either an almost technical, quite blameless, and profoundly interesting aesthetic fact, more often met with where art aspires beyond the bounds of human expression than elsewhere; or else the meaning is that a device has been used unintelligently and without definite purpose. And it makes not an atom of difference whether this use is early or late: thus the device of the canon is, more often than not, vilely conventional in the late fifteenth and early sixteenth centuries, and extremely beautiful wherever it occurs in Schumann and Brahms. So long as a thing remains the right thing in the right place, custom has simply nothing to do with it. Custom may help us to understand what might otherwise be distressing in its remoteness from our humdrum ideas; and custom frequently is an unmitigated nuisance, making us feel towards classical works as an overgrown choir-boy whose voice is cracking must sometimes feel towards the forms of worship which have become too familiar to impress him—but custom never makes good criticism or in any way ministers to the enjoyment of art, so long as it is allowed to dictate to us.

This digression was necessary here, because all the concerto forms show an unusual number of constantly recurring features, and it is of great importance that we should never be misled into estimating these features as conventional merely because they are frequent. Indeed, the really conventional composer abolished them long ago. After using them in a hopelessly unintelligent way for some centuries, he naturally concluded that what he could not understand was of no use to any one, and so he avoided them in the very same conventional spirit in which he had at first used them. The original composer is nowhere more triumphantly unconventional than when he chooses an old device because he knows its meaning, and applies it rightly, in the teeth of all popular criticism and current notions as to originality and genius. Let us see how far Handel and Bach bear this out.

The arias of Scarlatti and Handel (and, of course, all opera and oratorio writers between archaic periods and Gluck) obviously depend on the antithesis between a voice and an instrumental accompaniment. This accompaniment is generally conceived as orchestral; and accordingly (though the orchestra is not often very formidable except in warlike scenes where trumpets and drums are treated vigorously), there is almost always the contrast between the single voice and the chorus of instruments. In fact, wherever Handel is not either employing some special instrumental effect, itself of a solo character, or else writing merely for voice and figured bass, his usual direction for the top part of the accompaniment is 'tutti unisoni'. But in any case the relation between voices and instruments is such that, as Gevaert teaches in his works on instrumentation, as soon as the living utterance of the voice strikes upon the ear, the orchestra falls into the background. This natural phenomenon is too powerful to be obscured by any perversions of modern taste. The callous and stupid use of it ought to have no influence on us. It has no influence on great artists, though they often shock contemporary critics, who have no better criterion of vulgarity than that it is what vulgar people do. As long as we know too much of what vulgar people do, we shall be worried and misled by the fact that, among other things, they ape their betters. Let us study their betters.

In great music, then, we may expect that such a contrast as that between a voice and an orchestra will always have its original value, and will be more, instead of less, impressive as the range of the art increases. Now it so happens that there is in a lesser degree just that kind of contrast between the quality of tone (not merely the volume) of a solo instrument and that of an orchestra. The solo player stands out from the orchestra as a living personality no less clearly, though somewhat less impressively, than the singer. Hence there was, in the period from Alessandro Scarlatti to Handel, the closest affinity, amounting in some cases to identity, between certain vocal and concerto forms. If we could understand a beautiful Handel aria so as to have some idea, however incomplete, of that wherein it differs from his hack-work, then we may hope to understand a Beethoven concerto.

When a voice or instrument is accompanied by something which it either thrusts into the background as soon as it is heard, or else fails to penetrate at all, a moment's reflection will convince us that the easiest way to give both elements their best effect is to let the accompaniment begin with a statement of the material, and then to bring in the voice or solo with a counter-statement. This arrangement brings out the force of the solo in thrusting the orchestra into the background, while at the same time the orchestra has had its say and need not seem unnaturally repressed as it probably would seem (supposing it to be at all powerful) if it were employed only to support the solo. Again, this ritornello of the orchestra will, as its name implies, return effectively at the end of the piece when the solo has reached its climax. The solo is probably more active, as well as more personal and eloquent, than the orchestra, and can therefore make a brilliant climax if it chooses; but it cannot make its climax very powerful in sound as compared with what the orchestra can obviously do with ease; and so this one missing element may be supplied, and the design rounded off, by bringing in the ritornello forte on the last note of the solo, thus ending the piece. Here we have the beginning and end of an enormous number of typical concerto forms. A single unbroken melody might be arranged in this way as a complete piece for a voice and orchestra, with no further elaboration and no other appearances of the orchestra except the opening ritornello and its recapitulation at the close; but generally the voice or solo goes farther afield and attains more than one climax in foreign keys, so that the orchestra introduces parts of its ritornello perhaps three or four times in such a movement.

Obviously much depends on the skill and sensibility of the composer in choosing different parts of this ritornello, bringing the solo into fresh relationship with it at each entry. Very early in the history of the operatic aria an important device was discovered, which is usually associated with the name of Alessandro Scarlatti. Its essential point is that the voice does not complete its first strain at once but allows the orchestra to finish it instead, and then begins again from the beginning, this time to continue. The device obviously has great value in establishing a more subtle relation between voice and accompaniment than is possible when they persist in alternating only in large and complete sections. It soon became 'conventional', that is to say a mere formula in the hands of composers who knew and cared nothing about the contrast and harmony of voice and accompaniment; and Mr. Fuller-Maitland, who describes it fully and accurately in the fourth volume of the *Oxford History of Music*, gives many instances of it in various stages of true feeling and decadence from Bach, in whose hands no device is more conventional than the very laws of nature, to Greene, who, in one of his anthems, shows its last trace in a futile piece of mechanism lazily indicated by a da capo sign.

And yet the device has never died, aesthetically speaking, though we may not be conscious of its ancestry. Wherever a solo depends for its effect on entering after an orchestral ritornello, there we shall find the trace of Alessandro Scarlatti's principle—that the solo should first be inclined to enter into dialogue with the orchestra—the speaker should conciliate the crowd before he breaks into monologue.

I do not propose here to trace how Bach was influenced by his predecessors in this matter. Bach is an original composer, and no conventional ideas about originality will prevent him from using the most hackneyed device in its fullest and oldest meaning. His

chief concerto form is in every particular derived from the typical
vocal aria form, at least as regards the first movement.

A little consideration of the new conditions involved will help
us to arrange the facts clearly. The opposition of solo and orchestra
began early to take a greater variety of forms than was possible
in the vocal music of the same periods. The main type of early
concerto was the *concerto grosso*, in which the opposition was
between such a number of solo players as could produce quite
a complete mass of harmony to oppose against the orchestra
proper. This opposition of the concertino against the orchestra or
*concerto grosso* (from which the form takes its name) could even
be reduced to a state of things in which all played together and
split into whatever groups they pleased; as in Bach's magnificent
Third Brandenburg Concerto, which is for a string orchestra which
plays in three parts in the ritornello, and divides itself into nine by
way of representing solo passages—no further indication of a distinction between solo and tutti being given. Still, apart from the
likelihood that Bach was writing for only nine players, and that
in performance by a larger band the nine-part passages should be
played by the leaders alone, this dividing of the orchestra at once
produces a fairly strong impression of that entry of individual tone
which we know to be the most expressive feature of the concerto
style; and this first movement of the only concerto throughout
which Bach does not write for a detached solo-group or single
solo, differs in no other way from the rest of his concertos.

We need only think of an aria enormously enlarged, with
its square-cut melody turned into a concentrated group of pregnant, sequential figures, such as befit a serious and monumental
movement that will not for a moment be confined within the
limits of lyric melody. We shall find all the other features of the
aria here: the ritornello, of course, states the main figures of
the movement in their most forcible shape; then the quasi-solo
of the orchestra divided into nine parts begins its version of the
theme, but, just as in Scarlatti's arias, bursts into a tutti before
the phrase is finished, though the greater scale of the movement
(and a higher organization in every respect) is indicated by the
fact that this interruption is in a new key. Another interruption
occurs before the resumed nine-part passages can deliver a longer
sentence; and we have to go some way into the movement before
these quasi-solos have any long uninterrupted discourse. Throughout the work the principles of alternation between quasi-solo and
tutti are most subtle and delicate in their adaptation to the peculiar
conditions of this band. Sometimes the three basses coalesce into
tutti while the six upper parts remain individual; in one most
impressive place, the basses do this in order to bring out a difficult

passage, thus retaining their value as solo parts. Sometimes basses and violins will each coalesce while the three viola parts flourish separately. In short, the combinations are endless, and are all in the highest degree expressive of the peculiar concerto opposition of forces. This is what Bach does under conditions in which the possibilities of concerto style are least obvious.

The Second Brandenburg Concerto is for four solo instruments and orchestra. Here the principles of the form are far more obvious. Yet they cannot be so strongly marked in a concerto for four instruments as in a concerto for one; and if Bach's extant concertos be studied as glorified arias, the vital aesthetic principles will reveal themselves in endless variety. (Incidentally these principles will help us to restore by conjecture the original forms of works extant only in arrangement.) Bach, far more than Handel, likes to organize both his larger arias and his concertos by making the solo enter with a different theme from that of the ritornello, so that when the orchestra breaks in on the first solo with Scarlatti's interruption (or something to that effect) the bit of ritornello so introduced has a new meaning. Sometimes he translates into these larger instrumental forms the things that happen in an aria where a solo instrument as well as a voice is opposed to the orchestra. Further details must be left to other analyses of Bach's vocal and instrumental works. Here we can only add that Bach, like the masters of later concerto forms, makes the relation of solo and tutti more intimate and less contrasted in middle and final than in first movements.

In short, Bach's concerto forms are completely identical with his vocal forms, except those that are dramatic, like some of Handel's, and those that employ the orchestra merely as a support, such as fugues and the severer forms of figured choral.

In the case of festive choruses, where form and brilliance are more important than fugue and solemnity, this identity is such that actual concerto movements have been arranged by Bach as choruses. And the arrangements are so amazingly successful that there is nothing but external evidence to prove that the chorus is not the original. The best illustration of this is the first chorus of a delightful cantata, *Vereinigte Zwietracht der wechselnde Saiten*, written to celebrate the election of one Dr. Kortte to a professorship. The very title of the cantata throws light on the concerto idea; for *Vereinigte Zwietracht* is a singularly accurate and forcible rendering of the root meaning of *concertare*; and Bach generally calls the solo part (*Cembalo*, *Violino*, or whatever the case may be) *certato*.[1]

---

[1] The true interpretation of this significant point is among my earliest recollections of that great musical scholar, A. J. Hipkins, whose kindness to me began in my childhood.

When we compare Bach's rendering of this 'united contest of turn-about strings' with the third movement of the First Brandenburg Concerto, we find that the framework, themes, and counterpoint are bar for bar the same, with the exception of an occasional expansion (two bars inserted here, half a bar there), to make the approaches to climaxes longer and more suitable to the grander massiveness of choral writing. But what will strike us most forcibly is that the chorus parts are derived, not from the horns and other wind-parts of the original, but entirely from the single solo part, a struggling violino piccolo (Quart-Geige, or kit), that has more difficulty in getting the upper hand of the orchestra than any other solo in the whole classical repertoire. The transformation of this thinnest of solo threads into massive and stirring four-part choral writing is one of Bach's most astonishing feats of easy and unerring mastery. Any ordinary man would have reasoned as follows: 'This movement is the only one in the concerto with a true solo, all the rest of the work being on the lines of the concerto grosso, and depending on the opposition of masses of strings, wood-winds, and horns. And this solo part is not very brilliant, nor does it give me any material I cannot get more easily from the winds. Therefore I will either neglect it, or absorb it into the arrangement I propose to make of the wind-parts, which shall become the chorus. And now that I look at the structure of the movement, I see that there is much repetition caused by this tiresome little solo part, the motive of which will vanish when my chorus carries all before it. So I will cut out all these conventional repetitions, and make the form of my chorus free and terse.' And so our *a priori* theorist achieves a breathless chorus in a jerry-built form. Thus the easygoing innovator (for all conventional minds are bursting with innovation) has arrived at the forms of many popular concertos of modern times. Bach's ways have nothing to do with *a priori* theorizing. In the true sense of the word he is the greatest of theorists, for he *sees*, he *understands*, and his vision is perfected in action.

Bach, or rather his chorus, seems to reply to our reasoner: 'You complain that the violin part is overshadowed, and you point out that the rest of the work is a concerto grosso. But this first movement is not; and your complaint only proves that the violin arrested your attention from the moment it appeared, and made you wish that the orchestra allowed you to hear it better. The violin spoke to you like a voice, and you found it too weak; it shall become a chorus, and you shall learn that the whole orchestra always was its loyal bodyguard. The repetitions you think conventional shall continue to mean here exactly what they always meant —the transformation of a formal statement into the living and

moving utterances of a personality; with this new splendour that
the personality is that of a happy multitude inspired by one joy.
The form of such a movement as this need no more change with
a reversal of its balance of tone than the forms of the mountains
change as the light falls at morning and evening. Let the horns
become trumpets, let us hear the thunder-clap and roll of drums
where the chorus sings of "der rollende Pauken durchdringender
Knall"; let the voices have more room here and there; but do not
dream of losing the vital beauty that not only gives the movement
its form, but is its very cause, the opposition of a *personality* to the
impersonal orchestra. It is no matter whether that personality be
an instrument, personal because isolated, or a chorus, personal
because having human speech. The moment it appears it rivets
our attention, and the orchestra itself becomes an eager listener
expressing its sympathy in harmonious assent.'

As if to demonstrate that the affinity between choral and concerto forms is no accident of an insensitive age, Handel once
adapted some non-ritornello choruses (such as 'Lift up your heads')
into a huge concerto. The results are absurd enough to make the
difference between right and wrong in this matter self-evident.

### THE SONATA-FORM CONCERTO

We have seen how the early aria form was adapted to the conditions of a concerto; though we did not enter into many particulars about the aria itself. We must be more careful with the forms
that underlie the concertos that are now to be discussed. The
best way to avoid a tiresome abstract of ordinary sonata form will
be for us to base our analysis on the difference between the sonata
forms and those of Bach. The cardinal difference between sonata-
style movements and those of the time of Bach is that the sonata
movement changes on dramatic principles as it unfolds itself, whereas the older forms grow from one central idea and change only in
becoming more effective as they proceed. Bach's grandest movements will show this no less than his smallest. You cannot, indeed,
displace a bar without upsetting the whole; but the most experienced critic could not tell from looking at a portion out of its context whether it came from the beginning, middle, or end of the
work. Yet almost any sufficiently long extract from the first movement of a sonata by Mozart or Beethoven would give a competent
musician abundant indications of its place in the scheme.

It would be convenient if we could say that the polyphonic idea
of form is the development of a single theme, while the sonata idea
is the development and contrast of several; but it would not be
at all true. The first movement of Bach's B minor Sonata for

cembalo and flute has fifteen distinct figures—which is more than can be found in the extremely rich first movement of Brahms's G major Violin Sonata—and yet it is a perfect example of the true spirit of polyphonic form; while Haydn often gives us quite mature sonata movements in which it is impossible to find more than one theme. Still, the great thing to bear in mind is that the themes of the old polyphonic movement, if there are more than one, flow one into the other. The movement grows without ever showing impressive preparation for the advent of something new; and its surprises, many though they may be to a sympathetic listener, are never much connected with new themes or indeed with anything we do not seem to have known from the first. But a Haydn movement sets out in search of adventures; and if there is only one theme, that theme will somehow contrive to enter in another place disguised as its own twin brother. There will always be a vivid impression of *opposition* of ideas, and of change as well as development. And Haydn's frequent use of one theme where orthodoxy expects two is a result of amazing invention working on a deceptively small scale and seizing every conceivable means of making the dimensions of his work seem spacious, and its outlines free.

Hence the early instrumental forms were such that a short pregnant ritornello could sum up the principal material of a movement in a single line, while the solo was under no need to introduce more fresh matter than suited its disposition. But the material of sonata forms cannot be so briefly summed up; the ritornello, if it is used at all, must be larger and must contain more than one paragraph.

The great masters of sonata form were not to be persuaded to abandon the ritornello. The larger range of sonata movements, the treatment of the orchestra on lines as dramatic as those of the new forms, and the rise of a corresponding style of solo playing—all these facts conspire to make the ritornello more instead of less necessary than before. Bach's concerto orchestra was almost always merely a string band; when he adds wind instruments to it, these show a strong tendency to detach themselves as subordinate solo parts; and so completely does he falsify the current idea about the parity of his orchestral and solo parts, that his great Double Concerto in C major for two cembalos reduces the string-band to a mere support, necessary and effective, but in no way opposed to the cembalos, who wrestle only with each other. Under these conditions Bach even abandons the ritornello. Not so the masters of sonata form: their orchestra uses wind instruments in every possible combination with the strings, sometimes opposed in groups, as in the old concerto grosso, sometimes in solos, and constantly in perfect blending of tone with the strings as part of the compact chorus. Such an orchestra cannot be allowed to remain permanently in the background. On the other hand, the solo will need to be more brilliant than ever before, if it is to stand out against this orchestra which has already so much contrast of its own. The modern concerto form must rest more than ever on the old and natural concerto idea, the entry of a personal voice instantly arresting attention, and by mere force of its individuality thrusting even the most elaborate orchestra into the background. And the more rich the orchestra, and the greater the number and range of themes, the longer and more effectively may the appearance of this individual voice be delayed by an orchestral ritornello, if only this remains truly a ritornello and does not merge into pure symphonic writing. Here we have the key to the true method of conveying sonata form in terms of a concerto. The ordinary account of the matter, as given in standard treatises, is that the orchestra gives out the first and second subject with most of their accessories, more or less as in a symphony, but all in one key, instead of the first being in the tonic and the second in the dominant; that the solo then appears and restates these subjects somewhat more at leisure and in their proper complementary keys; after which there is a shorter recapitulation of part of the tutti in the new key, whereupon the solo again enters and works out an ordinary sonata development and recapitulation more or less in combination with the orchestra; after which the movement ends with a final tutti, interrupted by an extempore cadenza from the solo player. Now this scheme is, no doubt, rather like a concerto as it sounds to us when we are not listening; but it is falsified in all its most important particulars by nearly every concerto in the classical repertoire except Beethoven's in C minor; and the whole subsequent history of Beethoven's treatment of the form indicates that he learnt to regard the structure of the first tutti of his C minor concerto as a mistake.

Let us try to discover the true concerto form by analysing a great work of Mozart, the Pianoforte Concerto in C major (Köchel 503), referring to parallel cases wherever they may help us.

Mozart begins with a majestic assertion of his key, C major, by the whole orchestra, with mysterious soft shadows, that give a solemn depth to the tone (Ex. 1).

Ex. 1.

Allegro maestoso.

The second of these sombre changes passes into C minor with extraordinary grandeur and breadth, and a new rhythmic figure (Ex. 2) rises quietly in the violins.

Ex. 2.
C minor.

(a)

This new figure bursts out forte in the bass[1] with a counterpoint on the violins (Ex. 3), in the major again, and with the full orchestra.

Ex. 3.

Bass 8ve. *lower.*      (a) *inverted.*

It modulates broadly and firmly to the dominant, which key it explores triumphantly, and finally annexes by trumpeting the rhythmic figure three times on G. Now this is not quite in the manner of a symphony. True, many of Mozart's earlier symphonic first themes consist, like Ex. 1, of little more than a vigorous assertion of the tonic and dominant chords; but they continue in a style that only slowly becomes more epigrammatic and melodious, and hardly rises to any surprising harmonic effect throughout the whole movement; whereas this concerto opening is mysterious and profound in its very first line. It shows at once a boldness and richness of style which is only to be found in Mozart's most advanced work. A symphony in this style would certainly begin with something more like an articulated regular theme, however openly it might be designed to emphasize the tonic and dominant of the key. (Compare the opening of the Jupiter Symphony. The Jupiter Symphony is the *locus classicus* for an architectural opening, but it takes no such risks as the opening of this concerto.) These solemn procedures have much the effect of an *introduction*. That impression is somewhat modified as the music carries us out with its tide, and we realize that we have indeed begun a grand voyage of discovery. This cannot be an introduction that leads to something with a beginning of its own, but

[1] In the only printed parts accessible (published, to its lasting disgrace, in connexion with the complete critical edition), all this is blurred by a stupid crescendo. The parts are simply plastered all over with additional marks of expression that show a total deafness to fine orchestration, dignity, and vividness of style, and only one faint gleam of intelligence, that the editor does not give his name. The only way to avoid hours of labour in clearing up this mess is to play from manuscripts faithfully copied from the score.

it must be a preparation for some advent; and we can best realiz
how grand it is if we try to imagine the effect with which a choru
might enter at this close on the dominant (end of the passag
beginning at Ex. 3). The entry of a chorus, singing the psaln
*Dixit Dominus*, would be almost perfectly appropriate; indee
Mozart's church music, which is mostly of an earlier period
rarely attains to such power and solemnity as this opening. If w
turn to Brahms's *Triumphlied*, we shall find that the orchestra
introduction, though not nearly so long as these first fifty bars
is not unlike them in the way in which it covers its ground an
seems to be leading up to something. But of course a choru
thrusts the orchestra far more into the background than a sol
instrument can. Our opening tutti must develop further, for th
orchestra will not sound relevant if repressed by the feeble tone of
single instrument before it has stated several contrasted themes.

We have, then, paused on the dominant. Observe again tha
the modulation to the dominant is not like the normal early modu
lations of symphonies. Though, if taken out of its context, th
close of this passage would seem to be clearly in G, yet it her
sounds only like very strong emphasis on the dominant of C. True
in symphonies of an earlier period Mozart would have followe
his close by a second subject in G; but the effect of doing so i
always a little epigrammatic—the taking advantage of a natura
emphasis on the dominant so as to turn it into a new tonic; an
I believe that Mozart differs, even in his earliest works, fron
ordinary composers in seeing that the device *is* epigrammatic
whereas they only saw that it was convenient and obvious. Bu
it certainly would not tell in a work in the advanced style of thi
concerto. The only way to prepare the mind for G major after thi
grand opening would be to go to *its* dominant and pause on that
But the present close in G (in spite of the F sharp and all th
firmness and emphasis) has not taken our minds out of C at all. W
feel that we are *on* the dominant, not *in* it. Again, if this wer
a symphony and Mozart wished to begin his second subject, o
preparations for it, at this point, he would be almost certain to plung
into a remote and quiet key, most probably E flat, rather than us
the old colourless device described above. And it is interesting t
note that this is exactly what Beethoven did in the same circum
stances in his C major concerto, when he had not yet realized th
difference between symphonic form and the form of the concerto
ritornello. (Another reason for making particular note of thi
possibility of E flat will appear later.)

What does Mozart do? He remains in C; and this fixity of ke
stamps the introductory ritornello character of the music mor
and more firmly the longer it continues. Out of that Beethovenis

rhythmic figure ┐ ♪♪♪ | ♩ arises a quiet march in C minor, half
solemn, half gay, and wonderfully orchestrated (Ex. 4).

Ex. 4.

&c.

This is repeated by the wind, with soft trumpets and drums, in
the major. 'Here', explains the believer in standard accounts of
concerto form, 'we evidently have the second subject, which the
solo will eventually restate in the dominant.' Wait and see.

After this counter-statement there is a delightful kind of
Hallelujah Chorus (Ex. 5), which settles with majestic grace into
a quiet cadence-figure (Ex. 6);

Ex. 5.

&c.

Ex. 6.

&c.

&c.

Light semiquaver accompaniment.

and the grand pageant of themes closes in triumph. Then the strings
seem to *listen*, for one moment of happy anticipation. As they
listen the pianoforte enters, at first with scattered phrases (Ex. 7).

Ex. 7.
Strings.      Pfte.

These quickly settle into a stream of florid melody, which
grows to a brilliant climax in accordance with the artistic necessity that the solo should hold its own by doing that which most

distinguishes it from the orchestra, and should therefore be florid just in proportion to the amount of orchestral impressiveness.[1]

On the top of this climax the full orchestra re-enters with Ex. 1, on the same principle as the bursting in of the ritornello upon the first utterances of the voice or solo in the polyphonic arias and concertos. The impressive soft shadows of this theme are now beautifully illuminated by running passages in the piano-forte, which continues the theme in close dialogue with the wind-band. Ex. 2 follows, yet more impressive, thrilled with the rise and fall of pianoforte scales. Instead of leading to a triumphant outburst in the major, it is continued in the minor with very dark colouring and great breadth of rhythm, and culminates on the dominant of C minor, which the full orchestra sternly em-phasizes with the rhythmic figure (a) ♩ ♫ ♩· . Here, then, we have another pause on the dominant, not unlike that which we had shortly after Ex. 3. What does the pianoforte do now? It quietly modulates to E flat, exactly as we saw that Beethoven was tempted to do in the opening tutti of his first concerto. And that modulation, which is a mistake in a ritornello[2] because of its symphonic char-acter, is for the same reason beautiful when the solo has entered and established its relation to the orchestra. Here Mozart gives the pianoforte a new theme (Ex. 8) pervaded by that omnipresent rhythmic figure (a).

Ex. 8.

Transition Theme.

(a)                                                                            &c.

[1] Hence the source of all our delusions as to the relation between the concerto and the bravura styles. A modern concerto *must* be technically difficult, because all the easy ways in which a solo can stand out against an orchestra are harmonically and technically obvious, being the elementary things for which the instrument must be constructed if it is to be practicable at all; and as the orchestra becomes more varied and powerful, the soloist must dive much deeper into the resources of his instrument. Hence the concertos of Mozart are in general far more difficult than any earlier ones; those of Beethoven the most difficult of all except those of Brahms; while the concertos of the virtuoso-composers, which exist mainly for technique, are easier than any others, since whatever types of passage they employ are written on progressions schematic at best, so that they can in time be mastered once for all like the knack of spinning a peg-top; whereas the great composer's passages never take your hand where it expects to go, and can be mastered by the muscle only in obedience to the continual dictation of the mind. Mozart's passages are in this respect among the most treacherous in existence.

[2] I continue to apply this term to the whole opening tutti of the largest concertos. The longest opening tutti does not, if rightly designed, lose the unity that characterizes the true ritornello, even if it contains many important changes of key.

This modulates to the dominant of G in a broadly symphonic style, thoroughly expressive of the intention to establish the new key with firmness. Contrast what we felt about the passage following Ex. 3. After dwelling on this new dominant with sufficient breadth, the pianoforte settles down into the second subject. This will come as a surprise to orthodox believers in text-books, for it has nothing whatever to do with Ex. 4, which seemed so like a possible second subject. Indeed the only part of it that has anything to do with the ritornello is a variation of Ex. 3, which obviously belonged originally to the first subject, though we may remember that the pianoforte had avoided it when it fell due after the solo statement of Ex. 2.

I need not describe the second subject in detail. Its new and main theme (Ex. 9) is first stated by the pianoforte—

Ex. 9.

and then counterstated and expanded by the wind instruments. The derivative of Ex. 3 follows (see Ex. 10) and leads brilliantly to a climax,

Ex. 10.
(cf. 3.)

(a) inverted.

with all that variety of colour and rhythm and continual increase of breadth which is one of the most unapproachable powers of the true classics, distinguishing them no less from the classicists, who do not know that they lack it, than from the romantic composers, the greatest of whom contrive to make their work depend on renouncing it in favour of epigram and antithesis.

On the top of this climax the orchestra, long pent-up, bursts in with Ex. 3 of the ritornello. And here Mozart contrives one of his most subtle and brilliant strokes. We saw that Ex. 3 originally led to G and closed emphatically in that key, but yet under circumstances that made us feel that we were all the time only on the dominant of C. But now, of course, it begins in G, and Mozart so contrives that it remains there, instead of going on to the present dominant, D, as it would if transposed exactly; and it ends with the *very same notes* for no less than ten bars, *as in its original occurrence*, but now, of course, with the strongest possible feeling of being *in* G, not merely *on* the dominant. Thus Mozart cannot even do a mere repetition without shedding a new light that could not possibly be given by any variation. There is no describing the peculiar and subtle pleasure this device gives. It depends on a delicate sense of key, but has nothing to do with the technical knowledge which enables us to name it; indeed, it is certain to be keenly enjoyed by any attentive listener whose knowledge of music is the result of relish for classical works, stimulated by frequent opportunities for hearing them under good conditions. On the other hand, it is quite possible that many persons skilled in the mechanics of what passes for counterpoint, and having at least a concert-goer's retrospective view of musical history, simply do not hear these effects at all.

The sense of key-perspective can never be made obsolete by new harmonic developments. In otiose styles, whether early or recent, it is in abeyance; but a genuinely revolutionary style is more likely to stimulate than obliterate it. Strauss's opening of *Also sprach Zarathustra* might almost pass for a paraphrase of the opening of Mozart's C major Concerto.

The orchestra ends, trumpeting the rhythmic figure (*a*) on G as a finally established key. The pianoforte re-enters, repeating the figure on the dominant of E. And now it goes straight on with the march theme (Ex. 4) in E minor, which is to furnish our development section. The concerto has been grand and surprising, leaving us continually mystified as to what is to happen, and now it takes shape.

This theme that so happily pulls the whole design together all the way back from its single previous appearance in the ritornello, now moves calmly through a long series of very straightforward sequences through various keys. But though the sequences are simple in their steps, they are infinitely varied in colouring, and they rapidly increase in complexity until, to the surprise of any one who still believes that Mozart is a childishly simple composer, they move in eight real parts.

These eight parts are in triple, or, if we count added thirds, quadruple canon, two in the strings, four in the wind with the added thirds, and two of light antiphonal scales in the pianoforte. No such polyphony has occurred since in any concerto, except one passage in the middle of the finale of Brahms's D minor.

Then there follows a majestic dominant pedal for the next eight bars, not at all polyphonic; the wind rises in a scale which the pianoforte crosses in descent, and just at the most satisfactory moment the full orchestra enters with the opening theme, Ex. 1; and we find ourselves in the recapitulation. The pianoforte shares the continuation, as in its first solo, and proceeds without alteration through the expanded version of Ex. 2 to the E flat theme, Ex. 8. This takes a new direction of very beautiful harmony and leads to the second subject. From this point the recapitulation bids fair

continue to follow its original exactly; but we find that the
ounter-statement of Ex. 9 is expanded in a new sequence of
modulations in minor harmonies, and suddenly we find ourselves again in the broad daylight of the major key, listening to
Ex. 4 as it was given in counter-statement in the ritornello! The
pianoforte has a brilliant part of its own in this incident. Then
the rest of the recapitulation follows, with Ex. 9 as if nothing had
happened. And, of course, at the end the orchestra enters with
Ex. 3, and comes to a pause on a 6/4 chord, whereon the pianoforte
extemporizes a cadenza. After this the orchestra crowns the work
with its final triumph of formal balance by repeating, what we have
not heard since the first entry of the solo, the closing themes,
Ex. 5 and 6.

It will be seen that this whole wonderful scheme entirely fails to
fit the orthodox account of concerto form. Evidently the opening
tutti has no connexion with the notion of a sonata exposition in
the key; it is a true ritornello, differing from that of an aria only
in its gigantic size. If further proof were wanted, Constance's
great bravura aria 'Martern aller Arten' in the *Entführung* would
furnish it, besides showing the use of auxiliary solos in the ritornello,
a device revived by Brahms in the slow movement of his B flat
concerto. Of course there are plenty of cases where the second
subject is represented in the ritornello, especially where the work is
not on the largest scale; but there is no foreseeing what the solo
will select from the ritornello. All that we can be sure of is that
nothing will be without its function, and that everything will be
unexpected and inevitable. I doubt whether three important concertos of Mozart (at least fifteen are important) could be found that
agreed as closely in form as Beethoven's three greatest concertos
(G, E flat, and the Violin Concerto). In one point they almost all
agree, even down to the smallest works; and that is the splendid
device of inserting in the recapitulation of the second subject a
theme from the ritornello that was not represented in the original
solo statement. In Beethoven's hands the concerto grew so large
that this device would no longer be weighty enough to pull the
design together, and so it has remained peculiar to Mozart.[1]

[1] Further investigation will show that this device is the result of a
larger principle which I had not grasped in 1903. The recapitulation
in the tonic is a recapitulation of the opening tutti as well as of the first
solo. It does not omit the features peculiar to the solo, but it adds to
them those features of the ritornello which the solo had not at first
adopted. In particular, it is likely to follow the course of the opening
much more closely than in the first solo; and the subsequent appearance
of a previously neglected theme is the most conspicuous result of this
tendency. In Beethoven and Brahms the main principle is quite as clear,
though it may not be marked by a special theme.

It is unnecessary to give a full account of the other movements
concertos, as they proceed, naturally use, like all sonata-works
more sectional forms, in which solo and orchestra alternate mor
simply than in the first movement. This is further necessitated b
the fact that it can no longer be effective to lay such tremendou
emphasis on the entries of the solo, now that it has so gloriousl
won its way into friendship with the orchestral crowd. Hence th
ritornello idea does not find such full expression in these late
movements, though Mozart is very fond of using a simple kind o
ritornello at the beginning of his larger slow movements, as in th
present work. I give the three main themes of this ritornello i
Ex. 11, 12 and 13.

Ex. 11.
(a)
(b)

Ex. 12.

Ex. 13.

The pianoforte turns Ex. 12 into a second subject and adds mor
themes to it; returning then by a really colossal passage on
dominant pedal to the main theme in the tonic, and a regula
recapitulation of both subjects. Ex. 13 is reserved to round o
the movement.[1]

Concerto finales are practically certain to be some kind o
rondo. Mozart soon found out how to make the rondo form brin
out the solo in the most appropriate way. He gives to the mai
theme (which is usually announced by the solo) a large number o
orchestral accessories, which do not recur with the returns of th

[1] In some of Mozart's andantes, notably that of the G major Concert
the themes of the ritornello are so closely welded together that it is a grea
surprise to hear what we thought was part of one melody blossom out in
new key as a well-contrasted second subject. (See Essay LXXXVIII.)

theme, until the very end where the solo shares in them as they round off the movement with fine effect.[1]

In the present instance, Mozart announces the main theme by the orchestra, and uses the accessories more extensively, making Ex. 15 modulate to A minor for the middle episode. But Ex. 16 appears only at the end of all, after a very big coda. In this finale the free-rhythmed connecting links between the main sections attain a breadth that was never approached until surpassed by Beethoven. Here are the remaining themes:

[1] Mozart found this use of accessory themes in the tonic valuable outside concertos. The finales of the two pianoforte quartets and of the great A major Violin Sonata are excellent examples.

## CONCLUSION

Only the analysis of individual works can adequately show the later developments of the true concerto form. These chiefly concern the first movement; for the other movements are not much prevented by the special conditions of concerto form from growing on ordinary lines. But the following generalizations may be useful.

1. Beethoven ceased making the ritornello come to a full stop before the solo entered. In his three greatest concertos the end of the ritornello is dramatic and expectant, so that the solo enters on a dominant chord and ruminates in broad passages of immense dignity and beauty before taking up the themes. These passages correspond to the new theme with which Mozart so often begins the solos of his larger concertos; but, with their entry on the dominant and their non-thematic character, they produce a far more thrilling effect. Mozart's nearest approaches to this are in the concerto just analysed, in the much earlier A major Violin Concerto, where the solo begins with a short, florid adagio, in the brilliant and witty Pianoforte Concerto in B flat (Köchel 450), see Essay LXXXVII, and in another big Concerto in C major (Köchel 467), where the solo enters on the dominant.

2. Beethoven did *not* 'emancipate the orchestra' as is commonly held: he could not possibly have made it more prominent and elaborate than Mozart makes it in such works as that described here. On the contrary, he treated the pianoforte much more constantly in full harmony, and this inspired him with the possibility of accompanying it by very incomplete harmony in the orchestra and so producing numberless wonderful effects that can be heard under no other conditions.

3. Beethoven had the art of inventing themes which pass continually through several keys. This enabled him to give the opening tutti of his G major Concerto great variety of tonality without becoming symphonic or losing its unity as a ritornello.

4. In the same work he secures the novel effect of letting the pianoforte begin, and making the orchestra enter *in a foreign key* with the next phrase, after which the ritornello proceeds on the orchestra alone.

5. In his E flat Concerto he discovered the possibility of a rhapsodical solo introduction before the ritornello.

6. In the same work he found out how to construct a gigantic coda out of a new recapitulation of the later themes of the ritornello, including even the entry of the solo. This removes the one real defect of the classical form, that it entrusts the organization of the coda to the player's extempore powers in the cadenza.

Brahms further developed the concerto form in the following ays.

7. He found a way of modulation that gives the ritornello ore than one key, and this, not by a series of transitions (like eethoven's in the G major Concerto), but by a real contrast of xed keys, all without loss of the necessary unity and flow.

8. He enlarged the notion of a solo introduction and made it both ematic and rhapsodic, thus saving space in the ensuing ritornello.

9. He did not, as used to be said, score too heavily for the solo; n the contrary he is demonstrably lighter than Mozart; but he ses the modern pianoforte in order to add greatly to the volume f a big tutti.

10. He discovered that if the solo takes most of its material rom the orchestra, the orchestra may take some fresh material rom the solo; and thus he obtained many new contrasts.

11. He found out how to write a symphonic scherzo for piano- rte and orchestra.

Such innovations do not make a formidable catalogue, but they re the outward signs of spiritual forces that are not concerned in he gyrations of the up-to-date weathercock. In the classical oncerto forms the orchestra and solo are so organized that both re at their highest development. The conditions of such a prob- m do not admit many obviously different solutions; and the oncertos that abandon the classical form obtain their unlimited ariety by being structures of a much looser and less ambitious rder. They stand on their own merits, and can be defined only y individual analysis. Beethoven had no reason, for example, o despise Weber's *Conzertstück*; and later composers, from Mendelssohn onwards, would have seen no reason why it should ot have been called a concerto. It is manifestly better than Veber's regular concertos; and composers may as well write the est music they can, without being worried by a terminology that vould confine the word 'concerto' to a form which exists in hardly hirty perfect examples.

# MOZART

## XXXVI. PIANOFORTE CONCERTO IN A MAJOR (KÖCHEL'S CATALOGUE, NO. 414)

### 1 *Allegro*. 2 *Andante*. 3 RONDO, *Allegretto*.

This is one of a group of three small pianoforte concertos which Mozart wrote not long before *Figaro*, during the period of the six tring quartets which made Haydn acknowledge him as the greatest omposer he had ever heard of. These concertos are small as he wild strawberry is small; they are no stunted growths, nor

are they school-pieces of 'educational' value; they are highl
characteristic and mature masterpieces. The smallest is in F majo
and its character is somewhere between that of an Aberdeen terri
and a Dandie Dinmont; it does not happen to show fight, but i
quiet sagacity is no sign of weakness. The largest is in C major. T
the little old orchestra of strings, two oboes, and two horns, fo
which all three are written, it adds trumpets and drums, with whic
it makes dramatic jollifications; the slow movement reacts fro
these in a style which is the source of Mendelssohn's Songs withou
Words; and the finale is a fairy-tale in which a melancholy adag
twice introduces the marvellous into the design.

The little A major Concerto is in style midway between thes
two; and it would be difficult to find another work of Mozart i
which practically every single theme is so typical of his style. Eve
small works of art in these large forms usually assert a composer
style more in their treatment of themes than in any large proportio
of the themes themselves. Those of the little F major Concerto a
almost all common formulas, and so are more than half of those o
the little C major; but here it almost seems as if Mozart had con
centrated the most personal features of a dozen compositions o
this single work. He appears to have been fond of it himself and t
have played it or taught it often to his favourite pupils, for he ha
left two complete sets of cadenzas for it, by no means as perfunctor
as his written cadenzas usually are. As a rule it may be taken tha
Mozart's written cadenzas do not adequately represent what h
would extemporize in the places where they are required; but th
concerto gives us the exceptions. They are very short, but full o
valuable features in design.

The opening tutti of the first movement gives, as usual, th
principal themes of the first subject—

Ex. 1.

followed by a vigorous transition theme which I do not quote; an
the second subject, a gallant little march, full of Mozart's Tyroles
raillery.

Ex. 2.

esides these we have an important feature in Mozart's mature
·ncerto form; a prominent theme which is ignored by the solo
·strument when it first gathers up the threads of the opening
·tti, but which pulls the whole form together when the recapitula-
·on follows the lines of the tutti more faithfully, and puts this
·eme in its proper place.

Ex. 3.

·astly, there is the final cadence-figure which (as in the earlier
·te concertos and elsewhere) the solo has a way of neatly turning
·to a new transition theme. I need not quote it, as this description
·ill suffice to identify it.

There are people who still believe that Mozart's whole idea of
·anoforte playing was confined to a pretty tinkle. It may surprise
·em to hear that Mozart's friends were fond of asking him to
·nake the pianoforte sound like an organ', and that he delighted
· so obliging them. What they meant thereby is shown by the
·rst theme of the slow movement, which the pianoforte, when
·s turn comes, gives in very full chord.

Ex. 4.

Another theme, which afterwards constitutes the second subject,
· remarkable for its likeness to the first theme of the first move-
·ent (see Ex. 1).

Ex. 5.

·ich resemblances come too often and too prominently in Mozart's
·ncertos to be accidental. They are sometimes placed where they
·ve exactly the same function in each movement, and are always
·aced where they must attract attention.

The finale, beginning with a lively little formula-tune—

Ex. 6.

·ntinues with an excellent theme full of sly resource, which brings
·out most of the action throughout the movement.

Ex. 7.

The pianoforte, which, after stating Ex. 6, gave way to a tutti
full of accessory themes, re-enters with a new cantabile transition
melody, which I need not quote, though it is the source of some
pretty dialogue in the coda. It leads to the first episode (or second
subject), in which, among other themes, Ex. 7 is developed. Like
nearly all concerto finales this movement is a rondo; and so in due
course Ex. 6 returns, and then Ex. 7 leads to the middle episode
beginning with a playful tune in D major. Look out for the violas
with their mocking imitations.

From this middle episode Mozart returns, not to the first subject
but to the solo cantabile transition theme, and so to the recapitulation of the second subject. Then follows a coda in which Ex. 7, the
transition theme, and all the accessories given by the first tutti round
off the whole design with delightful freedom. Notice, for example,
the whimsical pauses in the transition theme when, after the
cadenza, it enters into dialogue with the orchestra.

## LXXXVII. PIANOFORTE CONCERTO NO. 15, IN B FLAT MAJOR
### (KÖCHEL'S CATALOGUE, NO. 450)

1 *Allegro.* 2 *Andante.* 3 *Allegro.*

Ludwig Deppe, the originator of the method of pianoforte playing
on which I was trained, used to call Mozart's fifteenth concerto
'the most difficult concerto in the world'; as readers of Amy Fay's
*Music Study in Germany* may remember. In the days which that
book commemorates it was still possible for a responsible critic to
remark (as Beethoven himself would have remarked) that we should
regard Mozart's cadenzas and passages as child's-play. Amy Fay
already thought that 'such a critic ought to go to school again'.
Mozart's own opinion is interesting. He produced this concerto
as one of three, together with the great Quintet for pianoforte and
wind-instruments, in March 1784; having early in February produced the Sonata for two pianofortes. Of this concerto, with its
soldierly brother in D major and two others, he writes to his father
on 24 May: 'I cannot come to a decision between those two concertos in B flat and D. I consider them both concertos that make
one perspire; but in difficulty the one in B flat beats the one in D.
Besides, I am very anxious to know which one of the three concertos, in B flat, D, and G, you and my sister like best; for the one
in E flat is not at all in the same class, being a concerto of quite a
peculiar kind and written rather for a small orchestra than for a
big one.'

The Concerto in G is a large work written in April of the same
year.[1] From Mozart's letter we learn that the difference between

[1] *Vide* following analysis.

small and large orchestras is not a matter of trumpets and drums. Our Dresden-china Mozart is a fiction which we may remorselessly hand over to the most panclastic of scullery-maids.

Of a symphony smaller than the Linz Symphony Mozart writes that it went '*magnifique*' with forty violins, ten double-basses, six bassoons, and all the wind doubled. This treatment would not suit even a heroic concerto, but the fact puts an end to miniature views of Mozart's style.

The opening theme of this B flat concerto—

Ex. 1.

shows Mozart in his most *schalkhaft* (or naughty) mood, and the change of accent at * shows that his naughtiness is stimulated by his most dangerous wit.

The raillery is continued even more quizzically. But soon Mozart, though refusing to leave the tonic chord, plunges into the usual forte theme which comes to the usual half-close. Then, thinks the usual theorist, we have the usual second subject.

Ex. 2.

But, as we have seen before, it is impossible to tell which, if any, of the themes of a Mozart tutti is going to belong to the second group.

Another tutti theme, beginning with a conspirator's crescendo, leads to the cadence-figure of the whole ritornello. On the stage this would imply a ribald gesture addressed to deluded husbands. See *Figaro*, Act IV, No. 26 '*gia ognuno lo sa*'.

Ex. 3.

While the orchestra is finishing some final chords, the pianoforte enters with a declamatory running figure, which it turns into an introductory cadenza. It then states the main theme, Ex. 1. Having completed this, it proceeds on entirely new lines, and modulates broadly to the dominant, where it gives out a second subject, consisting, with all its accessories, of themes that have never been suggested by the opening tutti at all.

Ex. 4.

At the end of this the orchestra bursts out with a dovetailing of the two forte themes of the tutti; ending, of course, with the cornute gesture of Ex. 3. The latter figure of this theme is turned into a chromatic run by the pianoforte, which thus begins a short but adequate development. This becomes dignified in becoming episodic; and the return to the first subject is, as always in Mozart, delightfully comfortable in the impression it gives of accurate timing.

With the recapitulation we see the full breadth of Mozart's concerto form. It is quite as much a recapitulation of the first tutti as it is of the first solo, and consequently it gathers up threads which the first solo had left unused. Thus it uses the first tutti forte before preparing for the second subject, and in the course of the second subject it inserts Ex. 2. Lastly, it follows the end of the solo not by a forte but by the original conspirator's crescendo. Even after the (presumably extemporized) cadenza, the orchestra turns its last chords to fresh account, no longer overlaid by the pianoforte.

The slow movement is a set of ornamental variations on one of Mozart's most beautiful themes.

Ex. 5.

Two double variations (i.e. variations in which the repeats of the two halves of the theme are themselves varied) suffice with a short coda to make a movement of great breadth and of almost solemn tone.

With the finale Mozart becomes *schalkhaft* again. Says the Fool in *King Lear*—

'This prophecy shall Merlin make, for I live before his time,'

and in the same spirit we may suppose Mozart to have foreseen that one day Schumann would write a pianoforte quartet with a slow movement which takes Mozart's naughtiest theme seriously.

Ex. 6.

Mozart.

Schumann.

o concerto-rondo by Mozart can do with less than seven different
themes.  Of these I must quote, besides Ex. 6, two themes from
the tutti—

and (omitting the cantabile transition theme, with which the pianoforte re-enters, and the theme of the middle episode) the beginning
of the first episode (or second subject) with its more than intelligent
anticipation of Liszt's dovetail-hand technique.

The returns to the main theme (Ex. 6) are particularly witty.
For the first return Mozart wrote an extra cadenza (not given in
the score); and the second is reached from the extreme distance of
minor by a dialogue between pianoforte and oboe.

At the end of the movement Ex. 7 and Ex. 8 are combined in an
amusingly dramatic way.


## LXXXVIII. PIANOFORTE CONCERTO IN G MAJOR
### (KÖCHEL'S CATALOGUE, NO. 453)

1 *Allegro.* 2 *Andante.* 3 *Allegretto, with Presto* FINALE.

The Concerto in G, written in 1784, is one of Mozart's richest
and wittiest.  The slow movement is full of deep and tender
feeling, with a certain gravity in its sweetness and light; but the
first movement and finale are in the most intellectual vein of high
comedy, culminating in an epilogue of pure *opera buffa* on a more
expansive plan than almost any other of Mozart's codas.  The
scoring, for small orchestra without clarinets, trumpets, or drums,
is as consummate as that of the three great symphonies; and the
pianoforte part is highly polished, without any of the problems
Mozart sometimes presents by leaving it in a sketchy state to be
filled out extempore by himself as the pianist.  He even wrote two
separate sets of cadenzas for the first two movements.  Both sets
are far from perfunctory, and it is difficult to choose between them.

Of the first movement I quote, first, the opening theme—

Ex. 1.

and (passing over its forte sequel) the wistful cantabile whic
afterwards becomes the second subject.

Ex. 2.

&c. leading to—

A dramatic incident in a dark key—

Ex. 3.

will show later on that the development is not quite so episod
as it seems. The ritornello ends with three contrasted themes, c
which I quote the first, with its *Don Giovanni* sharpened octave

Ex. 4.

The pianoforte enters with Ex. 1 and follows the course of th
ritornello closely until it sees opportunity for modulating broadl
to the dominant. Here, however, it introduces the second subje
with a quite new theme—

Ex. 5.

&c.

fter which the cantabile (Ex. 2), with its introductory quaver
igure, appears. It is followed by a series of running and arpeggio
hemes, until the orchestra caps the climax by entering with its
irst (unquoted) forte theme. The development has an air of being
pisodic throughout; but its first part is suggested by Ex. 3. At
he end of the recapitulation, this intervenes dramatically in its
riginal shape.

The slow movement is one of those profound utterances of
Mozart in terms which are almost confined to formulas; the
anguage of the *Zauberflöte*, the last (so-called 'Jupiter') Symphony,
nd the *Requiem*. Few casualties of criticism are more amusing
han the collision between such works of art and the plausible
logma that 'every important musical composition must have
trongly original themes'. The truth is that nobody knows exactly
vhat a theme is, or how many themes make an idea, or even how
nany ideas may go to a theme and whereabouts in the theme they
nay be situated.

Externally and conventionally the main themes of this wonderful
ndante are, first, a solemn pleading phrase, which breaks off with
pause (Ex. 6) and is followed by an arioso formula for oboe with
long swelling first note. This my quotations omit, and I give in
Ex. 7 the dialogue for three instruments which arises from it.

Ex. 6.

Ex. 7.

&c.

Vho would have thought that this dialogue is going to become the
econd subject in a highly developed sonata form?

A majestic forte theme joins the procession, and the tutti con-
ludes with the one obviously 'original' theme of the movement, a
profoundly expressive blend of minor and major modes.

Ex. 8.

&c.

The modulations throughout the movement are in a grand dramatic
ein, the dramatic note having been already indicated by the
nusual pause after the opening phrase (Ex. 6).

Classical concertos contain few examples of the variation form
there are only four in Mozart (the present finale, that of the (
minor Concerto, the slow movement of a concerto in B flat, and
so-called rondo written as a new finale to an early concerto in D
The variations in the G major Concerto are among the most witt
and ingenious achievements in this form before Beethoven. Th
wit begins with the theme, of which Ex. 9 is the first strain.

Ex. 9.

From Mozart's petty-cash book we learn that this tune attracte
not only the notice of the general public but also that of the birds
or at least that of the bird-fanciers, for he spent thirty-fou
kreutzers on a starling which delighted him by producing his tun
in the following Cloud-cuckoo-land version:

Ex. 9a.

The variations, most of which are double (i.e. with varied or totall
contrasted repeats), attain to great remoteness from the externa
melody; the fourth, in the minor mode, being a mysterious piec
of counterpoint on a quite new idea strictly following the structur
of the theme.

The fifth and last variation (a double variation with violen
contrasts) expands into a coda which leads to the presto finale o
epilogue, a comic wind-up big enough for *Figaro* and unique ii
Mozart's instrumental works. Most of its themes are new. Tw
of them I quote.

Ex. 10.
Presto.                                            Horns.

Ex. 11.

The original theme (Ex. 9; not 9a) romps in among the othe
conspirators as if it had known them all its life.

## XXXIX. PIANOFORTE CONCERTO IN A MAJOR (KÖCHEL'S CATALOGUE, NO. 488)

### 1 *Allegro.* 2 *Andante.* 3 *Presto.*

The three months of June, July, and August 1788 are famous for the creation of Mozart's three greatest symphonies; but they are not more wonderful than the single month of March 1786, in which the two pianoforte concertos in A major and C minor were written. These works are in no way inferior to the symphonies, nor are they less sharply contrasted with each other. The pathos of the C minor Concerto is even more profound than that of the G minor Symphony, though the texture is less concentrated. The A major Concerto is, with the additional element of pathos in its remarkable slow movement, as eminently a study in symphony as is the E flat Symphony, which it further resembles in revealing the clarinets as Mozart's favourite wind instruments, and omitting the oboes. Before the year was out Mozart had produced another concerto (in C major) which fully equals the Jupiter Symphony in triumphant majesty, and even in contrapuntal display. (See the analysis in the Essay on the Classical Concerto.)

As there is no rule without an exception to prove it, I readily admit that the first eight and a half pages of this A major Concerto completely tally with that orthodox account of classical concerto form which I have taken such pains to refute every time I have discussed a classical concerto. And if a single concerto, and that a work which the text-books have not selected as specially typical, can establish a form as 'normal' in points wherein all the other classical examples differ from it and from each other so radically that these points can hardly be identified at all; then perhaps Mozart did here produce an orthodox first movement—as far as the middle of the ninth of its twenty-two pages. But at that point things begin to happen which cannot be found in any other concerto.

However, it is perfectly true that of the five themes (or more, according as you take broad phrases or single clauses) which the orchestra gives in its opening tutti, the pianoforte takes up the first four quite faithfully in their order, making Ex. 1 the first subject;—

Ex. 1.

continuing the forte orchestral sequel (which I do not quote) as a regular transition leading to the dominant; transposing to that key (with the aid of only two extra bars) the exquisitely graceful and

gallant theme which the orchestra had already in the first instance
marked off by a formal preparatory half-close—

Ex. 2.

and following it with the next theme.  This is a somewhat more
dramatic paragraph, in which three bars, with rustling inner movement tinged with minor harmony, are answered by a spirited major
close, which in its turn gives way to a plaintively quizzical question
and answer in the 'relative minor' (F sharp in the tutti, C sharp
when we have it in the solo statement).  The continuation of this
is the only part of the first tutti which the pianoforte expands
into a longer and more brilliant passage so as to prepare for a
big re-entry of the orchestra, instead of passing on to the formal
little orchestral cadence theme with which the first tutti has
closed.

But quickly upon this big re-entry of the orchestra there comes
the inevitable shock to orthodoxy.  The need for such a shock is
more pressing than any matter of terms or technicalities.  The
objection to the 'orthodox' accounts is that they inculcate spurious
forms, and so induce composers to revolt from the study of classical
music because it is identified in their minds with what they instinctively feel to be bad.  Now in the present instance, if Mozart
had not at this point some stroke of genius in preparation—if his
only intention were to write a development on the preceding themes
and return to a regular recapitulation—his form would be orthodox
but stiff; at all events no better than Spohr's concerto form, and
considerably less good than the best of so modest a master as Viotti,
who (as Joachim and Brahms agreed) was quite capable of intelligent experiments.  By what possible means can Mozart, as far as
we have followed him here, manifest the principle governing
the recapitulation of all his other concertos, that the solo recapitulates, not its own version of the first and second subject, but
a fusion of its version with that of the original tutti?  Here the
two are as nearly as possible identical.  Well, let us see what
happens.

The orchestra has hardly got beyond the beginning of its resumption of the first forte of the opening tutti when it breaks off
and after a half-bar's silence softly gives out a quite new theme
which brings a deeper and graver mood to add to the grace of the
whole work.

Ex. 3.

The pianoforte takes this up in a florid variation, and with the aid of another new episodic theme in semiquaver movement, works out a broad development in dialogue with the orchestra. Thus, when the recapitulation is reached, the old themes return with complete freshness. And, what is perhaps more remarkable though less obvious, the development had none of the looseness of effect that in ordinary sonatas is apt to result from basing it mainly or entirely on 'episodes'. The episode was here a thing of absolute dramatic necessity. And after the now inevitably and rightly regular recapitulation, Mozart paradoxically vindicates his principle of making the solo refer more closely to the orchestra than to its own exposition of the themes. For when he comes to the last climax of pianoforte passages, it is the pianoforte that breaks off and, after a half-bar's silence, gives out Ex. 3 in its original simplicity and gravity. Afterwards the orchestra too has its say. And the poor pianoforte player has the appalling task of making a cadenza that shall not set the Mozart-lover's teeth on edge. Mozart has written a cadenza for this concerto, but a more than usually perfunctory and inadequate one. It is doubtful whether he would have regarded any of his written cadenzas to first movements as adequately representing his way of extemporizing, and it is quite certain that he could not wish to be represented by this one; though, like all his cadenzas, it conveys at least one useful hint.) Finally the orchestra rounds off the movement with its little cadence theme which has not been heard since the end of the first tutti.

The slow movement (Mozart's only composition in the key of F sharp minor) is of the most touching melancholy. Its first theme—

Ex. 4.

is stated by the pianoforte alone, and shows in its second bar a feature of late eighteenth-century style which we accept as familiar, without curiosity as to its meaning. One of the most superb vocal gestures of the eighteenth-century singer was the display of an unerring aim in skips from one extreme of the voice to the other, especially when the notes were selected as being opposed to each

other in harmony, and so specially difficult to judge accurately
It was, as it ought still to be, the highest boast of the player o
an instrument that 'he made his instrument sing'; and Mozar
had an unrivalled reputation for that quality in his pianofort
playing. There is not the slightest difficulty in playing the lov
E sharp in Ex. 3 with the left hand and the next B with th
right; and even with one hand the risk of the skip in this slov
tempo would be quite unnoticeable; but the whole point of th
phrase is that the skip is conceived as an enormous change o
vocal register. The pianoforte is a supernatural singer with
compass of five octaves—not more, in Mozart's time; but fiv
octaves is more compatible with a vocal style than seven an
a half.

The orchestra introduces another theme—

Ex. 5.                                                          &c.

which the pianoforte takes up in a chromatic variation. This lead
to A major, in which key we have a lighter and perhaps happie
episode. I say 'perhaps', because the childlike new themes are ful
of prophecy of poor Donna Elvira when her affectionate simplicit
is bringing her back into the power of Don Juan. Here, howeve
there is no sardonic or comic background. The main themes soo
return, the pianoforte part being written in a skeletonic wa
which Mozart certainly must have filled out with ornamenta
tion. I claim to be an absolute purist in *not* confining myself t
the written text. With Beethoven the case is already different; ye
even Beethoven absent-mindedly sent the score of his C mino
Concerto to the publisher after it had been performed, and th
publisher returned it rather angrily, pointing out that the piano
forte part had never been written at all. This is the extreme cas
which decisively shows that the autograph score of a Mozart con
certo is not always the best place to look for the pianoforte part a
he would have it played.

The most difficult point comes near the end, where the moo
is almost that of Wordsworth's—

> Roll'd round in earth's diurnal course
> With rocks, and stones, and trees.

Here there is no doubt that Mozart intends to use the effect of
singer's display of the extreme compass of his voice; and whateve
ornamentation one attempts must show this instead of disguising it

In concertos Mozart's rondo form contains features which he uses elsewhere; and the finale of the present concerto is remarkably like the finales of the great A major Violin Sonata, the two pianoforte quartets, and that most wonderful neglected masterpiece, the Sonata in F for four hands. The essential feature in the concerto-finale is that the solo player states the theme, and the orchestra gives a counterstatement, to which it appends a long string of other themes, none of which is destined to reappear until the last stages of the work, where they all troop in and make a triumphant end. Mozart was delighted with the effect, in other works than concertos, of this string of themes in the tonic and the resulting delay before any new key is established. He then establishes his new key rather abruptly, and enjoys another luxurious string of themes in it. Richard Strauss, one of the greatest Mozart-lovers of modern times, has produced some of the essence of this effect in the structure of *Till Eulenspiegel*. I cannot quote more than three of the themes of the present finale; but there are no less than ten perfectly definite and important ones, not counting various running passages that could easily be distinguished from each other. The end of the tutti distinctly recalls the quizzical F sharp minor incident at the corresponding point in the first movement.

Here is the first of the four themes in the first subject:

Ex. 6.

I do not quote the two transition themes which the pianoforte gives out after the orchestra has had its say. From the second subject I quote its first theme—

Ex. 7.

which in the recapitulation is given in the major, and its irrepressible third theme which figures largely in the coda.

Ex. 8.

The middle episode contains at least two more themes, one i
F sharp minor, the other in D major; and when the time com
for returning to the tonic, it is not the main theme but the trans
tion themes that turn up. The main theme is thus all the mo
welcome when it reappears, and is followed by its train of ac
cessories, divided between the pianoforte and the orchestra. I
addition to this, there is a big coda, towards the end of which Ex.
sails in with a grandiose subdominant colouring that adds to it
glorious effrontery.

### XC. PIANOFORTE CONCERTO IN C MINOR (KÖCHEL'S CATALOGUE, NO. 491)

1 *Allegro.* 2 *Larghetto.* 3 *Allegretto.*

I do not propose to repeat here what I have said elsewhere o
classical concertos. But besides quoting certain themes I hav
three general points to make, one special point, and one anecdote

My first point concerns Mozart's own special treatment of th
form of the first movement of a concerto. In no other form doe
he show so much variety, and I cannot recall any two cases i
which his procedure is the same through the whole movemen
But there is one interesting general principle. As every concert
goer knows, the first movement begins with a long orchestra
ritornello, and the accepted text-book theory (which is ver
incorrect) asserts that this ritornello contains the first and secon
subjects all in the main key, and that when the solo instrumen
enters, it restates and expands these, distributing them into thei
proper keys and, in co-operation and alternation with the orchestra
building them up into a more or less normal development an
recapitulation, the bulk of the coda being, unfortunately, left to th
mercy of the solo-player's gift of extemporizing. Now you canno
possibly tell which of the many later themes of the opening tutt
is going to belong to the group of first subject, and which to th
second. Most people would confidently guess that in the presen
case the theme which begins in the middle of Ex. 2 belongs to th
second subject.

Ex. 1.

Ex. 2.

rising to

But the pianoforte seems to know nothing about it, or indeed about any of the orchestral themes except Ex. 1, and even this it only takes up in continuation (from figure (*b*)) when the orchestra violently forces it on the attention. The first pianoforte theme is a long, slowly-moving cantabile which I do not quote. Then the orchestra, as we have seen, intervenes with Ex. 1, which the pianoforte, disregarding the first four bars, develops into a transition passage. This leads with great deliberation to an immense second subject containing any number of new themes, of which Ex. 3—

Ex. 3.

is the second and most important. Besides this there is a rich passage in which the flute gives Ex. 1 in E flat minor, accompanied brilliantly by the pianoforte. There are several other themes and passages, all of them new, thoroughly in the manner of second-subject material, and all utterly subversive of the doctrine that the function of the opening tutti was to predict what the solo had to say. At last the full orchestra enters with what sounds, in retrospect, like a free version in E flat of the original last phrases of the tutti. As a matter of fact this also, except its touching soft close, is really new as well as free.

The development is begun by the pianoforte with its own (unquoted) opening cantabile. Then the orchestra intervenes with Ex. 1 in F minor, and a broad and simple development ensues, arising mainly from figure ($b^2$). The middle stage of this is marked by a passage of fine, severe massiveness, in which the majestic anger of the orchestra is answered by rolling arpeggios from the pianoforte. At last the recapitulation is reached. And now we can see very clearly one of Mozart's peculiar principles of concerto form; a principle far less easily traced in either Beethoven or Brahms, though both these masters use it. With Mozart the principle is definitely this: that the recapitulation recapitulates not so much the first solo as the opening tutti. Here we have the extreme case, in which the first solo (and hence everything that has to do with the second subject) has been entirely new. Hence we are struck with the full force of the fact that now in the recapitulation the orchestral and solo materials are for the first time thoroughly combined. Of course the result is quite impossible to fit in with any ordinary text-book theory of sonata form; the second subject is ruthlessly compressed, the order of its themes altered, and there is nothing to correspond with the flute passage founded on Ex. 1. But Ex. 2 appears in full, and pulls the whole design together as nothing else could do. This device of holding one of the most prominent tutti themes in reserve for the recapitulation is peculiar to Mozart, and is retained by him even where there is no other evidence of the principle we have just seen illustrated.

My second point illustrates some characteristic differences in the emotional ranges covered by Haydn, Mozart, and Beethoven. Neither Haydn nor Mozart produced more than a small proportion of works in minor keys; and while their ways of characterizing the minor mode are by no means conventional, nearly all their works in minor keys have a special character. Tell me that a mature but unknown large work of Mozart is in a minor key, and I will confidently assert that while it may have humorous passages it will certainly have both passion and pathos, and that while the pathos will almost certainly not amount to tragedy, it is very likely that much of the work will border on the sublime. If a large work of Haydn is in the minor mode it is almost sure to conceal pathos beneath a blustering temper in its quick movements. With Beethoven we reach the world of tragedy. Now the recapitulation of a second subject in a minor movement is likely to make these distinctions very clear. For, if the second subject was, as usual, originally in a major key, what is to become of it when it is recapitulated in the tonic? Haydn, in his later works, nearly always indulges in a 'happy ending' by turning the whole thing into the tonic major. Mozart (except in the finale of the D minor Concerto, where he achieves both his own and Haydn's method by adding a happy epilogue) always makes a pathetic transformation of his originally happy second subject into the tonic minor. This is pathetic but not tragic. Beethoven seems, at first sight, to return to Haydn's practice, but really he has transcended Mozart's; his major recapitulation has all the power of tragic irony, and the catastrophe follows in the coda.

Near the end of the first movement of this concerto a curious detail occurs. The cadenza comes in the usual place, after the recapitulation: there is the usual pause of the orchestra, and blank space left for the extempore solo; but the usual concluding shake

not indicated and the orchestra re-enters with a connecting
passage of two bars which is not to be found elsewhere in the
movement. After much thought I have come to the conclusion
that the omission of the shake is not an oversight, and that Mozart
had in view a novel way of ending the cadenza in this case. It is
a pity that this concerto is not one of those for which he wrote
down his own large collection of cadenzas, for these, though perfunctory like all similar attempts to write down what should be
extempore, are priceless evidence as to the style and technique of
his difficult lost art. As it is, I am reduced to guesswork.

The first theme of the child-like slow movement—

Ex. 4.

raises in its fourth bar my last general point, the most difficult of
all the problems that beset the interpreter of Mozart's concertos.
At first sight it seems hard to realize that the naivety of that fourth
bar can be intentional. Yet Mozart must have thoroughly impressed
upon his young pupil Hummel that its whole point was its utter
simplicity; for many years afterwards Hummel, having become the
most brilliant and authoritative pianist-composer in Europe, published an arrangement of eight of Mozart's greatest concertos, in
which he rewrote almost every bar of the pianoforte passages and
brought them up to date. Yet he did not dare to touch this bar,
until at its fifth and last appearance he added one little turn. But
this raises the whole question of extempore ornamentation in
Mozart's concertos. I am far from pretending to settle the problem.
Hummel's ornamentation will certainly not do; but it should be
studied, for he had all the knowledge we have not, though his
temperament was inflated rather than inspired. It is quite certain
that the plain text of Mozart's pianoforte part is often incomplete; for instance, you find a clarinet and a bassoon varying
their repetitions while the pianoforte part at the same moment
has always the old bare outline. Clearly the orchestral players
could not be left to extemporize variations, and the pianist could.
But one is thankful to do as little as possible; for any deviation
from Mozart's style, even a deviation into early Beethoven, sets
one's teeth on edge. I am inclined to think that the problem set by
this slow movement in particular is the reason for the otherwise
inexplicable fact that this C minor Concerto, perhaps the most sublime of all Mozart's instrumental works, is less known at the present
day than the D minor, which happens to look less incomplete.

In Beethoven's young days these things were not difficulties but
opportunities. Players and singers were judged quite as much by

their taste in ornamentation as by their capacity for making th
best of what the composer wrote down. According to Danr
reuther, even the word *semplice* in the recitatives in Beethoven'
D minor Sonata is a special warning to the player not to add orna
ments; and we actually find Chopin, in an early posthumous set c
variations, inscribing the theme *semplice e senza ornamenti*.

Be this as it may, Mozart's C minor Concerto was in Beethoven'
time one of his most famous works, and it made a profound im
pression on Beethoven. The theme of the finale can only be calle
sublime.

Ex. 5.

In the first stages of sketching for his C minor Symphony
Beethoven was thinking of making a pathetic finale, and he jotte
down a theme in 6/8 time that was little more than a variation c
this, a variation that would have passed almost unnoticed amon
the variations Mozart's finale actually consists of. Some of thes
variations are pathetic, some childlike (e.g. the cheerful episod
in A flat, and the graceful one in C major), and some majesti
as the orchestral fortes and the one in flowing four-part polyphon
for the solo. But, as with Greek art, the subtle sublimity is
function of the simplicity and clearness of the surface; until a
last the whole pathos of Mozart's work is summed up in the las
variation, in 6/8 time.

Ex. 6.

It must have been the haunting second phrase of this (bars 5–8
that made Beethoven exclaim to Ries as they listened to it durin
a rehearsal: 'Oh, my dear fellow, *we* shall never get any idea lik
this.' Perhaps this was true enough of Ries. But even of Beethove
himself it is true that he did not strike this particular vain of patho
and romance until his art had gone beyond all possible reach o
Mozart's direct influence. Then indeed, in the finale of th
Quartet op. 95, Beethoven did produce a heart-rending theme o
the same incomparable simplicity.

## CI. FLUTE CONCERTO IN G MAJOR (KÖCHEL'S CATALOGUE 313)

1 *Allegro maestoso.* 2 *Adagio non troppo.* 3 RONDO: *Tempo di Menuetto.*

The two flute concertos of Mozart appear to have been written, together with the Concerto for flute and harp, in 1778. This, in G major, is not less witty and beautiful than the one in D major. In an interesting series of articles in the *Chesterian*, Louis Fleury commented upon the tendency of the flute composers of a hundred years ago to write pretentiously and pompously for this childlike and elfish instrument. The crushing solemnity of the nineteenth-century virtuoso musician certainly did produce depressing developments. Kuhlau wrote magnificent sonatas and duets and concert pieces, which earned him the title of the Beethoven of the flute. We have still to learn that Beethoven was at any time known as the Kuhlau of the orchestra. Mozart had a gentle vein of irony which often goes with a long range of prophetic vision, and we may take it that when he inscribes the first movement of this Concerto in G major *allegro maestoso* he writes the inscription with his tongue in his cheek. He is in fact doing very much what Mendelssohn did in the *Midsummer-Night's Dream* music, when Pease-blossom, Cobweb, and Mustard-seed make their bows to Bottom the Weaver to the accompaniment of a flourish of trumpets on two oboes, while two flutes execute a roll of drums. I quote enough of the first and second subjects of the first movement to show the range of contrast between the majestic attitude of the opening, where you are requested to keep grave—

Ex. 1.

*Allegro maestoso.*

and the second subject, which begins in an unexpected part of the scale and continues in epigrammatic vein.

Ex. 2.

The slow movement is the richest and most beautiful movement in these flute concertos. Here Mozart has boldly substituted two flutes for the oboes which constitute with the horns the usual wind band in his smallest concertos. Thus the solo flute is now

standing out against a background largely of the same colour
But the strings are muted; and the horns, in a lower key than
in the first and last movements, provide a darker tone. The solemn
opening figure, in which the flute has no share, intervenes with
dramatic weight at the turning points of the structure.

Ex. 3.

The movement is in the usual arioso sonata form.

The finale is one of those graceful *tempo di menuetto* rondos which
Mozart seems to have given up writing in his later works.

Ex. 4.

In spite of its leisurely tempo it gives the flute more scope for its
characteristic fantastic agility than the rest of the work. It is
broadly designed without any unusual features, and ends quietly
like almost all Mozart's examples in this tempo.

## XCII. FLUTE CONCERTO IN D MAJOR (KÖCHEL'S CATALOGUE NO. 314)

1 *Allegro aperto.* 2 *Andante.* 3 *Rondo. Allegro.*

It is very good for an artist to make the best of a task he dislikes; so
long as there is a good best to be discovered for it. It is said that
Mozart could not abide either the flute or the harp; yet, as we shall
see, when at the command of a Duke in Paris he had to write a
double concerto for those instruments, he dissembled his love in
a long and charming work, and only on the last page ushered the
harp downstairs in an exposed passage which neatly contained the
two perfectly simple things which no harpist, ancient or modern
can play.

As for the flute, whatever he may have said about it, he liked it
well enough to write two concertos, an andante with orchestra
which is conspicuously lovely in tone and feeling, and two quartets
for flute and strings which are by no means perfunctory. These
five works are all comparatively early, ranging from 1777 to 1778
but Mozart was a mature artist in most art-forms at the age of

welve; and not even an opera can be dismissed as an 'early work'
f he was twenty when he wrote it. He took the flute seriously
nough in these highly-finished little works: more so than in his
upreme masterpiece *The Magic Flute* (which indeed has only two
pisodes to justify its title).

Of course, he is incapable of such a blunder as to write for a big
rchestra with a long and heroic opening tutti, by way of preparing
or the entry of his Puck or Ariel. His opening tutti is short,
hough it summarizes the whole movement from the first subject—

Ex. 1.

o the second, with its warning notes such as usher in a change of
ey in a Viennese waltz—

Ex. 2.

nd its mischievous cadence-theme—

Ex. 3.

he last bar of which (figure (a)) the flute has a characteristic way
f detaching for purposes of its own. At the end of the movement
his figure tricks the Eminent Critic into giving the performers the
xquisite pleasure of being blamed for deficient ensemble when
hey play the last bars accurately. Throughout the movement the
econd violins behave with an opera-buffa malice which Mozart
articularly cultivated at this period: it makes all his early concerto-
uttis crowded with contrapuntal and operatic life; and it almost
onjures up an awful vision of an early Rossini whom one could
ike seriously, much as, according to Professor Saintsbury, the
ymed headings to the pages of *The Rose and the Ring* evoke the
host of a Milton with a sense of humour.

As for the flute, Mozart may not have been the earliest to under-
and its fantastic agility—these questions of priority interest
obody who wants to listen to music—but no one before or since

has better seen the point of its qualities: the agility that can in the same breath give and deny local habitation to whatever airy nothings it is pleased to name; and the innocence which can seem superhuman rather than cold, so long as the composer does not give it phrases indicating passions of which it is ignorant. None of Mozart's flute-music happens to be pathetic, except the slow movement of the D major Quartet: the exception shows that there was nothing either in the Flute or in Mozart's idea of it to prevent his being as pathetic as Gluck in the Elysian scene of *Orfeo*, or Brahms in the finale of his Fourth Symphony. There is no limit to the beauty and pathos of childhood, so long as it is true to the nature of childhood. It so happens, however, that in this concerto the only serious note is to be found in the serenity with which the flute answers the quasi-heroic gestures of the first theme of the slow movement—

Ex. 4.

and in the second subject in dialogue between flute and orchestra

Ex. 5.

As for the finale, two quotations from its numerous collection of themes will show its lightness of heart, its flexibility of rhythm—

Ex. 6.

(note in Ex. 6 that the theme, though it foreshadows Blonde's lively air in the *Seraglio*, has none of that young person's squareness of phrasing), and its richness of counterpoint—

Ex. 7.

in a central episode complicated enough to get the copyist of the earliest extant band-parts into a thorough muddle.

It is in some ways a pity that music of this order never gets the kind of vulgar valuation that comes to pictures and beautiful pieces of furniture. This Flute Concerto is supremely artistic in every way; its slightness and smallness are functions of its greatness; and we might expect it to fetch a fabulous price if it were an escritoire, or a porcelain dinner-set, or any other form of art which daily useful-ness has caused to be produced anonymously in good periods as well as in bad.

### XCIII. ANDANTE FOR FLUTE WITH ORCHESTRA
### (KÖCHEL'S CATALOGUE, NO. 315)

The last and perhaps the most beautiful of Mozart's flute works, this Andante may possibly have been intended as a substitute for the andante of the Concerto in G. The very beautiful and elaborate slow movement of that work requires two flutes in the orchestra besides the solo player, and Mozart may have found that this was inconvenient. The other cases in which there is a single movement, slow or quick, for a solo instrument with orchestra are all known to be cases of reviving an old work and substituting the new movement for the corresponding old one. Be this as it may, the new movements are at their best by themselves, and the original works are best in their early form. The production of a concerto at a public concert in Mozart's, and even as late as Chopin's time, was one of those best of all possible events in which every detail was a necessary evil. The first movement was produced in one part of the concert, the slow movement and finale were produced about an hour afterwards when the audience had been gratified by other items which might now find place in a rather primitive variety entertainment. Nothing more clearly proves the genius of the greatest masters of eighteenth-century music than the un-doubted fact that their concertos and symphonies have an inviolable unity, which at the time of their composition was appreciable by the composer alone, or to the few who studied the works in private.

More than anything else in the flute works of Mozart, the style and themes of this andante are prophetic of his yet more magic flute of thirteen years later. The position and melodic type of the first theme is very like that of the tune with which Tamino in *Die Zauberflöte* first tries the power of the magic flute, with the effect of bringing on to the stage a complete menagerie of fascinated birds and beasts.

My quotation indicates the picturesque introductory chords for

oboes, horns, and pizzicato strings, which are cunningly develope‹
later on into a second subject. The movement is worked out in t‹
typical arioso sonata form, and is one of the ripest examples ‹
Mozart's style at its comparatively early date of composition, 177

### XCIV. CLARINET CONCERTO IN A MAJOR
### (KÖCHEL'S CATALOGUE, NO. 622)

1 *Allegro.* 2 *Adagio.* 3 RONDO: *Allegro.*

As far as the art of writing for the instrument is concerned, Moza‹
may well be considered to have invented or at least discovered t‹
clarinet. His three compositions in which the clarinet is the leadi‹
wind instrument, namely the Clarinet Concerto, the Trio for pian‹
forte, viola and clarinet, and the Quintet for clarinet and string‹
belong to the last year of his life and are among his most beautif‹
works. The concerto is in the full-sized classical form and by ‹
means on a small scale. If it were a pianoforte concerto, it wou‹
be among the more important ones, though Mozart has avoid‹
involving his sharply characterized solo instrument in any pol‹
phonic discussions with the orchestra. Mr. Forsyth in his admi‹
able book on orchestration has quoted copiously from both Sta‹
ford's concerto and Mozart's by way of showing among oth‹
things how the essentials of clarinet-playing remain the san‹
to-day as they were in Mozart's time. It is interesting to con‹
pare the orchestra of the two works. It stands to reason that ‹
neither of them will clarinets be present in the background, b‹
Mozart's solo clarinet is in a different relation to its backgrou‹
from Stanford's, for Stanford relies upon oboes as a contrast to h‹
solo instrument in wind tone, whereas Mozart has only flute‹
bassoons, and horns. He thus surrounds his clarinet with no stro‹
contrasts of tone at all, and yet there is no lack of relief. The softne‹
of the flutes rather enhances the vitality of the clarinet. I quo‹
three of the many themes of the first movement.

Ex. 1.  1st Subject.

Ex. 2.  Transition.

Clarinet.

&c.

Ex. 3.

The slow movement will be recognized as well known by many listeners who have never before realized where it came from. I have heard it as a horn solo and as a violin solo, and in almost any form except that in which Mozart wrote it.

Ex. 4.

The finale is a full-sized rondo of which the following are the main themes:

Ex. 5.

A point as fine as any in Mozart's chamber and orchestral music is the freedom with which the second subject (Ex. 6) is treated in its recapitulation before leading to the spacious coda.

## XCV. VIOLIN CONCERTO IN D MAJOR
### (KÖCHEL'S CATALOGUE, NO. 218)

1 *Allegro.* 2 *Andante cantabile.* 3 RONDO. *Andante grazioso, alternatin*
*with Allegro ma non troppo.*

Of Mozart's violin concertos the fourth, in D, and the fifth, in A
show the style of his adolescence at its wittiest. The fourth is i
higher animal spirits and therefore has less leisure for meditatio
than the A major; but it is not less witty, and, like the A major, i
has its surprises in dramatic incident and form.

As the orchestra is without trumpets the opening theme imitate
those heraldic perquisites with great vigour.

Ex. 1.

The main theme of the second group is graceful, with the peculia
tang of Mozart's style at the age of nineteen.

Ex. 2.

There are as many other themes as there are musical sentence
so that this opening tutti contains at least four more that woul
deserve quotation. And the solo violin has many more of it
own. But the most interesting matter is the question of how
can deal with Exx. 1 and 2. To those who do not know this concert
I will not divulge the secret of how the solo violin, like the sonne
in Milton's hands, becomes a trumpet; but there is no harm i
remarking that it delivers Ex. 2 in a deep bass voice.

The slow movement is serious in manner, but not less inveter
ately witty in detail. Its main theme is grave.

Ex. 3.

Its second group is heralded by an ornate theme.

Ex. 4.

Mr. Fox Strangways, in an interesting analysis of certain criteri of melodic beauty, crowned his argument with a gesture of humorous despair induced by a phrase in the coda of this movement, where the violin (like the Duke of York with his 20,000 men) simply walks up a scale and then walks down again. But Mr. Fox Strangways knew all the time that this phenomenon was the surface of a harmonic process without which it would have no meaning. Still wittier is the way in which the movement ends with a phrase that had hitherto always appeared to be merely medial.

The contredanse of Mozart's time was a dance with abrupt alternations of tempo; and there were also minuets *mit eingelegten Contredansen*. From such origins arises a special kind of rondo, to be found in more than one of Mozart's violin concertos, and also in his D major Violin Sonata, the rondo of which is twin brother to that of the present work.

The main theme asks wistful questions in a slow tempo (*Andante grazioso*).

Ex. 5.

And the questions are answered quizzically in a quick movement (*Allegro ma non troppo*)—

Ex. 6.

which leads to the dominant, where a second group begins with the following theme—

Ex. 7.

The two tempi alternate in consequence of the rondo form. But the second episode, beginning in B minor, leads to another change of tempo in the shape of a slow gavotte in G major—

Ex. 8.

which is continued with a delicious theme over a drone-bass.

Ex. 9.

When Ex. 5 returns, it is worked out in regular recapitulation with Exx. 6 and 7, and the concerto ends, like its middle movement with a sudden dying away in mid-phrase.

## XCVI. VIOLIN CONCERTO IN A MAJOR
### (KÖCHEL'S CATALOGUE, NO. 219)

1 *Allegro aperto.* 2 *Adagio.* 3 *Tempo di Menuetto.*

Mozart's five authentic violin concertos were all written in Salzburg in 1775 when he was nineteen years of age. The Concerto in E flat which is the most frequently played, and which purports to be the sixth, may be based on genuine material, but no competent musical scholar believes that it can possibly be genuine in the form in which it is known to us. The seventh concerto was discovered early in the present century, and has been often played with success. It is not in a perfectly satisfactory state of preservation; but, if it is a forgery, it is an exceedingly clever one, and it does not make the mistake of imitating a generalized Mozart of no particular period. No composer has had so many forgeries foisted upon him as Mozart. There are five spurious masses, including the celebrated Twelfth Mass; a concertante for four wind instruments and orchestra, purporting to be the lost work known to have been written in Paris for a rather different combination; a number of spurious songs; several sonatas and smaller pieces; to say nothing of the peculiar disaster of instrumental parts added to genuine works so unskilfully that the authenticity of the whole seems questionable until the additions have been removed. What is known, then, about Mozart's violin concertos is that in 1775 he made a brilliant beginning in this most difficult art-form, and never afterwards followed it up. It is noteworthy that the three greatest violin concertos in existence are all peculiarly happy but solitary efforts of their composers: Beethoven, Mendelssohn, and Brahms. It is not so remarkable that Mozart produced five violin concertos in one year as that he produced them early in his career. It was natural to produce several, since the scale of the form at that period was not large. I have had occasion, in commenting upon the flute concertos which belong to the same period, to call attention to the special vein of epigrammatic comedy which characterizes Mozart's style up to the age of twenty-three. In the A major Violin Concerto it attains its height, and is also combined with a specially fantastic kind of childlike beauty. Mozart's form at this period was almost as full of experimental features as Haydn's, and the work is full of surprises.

The opening theme as given out by the orchestra seems to be merely a formal assertion of the chords of the key in the

sual eighteenth-century style, but I quote together with it a
totally new idea which the solo violin is eventually going to build
pon it.

Ex. 1.

The theme which afterwards becomes the second subject is one
that could walk into the House of Lords with the same friendly
self-possession as into its own kindergarten.

Ex. 2.

And who would have thought that the formula which ends the
orchestral tutti—

Ex. 3.

could so coolly become an important transition theme when the
solo violin takes it up?

Ex. 4.

The entry of the solo violin itself is one of the greatest surprises
ever perpetrated in a concerto. We expect it to begin either

directly with a statement of the opening theme, or else, if Mozart
is inclined to anticipate Beethoven, with some preliminary running
passages. We certainly did not expect that the violin would begin
with a sustained arioso in a very slow adagio time with a running
accompaniment. There is a childlike grandeur in this gesture
which almost overawes the sense of humour to which Mozart was
undoubtedly appealing. You may take this as a measure of the
poetic power underlying all the fun. For the rest of the movement our four quotations will suffice. It was surprising enough
when Ex. 3 developed into the solid structure of Ex. 4, but it is
still more surprising when it turns out to be the absolutely abrupt
end of the whole movement.

The slow movement is not less notable for the terse and epigrammatic character of its themes. The essentials of them are all stated
in the opening tutti, the substance of which is expanded by the
solo violin much on the lines of the first movement in sonata form.
I quote the two figures in the stream of melody which become
articulated into first and second subject.

Ex. 5.

Adagio.

Ex. 6.

The finale is, like most concerto finales, a rondo. In a moderate
tempo di menuetto it begins as if it was going to pass all its existence
in graceful ease. I quote the first theme with its codetta.

Ex. 7.

Tempo di menuetto.

Ex. 8.

bis.

The first episode on the dominant presents just the kind of contrast
one would expect; and the return to the main theme follows in due
course. The second episode, beginning in F sharp minor, with
darker colouring and a somewhat wider range of key, is again just
what the situation seems to require; and in the second return of
the main theme the attentive ear may note that there is a little more

etail in the accompaniments, whereby the design is unobtrusively
ept alive. The next thing to expect would be a recapitulation of
he first episode in the tonic, with some slight modification of the
ransition leading to it. But suddenly we have a contredanse in
A minor (2/4 time), scored with the grotesque effects characteristic
f the real dance-music of the Viennese public ball-rooms in 1778.
Mozart gives this full scope to express itself with all manner of
epeats and alternating sections. It enlarges the range of the finale
s triumphantly as that impressive adagio arioso enlarges the range
f the first movement. After this the rondo theme returns and
eads to the orthodox recapitulation of the second subject and to
 final return, the accompaniments naturally varying in detail each
ime; and to crown all, this broadly designed movement ends with
he simple abruptness of the codetta to the theme (Ex. 8).

It is not surprising that this work was a great favourite with
oachim, who wrote cadenzas for it that are among the most
erfect that have been written for any concerto.

## XCVII. ADAGIO IN E, FOR VIOLIN WITH ORCHESTRA
### (KÖCHEL'S CATALOGUE, NO. 261)

This broad and dignified aria for violin was produced by Mozart
s a substitute for the more kittenish slow movement of his A
major Violin Concerto, on an occasion when that work was played
by a violinist named Brunetti, who, we may infer, wanted an
pportunity of displaying his full range of tone. We need not
nfer that Mozart wished the new adagio to remain permanently
s a part of the A major Concerto, the childlike humour of which
t would only embarrass. Public performances of concertos, even
s late as Chopin's time, were given in conditions that make it a
marvel that the great composers showed any sense of unity of
mood and style; and Mozart had more to gain than to lose by
pleasing Brunetti in a performance where the first movement was
o be given in the first part of the concert and the rest in the second
part after several other items. On the other hand, we gain a rare
addition to the small number of single movements for violin and
orchestra; a piece at least as important as the violin romances of
Beethoven, and, for all its seemingly automatic handling of forms
already highly conventionalized, far more distinguished in style.

The orchestral violins (but not the lower strings) are muted, and
the wind-band consists of two flutes and two horns. The A major
Concerto has oboes instead of flutes, and thus Mozart seems to be
taking special measures to throw the solo violin into higher relief
in this movement. With this tiny orchestra he achieves many
remarkable tone-colours by a few unexpected holding-notes and
by sforzandos in the inner parts.

Ex. 1 shows the main theme; Ex. 2 a characteristically pregnant
connecting link; and Ex. 3 is the beginning of the second subject.

Ex. 1.

Ex. 2.

Ex. 3.

## XCVIII. CONCERTO FOR FLUTE AND HARP (KÖCHEL'S CATALOGUE, NO. 299)

1 *Allegro*. 2 *Andantino*. 3 RONDO: *Allegro*.

In 1778, during Mozart's visit to Paris, the Duke of Guines com-
missioned him to write a concerto for flute and harp. Mozart show
no great respect for dukes as such in his family letters, and so w
may believe him when he writes that the Duke plays the flute incomparably and the daughter plays the harp '*magnifique*'; th
resources of the German language apparently failing him a
English avowedly failed Dr. Johnson when he was '*pénétré* with
His Majesty's goodness'. Accordingly, though these instruments
were precisely the two that he could not abide, he soon began to
luxuriate in the fun of writing for them. The possibilities of th
single-action harp of the eighteenth century he exhausted in thi
work. Nothing could be done for it but to proceed on the lines o
very sketchy pianoforte music with an anxious avoidance of cantabile; but the flute reconciled him so far that after his Paris visit he
produced five by no means uncharacteristic works for it, of which
the three with orchestra (two concertos and an andante) are discussed in this volume.

It is not necessary to quote more than four of the sixteen themes
which Mozart sends streaming out in festive processions throughout and around this work. Although a developed style for the harp
cannot be said to exist within fifty years of Mozart's death, this
concerto is no exception to the rule that Mozart's imagination for
combinations of instruments and harmonies is infallibly accurate
and incomparably vivid. He has here to reckon with the fact that
the harpists in 1778 were preoccupied with making their instrument speak a language it could not properly pronounce; and he
makes no miscalculations. Even the daughter of a duke could not,
in spite of her *magnifique* playing, prevent the mischievous Mozart

om twice asking the harp to say 'shibboleth' at the end of the
ale. (And, by the way, the will to play practical jokes is dis-
nctly discoverable in Mozart's works. I, for my part, feel abso-
tely certain of his intention of getting the choir to mock the
ronunciation of some friend of his in a certain Mass, once well
nown, where the word 'Osanna' is set in close stretto to a synco-
ated rhythm, and a fortissimo mark is placed under the third
llable in all the voices and instruments at every single one of the
rty or fifty repetitions of the word.)

The technique of the flute, unlike that of the harp, was not only
ssentially mature in 1778, but had already reached a second
eriod of development. For Bach and Handel the flute was a can-
bile instrument well suited for principal melodies or polyphonic
reads played in its lower registers among an ensemble of soft
struments. But already in Mozart's time the habits of the flute
ad changed in order to enable it to assert itself in the new styles of
mphonic and dramatic orchestration, and he never loses an im-
ortant feature by writing low for the flute in a tutti, as Haydn,
ho also developed the new technique, continued often to do in his
test works. This being so, it is interesting to find that the Duke of
uines had a flute provided with holes (possibly also keys) for the
w D flat and C; which Mozart evidently could not count upon in
ny of his later flute works, as he never wrote those notes again.
his, at all events, indicates that it was not ducal stimulus that
duced him to write his remaining five solo works for the flute.
t was 96 ducats.)

Those extra low notes for the flute will be heard by the alert
stener about half-way through the first movement, during its
evelopment, where they are used as a bass to the harp! For the
st it will suffice to quote the opening themes; of the first move-
ent—

Ex. 1.

and of the luxurious slow movement, in which the style of the ha
is at its best within the possibilities of 1778, and the string orchest
is throughout enriched by division of the violas into two parts—

Ex. 2.

and the opening and closing themes of the five which are pour
out in the first tutti of the rondo.

Ex. 3.

The viola and second violin of this last theme contain one of t
shibboleths with which Mozart worries the harp on the last pag
a passage in which the hands and strings are brought into mutu
interference. There is no reasonable doubt that this is maliciou
and so is the other passage, in which Mozart goes out of his w
(altering, in recapitulation, a perfectly safe theme) to introdu
some chromatic steps for which even the modern harp is not co
veniently suited. Of course there is nothing embarrassing in the
jokes, which the composer expects to turn against himself in eith
of two possible events; for the passages will either be played wit
success, or something appropriate and more effective will b
substituted for them.

# HAYDN

## XCIX.  VIOLONCELLO CONCERTO IN D MAJOR

### 1 *Allegro moderato.*  2 *Adagio.*  3 *Allegro.*

The concertos of Haydn all date from his Esterhazy period, an
are on a small scale, like the horn concertos of Mozart. The
forms hardly deviate from those of the vocal aria on a large scal
but, even before the modern editor has enjoyed himself over then
they give remarkable scope for the art of the virtuoso player.

At present the only orchestral parts available for this concerto
are those of the venerable and voluminous Gevaert, whose reign
over the Brussels Conservatoire and whose treatises on ancient
music and modern orchestration sufficed in themselves to make
an epoch in musical education.

The worst of such thoroughness is that, where it re-scores the
classics, the results are like the leg that was so beautifully suited
for a top-boot—'Same size all the way up, sir!'

Haydn's scoring of this concerto was probably primitive,
possibly for strings alone, and certainly the better for a pianoforte
to exercise the obsolescent function of the continuo. That function
being now exercised by Gevaert with a wind-band in the style of
a full swell-organ, the orchestra must do its best to play the
accompaniments gently.

The first theme surprises us by being based on a *cliché* we would
have thought peculiar to Mozart. My knowledge of the lesser
contemporaries of Haydn and Mozart is severely limited by my
patience, and I have not found this *cliché* elsewhere.

Ex. 1.

But in the slow movement the same *cliché* is followed by one
equally peculiar to Haydn.

Ex. 2.

Nobody can tell me the exact notes of the tune of 'Here we go
gathering nuts in May'; but everybody agrees that the finale of
Haydn's 'cello concerto is suspiciously like it.

Ex. 3.

And perhaps the wicked people who, with the late Mr. Rudyard
Kipling among them, persecuted the miso-auto-bureaucrat Squire,
J.P., and M.P. for Huckley, may have reverted to the Haydn
archetype when they turned this innocent tune into *The Village
that Voted the Earth was Flat*. At all events, bars 5 and 6 of Ex. 3
irresistibly remind me of

> Flat as my hat,
> Flatter than *that!*

But we digress. And so does Haydn.

# BEETHOVEN

## C. PIANOFORTE CONCERTO IN C MAJOR, OP. 15, WITH BEETHOVEN'S CADENZA

1 *Allegro con brio.* 2 *Largo.* 3 RONDO: *Allegro.*

The first three pianoforte concertos of Beethoven show, in t]
opening tuttis of their first movements, a phenomenon almc
unique in his works. In other branches of music we may find sig
of a struggle with stubborn material, and Beethoven himself som
times admitted that for this or that problem of vocal and dramat
music he had 'not studied enough'. But in the first two pianofor
concertos all is facile and spacious, while in the third, in C minc
which he declared, before he wrote it, 'will be the best of the three
he not only made a great stride in the direction of his 'second styl
but set the model for the orthodox concerto form of his young
contemporaries and later theorists. Yet in all three concertos t]
nature of the opening tutti is radically misconceived; and that
the C minor Concerto (as is pointed out in my analysis of it) is a
advance upon the other two only inasmuch as Beethoven seems
discover the error at the moment of committing it, with the resu
that its tutti executes a charmingly dramatic *volte-face* in mic
career, as if to say 'But no!—I must not be the beginning of a syn
phony'. In his later concertos Beethoven realized and carried o
the purpose of Mozart's opening tutti, one of the subtlest an
grandest art-forms ever devised; but no sooner was he able to d
this than he was able to transcend Mozart in every line of instru
mental and harmonic form, so that contemporary and later orthe
doxy blundered far more grossly about his concerto form tha
any early failure of his to see the purport of Mozart's.

The composer or theorist may imagine that because Mozart
tutti is voluminous and flowing it is also discursive and can indulg
in passages of development. Or he may imagine that it can b
throughout like the exposition of a symphony, and that it shoul
accordingly display its first subject, transition, and second subjec
so that the listener knows beforehand exactly what the solo instru
ment is going to do. The first misapprehension is shown by Beet
hoven in his first two concertos; the second appears in the C minc
Concerto and is instantly corrected, but not until its impression ha
been made with such force that, until Brahms came to the rescue
the opening tutti of the classical concerto remained a mystery t
composers and theorists alike.

Now the C major Concerto (which is later than the B flat Con
certo published second to it as opus 19) seems to have been a

ject of more interest to Beethoven than he admitted. At all
ents he wrote no less than three cadenzas to its first movement,
d the third of these cadenzas is one of his most splendid successes
recording the style of an extemporization. It is fully in his
econd manner', and the compass given to the pianoforte shows
at it must have been written at least as late as the published score
the C minor Concerto; that is to say, later than the Kreutzer
onata, and not much earlier than the Waldstein Sonata, which
closely resembles in pianoforte technique. It is a wonderful
ception to the general style of the cadenzas Beethoven wrote for
s own concertos (he also wrote two for Mozart's D minor Con-
rto); and indeed I have not a word in favour of what he called
'*cadenza per non cadere*' for the Concerto in G, or of the curious
ianoforte version he made of his Violin Concerto. I remember that a
istinguished English pianist played the G major Concerto in Berlin,
1900 or 1901, with Beethoven's cadenzas, not having announced
e fact. The critics really hardly deserved their fate; but it was
nfortunate that they went so far as to call these cadenzas *geradezu
nmusikalisch*, though they might well think them hopelessly inade-
uate and frivolous. There is another set which is not bad.

But the case of this third cadenza to the C major Concerto is
tterly different: it affords a noble pretext for reviving a neglected
rly masterpiece which it harmoniously lifts to a higher plane of
usical thought. I cannot help wondering whether Beethoven
uld not have made something almost as great out of his first
adenza, which he left unfinished just after it had developed on
nes calculated to bring certain discursive passages of the tutti
to closer organic connexion with the whole. The speculation is
teresting, because the point, if achieved, would have anticipated
hat he does in the coda of his last concerto (the great E flat, called,
his profound if posthumous disgust, 'The Emperor').

The C major Concerto begins with quiet and martial energy.

Ex. 1.
(a)

A *forte* counterstatement leads to a grand pause on the domi-
ant, upon which a fragment of the second subject appears in a
emote key, and is carried through other keys in rising sequence.

Ex. 2.

III                                     F

This is very beautiful; but processions (or concerto tuttis) w
get into difficulties if they often thus digress in search of t
picturesque; and it is this passage which Beethoven worked
bodily into his, unfortunately incomplete, first cadenza.  The ne
passage, founded on Ex. 1, is also discursive—

Ex. 3.

and forms the opening text for all the three cadenzas.

At last the orchestra settles down to a cadence theme in Bee
hoven's most British-Grenadiers style—

Ex. 4.

and with a final paragraph on figure (a) of Ex. 1 the orchest
comes to a formal close.  Not until the G major Concerto d
Beethoven follow the example, twice set by Mozart, of letting t
solo enter on the dominant chord with an introductory passag
On the other hand he follows several examples of Mozart
beginning with an entirely new theme—

Ex. 5.

though, unlike Mozart, he omits to develop it later, not even findir
room for it in any of his cadenzas.  The orchestra intervenes wi
figure (a) of Ex. 1, and the dialogue now follows the orthodo
course of a concerto, the pianoforte working out a broad transitic
to G major, where Ex. 2 appears as a regular and complete melod
by way of second subject.  After a short digression, Ex. 4 follow
and brilliant passages then run an easy course, though som
energetic staccatos markedly anticipate a prominent feature of th
E flat Concerto.  The anticipation becomes still more noticeab
at the end, and amounts to more than coincidence, formal as th

assage is in both cases, and deeply rooted in the organization as
is in the later work.

Ex. 6.

Op. 15.

*queste note ben marcate.*

Op. 73.

&c.

The development is, as usual in concertos, largely episodic, the
pianoforte beginning grandly with another entirely new theme
which I need not quote. Perhaps one reason why Beethoven
abandoned his first cadenza was a feeling that if he once began to
pick up loose threads there would be no end to the task; and that
the true course was to accept the pleasure that the Mozartean Angel
of All Art-Forms allows to those who Really Can Extemporize.

The return to the recapitulation is gravely dramatic in Beethoven's best 'first style'; the pianoforte taking its final plunge there-
into by an octave-glissando; at which the modern pianoforte jibs.
The recapitulation itself is adroitly curtailed as to the first subject
and unaltered as to the second.

And now comes the pause for the cadenza. Beethoven's third
cadenza storms away in magnificent Waldstein-sonata style, at first
apropos of Ex. 3, then apropos of figure (*a*), which starts on a voyage
round the solar system. The second subject (Ex. 2) appears at last
in vastly remote keys, and drifts sublimely from the style of *La
Clemenza di Tito* to the style of *Fidelio*. Thunderous further
developments of figure (*a*) burst forth, and at last the usual final
shake is heard; but surely rather too much on the dominant of G?
Quite so; we have something to say in G major about Ex. 4; please
don't interrupt! This being said, the shake arrives again and
develops with great excitement—while the orchestra waits for the
final turn. Instead of which the shake trails off into runs. And at
last the cadenza ends without any shake at all.

Ex. 7.

*f*     *p* Well?     *ff* *Now then!* Orch.

The difficulties of the classical concerto form are almost entirel
confined to the first movement, and especially to its ritornello.  I
slow movements and rondos Beethoven was from the outset a
great a master in concertos as in other instrumental forms; an
a quotation of themes is all the commentary required for the re:
of this unjustly neglected work.  The largo begins with a three
strain melody (A, B, A), of which Ex. 8 is the first clause.

Ex. 8.

A broadly designed transition to the dominant gives an impres
sion that the whole may be developed into full sonata form wit
Ex. 9 as second subject.

Ex. 9.

But Beethoven prefers to keep space for a less crowded scheme
and he brings back his whole first melody with rich ornamentatio
and new scoring (in all his early orchestral works there is no othe
example showing such appreciation of the clarinet), and, withou
any allusion to the middle portion, concludes with a long-draw
coda full of solemn new ideas.

Beethoven never wrote a wittier paragraph with more Haydn
esque irregularity of rhythm than the main theme of the rondo o
this concerto.

Ex. 10.

The various transition themes need not be quoted.  The firs

isode, which is treated (as in all full-sized concerto-rondos) like
second subject—

Ex. 11.

ves rise to a romantic digression in E flat and G minor, such as
is made the second subject of the first movement of Beethoven's
irst Symphony famous; and it is remarkable in how many points
e First Symphony follows cautiously the steps this rondo had
ready taken firmly and boldly.

The returns to the main theme are effected by the following
chubertesque transformation:

Ex. 12.

&c.

The middle episode alternates two superb themes in contrast,
e one spirited (compare the corresponding theme in the Triple
oncerto)—

Ex. 13.

&c.

d the other quiet, chromatic, and polyphonic.

Ex. 14.

The rest of the movement arises naturally out of these materials,
d the coda is full of Haydn-Beethoven surprises, being (with the
ddition of several small undeveloped cadenzas) a glorified version
the later and less elaborate comic wind-up of the First Symphony.

## CI. PIANOFORTE CONCERTO IN C MINOR, OP. 37

1 *Allegro con brio.* 2 *Largo.* 3 RONDO: *Allegro vivace, Presto.*

eethoven's third concerto was projected at the same time as his
rst and second; neither of which, as he openly avowed, was so
nportant as this, for which he was reserving his best efforts. It
one of the works in which we most clearly see the style of his

first period preparing to develop into that of his second. Th
main theme—

Ex. 1.

is a group of pregnant figures which nobody but Beethoven cou
have invented. They would rank as important themes in his late
works; but he here states them, quite successfully and unselfco
sciously, in the tonic-and-dominant symmetries that still interest
him for their own sake in his first period. With the transiti
theme—

Ex. 2.

he emphasizes the barest harmonic formulas with a youthf
sententiousness peculiar to an artist who has grown conscious th
these formulas are still necessary but no longer interesting, an
that until some totally new light can be shed on them they are be
left undecorated. (Two other works in the same key, the C min
Quartet, op. 18, No. 4, and the C minor Violin Sonata, show th
same drastic simplicity at this juncture.)

Now comes a turning-point in the history of the classical cor
certo. The opening orchestral ritornello of the first movement i
the concerto form had been developed by Mozart on a scale tha
has not to this day been surpassed; with the result that the entr
of the solo instrument must, if it means anything at all, mean a
event impressive because long delayed. If, then, long delayed,
must be long expected; and the expectation must be roused by th
music and not merely by the title of the item on the programm
Mozart's opening tuttis are among the highest triumphs of a
in their command of expectant exposition; no two examples ar
identical in their own plan, or in relation to the solo. Nor ca
Mozart's forms be correctly said to have a restraining influenc
on Beethoven's early work. To him these forms were no mor
orthodox than the forms of Richard Strauss were to the youn
composers of 1900. Nor indeed have Mozart's concerto form
been codified even yet with any greater accuracy than that of

:hild's hieroglyph of the human form as a disk supported on
triangle with two five-pronged forks attached as hands.

At all events Beethoven had something better to do than to
:onsult text-books on the subject of concerto form. He did not
mmediately achieve Mozart's solution of the problem of the
pening tutti; indeed it is arguable that he did not at first grasp
vhat the problem really was. In his first two concertos the orchestra
njoys itself in ruminating developments which, like so many of the
1appy thoughts in Schubert's large instrumental works, stray away
rom the purpose of exposition. In the C minor Concerto, Ex. 2
akes direct dramatic action and leads to a long passage of pre-
)aration for the second subject in its destined new key. This is
heer symphonic exposition; it rouses no expectation of the entry
f a solo instrument, and, as we shall find, leaves nothing essential
or the pianoforte to add when its time comes. The second subject
nters—

Ex. 3.

&c.

cantabile midway between a Mozart heroine and the heroine of
3eethoven's *Coriolanus* overture. Suddenly the orchestra seems to
ealize that it has no right to take the drama into its own hands;
hat its function is not drama but chorus-like narrative; and with
modulation in itself dramatic, the melody calmly turns round to
C major and is followed by a series of cadence-phrases in the tonic
ninor (including derivatives of Ex. 1) which bring this, the longest
f all Beethoven's concerto tuttis, to a massive formal close.

The works of Beethoven that have had the most influence on
ater composers are rather such transitional compositions than the
:ompositions which Beethoven himself based on the experience he
3ained therein. It is the C minor Concerto that has ever since been
aken as the normal classical example, and not the G major and
E flat Concertos, which are supposed to introduce bold innovations.
Yet it is only in these later works, and in the violin concerto, with
:he voluminous preparatory exercise of the Triple Concerto, op. 56,
:hat Beethoven achieves Mozart's methods of handling the opening
:utti, plus his own methods of setting the solo free. Spohr,
Hummel, Chopin (in his F minor Concerto), and even Joachim
in his Hungarian Concerto, all took Beethoven's C minor Con-
:erto as their model for concerto form; and they all regarded
as an inimitable and individual stroke of genius the one feature
(the sudden shift back to the tonic during the announcement of
the second subject) by which Beethoven rectifies something that
dangerously resembled a mistake. This stroke being thus regarded

as unorthodox, the 'classical' opening tutti henceforth becam
accepted as an ordinary symphonic exposition, prefixed, for reason
impious to inquire, to a sonata for a solo instrument with orchestr;
accompaniment. No wonder the easy common sense of Mendels
sohn abolished this convention; but the possibilities of concerto
with no scope for orchestral organization became fascinatin
to the virtuoso jerry-builder; and until Brahms tackled the tru
problem again, the vitality of concerto forms was becoming th
vitality of undesirable things.

Beethoven, then, has in this C minor opening tutti recognize
and saved a dangerous situation in the nick of time. The pianofort
can now enter and restate the exposition that the orchestra ha
given. Beyond two introductory bars of scales, dramatically usefu
in later entries, and a slight expansion of the passage of preparatio
for the second subject, the pianoforte follows the opening tutti, ba
for bar, until the second subject (Ex. 3) has arrived. Here there i
of course no need for the *volte-face* made in the original tutti
the pianoforte is now at last free to expand the material into ;
brilliant group of new phrases. These consist mainly of develop
ments of figure (*b*) in Ex. 1 with running accompaniments, cul
minating in a long shake, below which clarinets and horns ente
with a triumphant version of the whole theme. Then the ful
orchestra bursts out with its cadence phrases, and soon proceed
to shed new light on the long passage of preparation for the second
subject (between Ex. 2 and Ex. 3) by giving it in G minor.

This is a genuine and important innovation, which Beethoven
uses with powerful effect in the E flat Concerto, and in the Violin
Concerto. Mozart never lets his second tutti modulate, and always
brings it to a full close. Beethoven's new experiment goes fa
to set his form free. The pianoforte enters with its introductory scales, not as a formula on a tonic, but as a dramatic
intervention on a dominant. It then settles down to a pathetic
cantabile development of Ex. 1, the figure (*b*) unifying the whole
design by persisting as an accompaniment. In broad and distinct
steps the threshold of C minor is reached, and, after suitable
preparation, the first subject begins the recapitulation fortissimo.
After the close of the second subject (the triumphant clarinets
beneath the final shake now becoming trumpets), the orchestra
enters in the minor and soon leads to the usual pause for a cadenza,
which Beethoven leaves to the player to compose or extemporize.
After the cadenza it was usual for the orchestra to conclude the
movement formally with the last few bars of the opening tutti:
but Mozart had already found ways of using the solo instrument
in the coda, notably in his C minor Concerto, a work which
influenced Beethoven profoundly and conspicuously both as a

ole and in detail.  And so here the final trill of the cadenza leads
an unexpected turn of harmony which, together with the quiet
try of the drums with figure (*b*), is one of Beethoven's most
pical strokes of genius.  The pianoforte retains the whole con-
ct of the coda, and ends the movement with scales recalling
first entry.

The largo is the most highly developed slow movement in all
ethoven's concertos, and *a fortiori* in any concerto.  In his later
ncertos the slow movements lead into the finales; gaining thereby
rious dramatic subtleties and depths by release from the necessity
completing their own design.  But in the C minor Concerto we
ve one of the great independent symphonic slow movements,
aching the climax of Beethoven's powers of solemn expression
his first period, and indeed quite in keeping with all that he
und to say in his second.  The shock of the first chord, in its
moteness from the C minor of the rest of the work—

Ex. 4.

in itself a feature of Beethoven's second period, though his
rlier works show some preoccupation with things of the kind.
he impulse came from Haydn, whose later works contain
amples of every possible key-relation.  The example of the slow
ovement of Beethoven's C minor Concerto has had a direct and
ovious influence on later composers, e.g. Brahms's First Symphony
d Third Pianoforte Quartet.

An ornate transition theme leads to a well-defined second subject
the dominant.

Ex. 5.

This is followed in due course by a sombre episode in dark keys,
ith cloudy pianoforte arpeggios accompanying a slow dialogue
the winds.  The episode, which has the function of a develop-
ent, drifts steadily towards the tonic, E major, and so returns
its own good time to the first subject.  Instead of recapitulating
e transition and the second subject, Beethoven makes a broad
oda out of the orchestral pendants to the first subject, having
lready redistributed the dialogue as between solo and orchestra.

The shock of E major after C minor is chiefly concentrated in
ne note, G sharp, the major third of E.  This is so near in pitch to
flat that on keyed instruments the same note has to serve for

both. Haydn, in the last and greatest of his pianoforte sonatas, ha
ventured upon this shock in a still more paradoxical form,
between the keys of E flat and E natural (equivalent in this ca
to F flat); he accordingly began his finale with a theme whic
first taps rhythmically at G natural, and, having duly explaine
this as third of E flat, proceeds to show that the next step is A fla

The first two notes of Beethoven's finale are a more immedia
and drastic summary of a similar process. Like Haydn, Beethove
has taken care that the last chord of the slow movement sha
display his Berkeleyan G sharp. Which Dr. Johnson refutes *thus*—

Ex. 6.

This great rondo is an admirable study in temper, worthy o
the wisdom that inspired the tragic style of the other movement
Among the works with which this concerto is always provokin
comparison by reason of its singularly direct influence on lat
composers, three finales are conspicuous—those of Joachim's Hur
garian Concerto, Brahms's First Pianoforte Concerto, and Mendel
sohn's C minor Trio. It is astonishing how closely both Brahm
and Joachim have followed the scheme of this finale, even in suc
details as the structure of the transition passages and the fugu
passage of development after the second episode. The interest i
comparing Mendelssohn's C minor Trio finale is different; it is
warning against giving tragic weight to emotions which in real lif
relieve themselves in a gust of temper. Mendelssohn's first them
is in much the same temper as Beethoven's, and promises a no
less spirited career. His second theme is in an enthusiastic moo
which would be rather shocked by an apparent lack of mora
indignation in Beethoven's energetic second theme.

Ex. 7.

And for the consolatory middle episode and triumphant end of hi
finale Mendelssohn unfortunately bursts into tears and a chorale
Beethoven's way of sounding the depths is more religiousl
consistent with his opening.

Ex. 8.

This comfortable and leisurely tune is followed by a little fugu
on the main theme (Ex. 6), beginning in F minor. The pianofort

ntervenes dramatically and carries us to a remote key which is the
nore impressive in that it happens to be that of the slow movement.
'rom this the steps back to C minor are broad and firm, and the
nticipation of the return to the rondo theme is duly exciting. The
ecapitulation of both main theme and second subject (Ex. 7) is
omplete and regular.

But the coda is utterly unexpected. In the tuttis of the main
heme the oboe had already made a splendid point by appearing
vith the theme in the major, transforming its initial G–A♭ into
3♯–A♮. Now the pianoforte, entering after an ornamental cadenza,
akes up this idea in the following new tempo and rhythm:

Ex. 9.

The rest of this presto is a brilliant series of fresh cadential phrases,
he last of which—

Ex. 10.

s a transformation of Ex. 7.

### CII. PIANOFORTE CONCERTO IN G MAJOR, OP. 58

(Meiningen Programmes, 1902, with alterations.)

1 *Allegro moderato.* 2 *Andante con moto; leading to* 3 RONDO: *Vivace.*

The G major Concerto is a work of a particularly prolific time in
Beethoven's career. Its opus-number places it between the so-
called 'Appassionata' Sonata and the three enormous string
quartets dedicated to Count Rasoumovsky; but Beethoven was
always at work on so many things at once, and so often allowed one
work to wait for years before completing it from sketches, that his
opus-numbers give little clue to the chronology of anything but
publication. In almost any four consecutive years of Beethoven's
life the chronology of his works is inextricable. The first idea for
a finale to this concerto was a graceful theme in semiquavers, which,
a year later, became the principal figure of the prisoners' chorus in
*Fidelio.* The present slow movement of the third Rasoumovsky
Quartet supplanted a wonderful idea in the same key which could
hardly have been developed properly by a string quartet, and which
eventually became the allegretto of the Seventh Symphony. Notte-
bohm's *Beethoveniana* and *Zweite Beethoveniana,* consisting of

copious extracts from Beethoven's sketch-books, will almost impe[l]
one to believe that Beethoven's whole life's work was as connecte[d]
as a single composition. We even find the theme of his last sonat[a]
op. 111, appearing in connexion with early sketches for the Violi[n]
Sonata in A major, op. 30, no. 3.

So much, then, for the chronology of this concerto. Beethove[n]
himself took the pianoforte part in its first public performance (o[n]
December 22nd, 1808); and, we are told by eyewitnesses an[d]
critics, played very impulsively and at a tremendous pace. Thi[s]
seems at first startlingly out of character with the first movemen[t]
but the explanation of Beethoven's 'tremendous pace' is simpl[y]
that, the tempo being allegro moderato, the rapid passages ar[e]
written in triplet semiquavers and demisemiquavers, and are thu[s]
nearly twice as fast as any that had been written before.

All three movements of Beethoven's G major Concerto demonstrate the aesthetic principles of concerto form with extraordinar[y]
subtlety. In the first movement Beethoven lets the pianoforte stat[e]
the first phrase—a quiet cantabile which is immediately taken u[p]
by the orchestra entering softly in a bright, remote key, a wonderful stroke of genius.[1]

Ex. 1.

Here the orchestra (a small one without trumpets and drums[)]
has the next sixty-eight bars to itself, and gives in rapid succession, with beautiful variety of crescendos and *fortes* and *pianos,*
the following themes—

Ex. 2.

A development of No. 1.

leading through a broad crescendo to another quiet theme belong-
ing (as we afterwards learn) to the second subject, and modulating
through a considerable range of keys—

Ex. 3.

[1] Mozart's interesting early Concerto in E flat (K.V. 291) anticipates
Beethoven in allowing the pianoforte to share the first theme with the
orchestra, but only in a jocular fashion with results no more than formal
and witty.

llowed by mysterious rising sequences on (*a*) and other figures

Ex. 4.

(*a*)

ulminating in—

Ex. 5.

&c.

very important theme, which leads to the final figures of the
tornello; viz.—

Ex. 6.

nd a new derivative of Ex. 1—

Ex. 7.

n which the solo enters with a meditative, long-drawn development of figure (*a*) which broadens and quickens into brilliant
unning passages.

Fifteen bars (no less) of this broad expanse lead to the re-
tatement of the material of the opening tutti, with the co-operation
f the solo instrument. The restatement begins with Ex. 2, and
he pianoforte interpolates a series of brilliant new figures while the
rchestra holds the thread with the rhythm ♩ ♪♪♪ | ♩ of (*a*), and
he bassoon and other wood-wind take up the theme in dialogue.

Suddenly the pianoforte becomes contemplative in a dark key—

Ex. 8.

8*va*..........

nd in a few bars of the highest beauty modulates to the dominant,
vhere there is a passage of preparation for the second subject. This
oon appears, beginning, to our surprise, with a new melody of
vhich the opening tutti had not uttered a note.

Ex. 9.

Strings.

This is answered by the pianoforte in a playful variation; and anoth
brilliant solo, in which again the orchestra holds the thread wit
♩ ♫♫ ♩, leads to Ex. 3, beginning in D minor, and soon enrich
with an ornate flow of semiquavers in the pianoforte. This lea
through Ex. 4 (as in the tutti) to Ex. 5, all with the most brillia
pianoforte accompaniment. These pianoforte figures seem, as the
have already done before, to force their way through the structu
till they emerge in a broad open expanse, and we hear the long tri
which classical composers have generally found the most co
venient way of ending the first solo in the exposition of the fir
movement of a concerto. Beethoven, however, does not end wit
the trill; he makes it lead gently to another repetition of Ex. 5 b
the pianoforte, beginning this time *piano* (so as to reveal the inna
tenderness of this majestic theme), but with a crescendo that bring
in the orchestra in triumph with the rest of the ritornello (includin
Exx. 6 and 7) just as in the opening tutti.

Beethoven has now well and truly laid the foundations of h
concerto form and is free to raise his edifice to heights undrean
of in earlier music. As the first essay in this volume shows, th
composer's main difficulties in the classical concerto are co
centrated in the opening tutti and the solo exposition of the fir
movement, the rest of the concerto presenting no special problem
Unless appearances have misled me (the chronology of Beethoven
Opp. 53–60 being so inextricable), the voluminous Triple Concert
Op. 56, is the technical exercise by which Beethoven experimente
with dry material in correcting the errors which he recognized i
his first three concertos. The obvious stroke of genius by whic
the pianoforte opens the G major Concerto and gives the orchestr
occasion to enter in a foreign key is not more wonderful than th
art with which the sequel retains and enhances the procession
character of the classical tutti; avoiding alike the dangerou
symphonic action which in the C minor Concerto threatens t
make the pianoforte an intruder, and the not less dangerou
discursiveness which in the C major and B flat Concertos leaves th
tutti at a loose end with matter almost more improvisatorial that
that of the solo. Contrast those expensive luxuries with th
wonderful modulating single theme (Ex. 3) which quietly takes it
place in the procession and yet covers a wide range of keys, onl
to confirm the home tonic more strongly.

Again, note the complete freedom of the solo exposition i
expanding in brilliant or ruminating passages and in introducin
new matter such as Exx. 8 and 9. Yet the material of the tutti i
quite as exhaustively used as in the C minor Concerto, where th
pianoforte was rigid in its translation of it. Every allusion to it i
creases by reflection the cogency of the original orchestral statement

imagine the solo version of Ex. 3 as it would sound if we had not heard the opening tutti : brilliant ornamentation for the pianoforte, with a melody on an oboe; beautiful in itself, but no contribution to the balance of forces. But the opening tutti has taught us to associate that theme with the orchestra, and its appearance on a single oboe now gives us the feeling that the orchestra is being properly represented by its most pathetic member; so we listen to the ornamental pianoforte part with worthier feelings than admiration of personal display.

The development begins with the pianoforte interrupting the quiet close of the ritornello (Ex. 7) by striking the rhythmic figure ♪♫♪|♩ on the minor third, F natural. Then follows a series of mysterious modulations, with an entirely new figure (x) springing out of (a) as if by accident.

Ex. 10.

Suddenly the pianoforte awakens to an energetic mood, which lasts for a considerable time, while the orchestra quietly works out (a) in combination with the new figure (x). At length we come to an impassioned climax in the extremely distant key of C sharp minor, and another mysterious process begins. Figure (a) is worked out again, from its rhythm ⅂ ♫♪ ♩ in the basses, to the following extraordinary transformation (the original tonic, G major, having been reached in two steps of a simple sequence)—

Ex. 11.

The new figure (y) will be seen to be a free diminution of the two bars of (a) that preceded it. It is now worked out very quietly as a fugue with a running countersubject. Beethoven does not expect us to recognize that we are in the home tonic, but the fact adds much to the mysterious effect of this very unexpected development. A short crescendo with the rhythm of (a) reasserting itself, first in its usual form, and then diminished ( ⅂♫♪♩ ), soon brings us in triumph to the recapitulation of the first subject.

This development is the most complicated passage in all Beethoven's concertos; yet it is perfectly typical of concerto style. Its breadth of sequence and its copious use of episodic matter that has not been heard in the exposition are natural results of the principles we have already seen in operation. The relation between

solo and tutti has made the repetition of material in the expos
tion specially impressive and characteristic, and the recapitulatio
and coda will make it still more so; and therefore the developmer
needs to be more simple and more contrasted than it would b
in a symphony or sonata, apart from the enormous difficulties c
balancing solo against tutti in a development on ordinary line
Accordingly we find that in classical concertos the develoment ma
be based either on the least weighty of the themes of the expositio
or on one that the solo had omitted (a brilliant device of Mozart's
or it may transform the themes almost beyond recognition (a
here), or may have much episodic matter (as here also).

Beethoven's recapitulation here follows the opening tutti muc
more closely than did the first solo; but Ex. 2 is interrupted by
sudden modulation to E flat, where a lofty contemplative passage
corresponding to Ex. 8, leads to the second subject (beginning c
course with Ex. 9) exactly recapitulated in the tonic. Where th
ritornello bursts in, taking up the thread of Ex. 5, we have a paus
on a 6/4 chord, as in all classical concertos; and the whole responsi
bility for the greater part of the coda is thrown upon the solo playe
who is supposed to extemporize the long cadenza that comes at th
point. Here we have the only really conventional element in th
much-maligned art-form; for obviously a bad cadenza is the ver
appendicitis of music; and unfortunately Beethoven himself sub
sequently scribbled some astoundingly bad cadenzas to this mos
ethereal work. Clara Schumann's cadenzas are better, but fever
ishly Schumannesque; and a good musician is justified in doin
his own best. Fortunately Beethoven has a wonderful way c
designing his movement so that a long spell of uninterrupted sol
in a style of development modified by the impulsive manner of a
extemporization, shall seem necessary and effective, whether it b
actually extempore or not.

Beethoven, knowing that some pages of solo will intervene
repeats Ex. 5, the theme he has just written before. Very quietly i
floats upward, and is followed by the final cadence theme Ex.
(thus omitting Ex. 6). As this dies away in the upper ether, we ar
roused by a rapid crescendo, with the rhythm (a) and its diminu
tion (as at the end of the development) surging up till it pervade
the whole orchestra, and the movement ends triumphantly.

If I am not mistaken, it was Liszt who compared the slov
movement of this concerto to Orpheus taming the wild beast
with his music. This is so apt that it is almost free from th
general objection that such comparisons tend at first to substitut
their own vividness for that of the music and then to lose thei
vividness in the necessity for tiresome qualifications of detai
But here the comparison is remarkably spiritual and free fron

oncrete externals. Note, in the first place, that, as in Liszt's own
symphonic poem *Orpheus*, it refers to the taming of wild Nature,
not to the placating of the Furies, though Liszt tells us that he
was inspired by the experience of conducting Gluck's *Orfeo*. But
the spiritual, or, if you prefer popular scientific jargon, psychological depth of the analogy is best shown in the one point of resemblance between this unique movement of Beethoven's and a very
different one, Orpheus's first sustained address to the Furies in
Gluck's opera. The pleadings of Orpheus are met phrase by phrase
with a thunderous *No* from the Furies in unison, until the last *No*
is a chord which shows that they will at length yield. In this
andante the orchestra does not imitate wild beasts or nature, and
the pianoforte does not imitate a lyre or a singer. But the orchestra
(consisting of the strings alone) is entirely in octaves, without a
vestige of harmony, so long as it remains stubborn and rough
in its share of the dialogue with the quiet veiled tones of the
solo. After its first soft pizzicato note it melts into harmony. In
the supreme moment of darkness at the end, the orchestra and solo
join in the same material (the chords in this rhythm ♩ ♪ | ♩ ),
whereas they had hitherto been totally contrasted.

The finale breaks in, pianissimo, with an intensely lively theme
in that prosaic daylight by which Beethoven loves to test the reality
of his sublimest visions. The daylight is the more grey from the
strong emphasis the theme gives to the subdominant chord, almost
producing the impression of C instead of G major.

Ex. 12.

The treatment of rondo form does not differ much in concertos
from its ordinary treatment on a large scale in other works. For
the main body of this movement, it will suffice to summarize its
form, and devote the rest of the analysis to the enormous coda
which (if we take it as beginning after the recapitulation of the
second subject) is exactly five-twelfths of the whole movement, not
counting the cadenza.

The first theme, after a variation by the pianoforte, has a counter-
theme.

Ex. 13.

III                                        G

The orchestra resumes Ex. 12 fortissimo, with trumpets and drum
appearing for the first time in the concerto. A transition theme-

Ex. 14.

leads to a very broad passage in triplet quavers on the dominant
D—taking its own time to bring us at last to the second subject.

This begins with a leisurely and serene melody for the pianofor
in extremely wide three-part harmony, of which the bass is a dee
tonic pedal. It intends to repeat itself.

Ex. 15.

8va...........................................................................................

The self-repetition impatiently breaks off, saying 'and all that
The orchestra unbanely gives a completed counterstatement, wit
intricate polyphony.

Then comes the lightest and simplest possible formula, i
brilliant arpeggios. We begin to think it unaccountably simple
when suddenly we wonder to find ourselves on the dominant of C
The orchestra explains, with these rhythms ♪♪ | ♩ ╷ | ♪╷ ♪╷ |
recalling (a) and (d) of the first theme (Ex. 12); and, after keep
ing us in suspense an enormous time (nearly forty bars) on th
dominant of C, Beethoven brings us back with a long rhythmle
run to our first theme. This and all its accessories are repeate
unaltered, but Ex. 14 is made to lead to E flat. Here we begi
the central episode with a new theme, consisting of nothing bu
energetic arpeggios of tonic and dominant chords. But this
made to alternate with rich developments of the first three figure
(a), (b), and (c). (Note especially the drums as a bass to the wind
with figure (a); and the treatment by the pianoforte of figure (c) i
triplets.)

This leads, through various keys, to the dominant of our tonic C
where a brisk chromatic passage for pianoforte brings us to th
broad expanse of dominant preparation that culminates in th
second subject, which we thus reach without having again returne
to the first. The recapitulation is exact until the end of the humo
ous arpeggio-theme, which this time lands us on a chord of E fla
where, as before the first return of the main theme, we seem t
be dwelling a long time while the orchestra hints ♪♪ | ♩. Bu
it gradually dawns on us that we are listening to the whole firs
theme in B flat on the violas.

Ex. 16. (Compare Ex. 12.)

The wood-wind become witty over figure (d); and suddenly the [fu]ll orchestra enters in a rage on a strange chord, working round to [th]e dominant of C, our old position for a return. The piano[fo]rte turns figure (b) into a slow arpeggio on that chord, taking, as [be]fore, an unconscionable time in getting back to our first theme in [its] original key. This time we have it in a new variation, and the [or]chestra comes blustering in with yet another, leading to the [tra]nsition theme (Ex. 14). Now the real business of the enormous [co]da begins. Figures (a) and (d) seem to be settling down in a [lei]surely tonic-and-dominant stride, when the dominant chord [se]ems to overstay its time and slowly changes to the vastly [di]stant key of F sharp major. Here we have the placid second sub[je]ct, Ex. 15, which calmly turns round to C major, and thence back [to] G, where it is gradually taken up by the whole orchestra with [a] crescendo, leading to a 6/4 pause for a cadenza. The cadenza [(w]hich Beethoven says must be short) is followed by more witticisms [in] figure (d) (augmented) in the horn; and then we settle down [co]mfortably to another variation (like Ex. 16) of the first theme, [wh]ich I quote in its still more delightful form as repeated in [a] remarkably close and persistent canon. It does not defeat its [ow]n by pedantic exactness.

Ex. 17.

Clarinets.

Brilliant semiquavers in right hand.

Pianoforte
(left hand).

[T]he music dies away in that upper ether which it has never left; [bu]t all the while we hear more witticisms on figure (d), which sud[de]nly quickens into presto quavers, with a crescendo. On the top of [th]is the full orchestra storms in with the principal theme, more

lively than ever in this quicker tempo. Of course, when it reach
figure (*d*), the irrepressible wood-wind and pianoforte have a lit
more to say before ending this audacious masterpiece of gigan
and inexhaustibly varied proportions with that astronomical pur
tuality which gives solemnity to Beethoven's utmost exuberance
high spirits.

### CIII. PIANOFORTE CONCERTO IN E FLAT, OP. 73

1 *Allegro*. 2 *Adagio un poco mosso, leading to* 3 RONDO: *Allegro*.

From the history of the 'Eroica' we know how Beethoven wou
have appreciated the vulgar title by which this concerto is known
the British Isles. So we will say no more about that, but atte
to the music.

The fifth concerto has a majestic introduction, in which the k
of E flat is asserted by the orchestra and pianoforte in a rhapsoc
outburst. This introduction reappears once at the beginning of t
recapitulation, and plays no further part in the narrative. As
the first movements of all classical concertos, including Brahms
the main threads of the story are set forth very broadly, but w
explicit avoidance of anything like development or combination,
the opening tutti, which is best called by its primitive title
ritornello. In this concerto the ritornello is specially formal a
voluminous; but we must be content with two quotations, thou
there are at least five distinct themes, and any number of importa
derivatives. Most of the derivatives come from the groups he
marked (*a*) and (*b*).

Ex. 1.

Ex. 2.

Obviously enough, Ex. 1 is the beginning of the 'first subjec
and it so happens that Ex. 2, which sounds exactly as if it were goi
to become the principal theme in the 'second subject', does r
deceive that expectation, as many an equally important theme k

:eived it elsewhere in Mozart, Beethoven, and Brahms. In fact
: whole procession of contrasted themes which this great tutti
·iews, in severe monotony of key, gives an unusually faithful
nmary of what the pianoforte is going to discuss. The severe
·notony of key provides a firm basis for the marvellous richness
the distant keys of B minor and B major (*alias* C flat), in which
: pianoforte is hereafter to present two variations of Ex. 2 before
: orchestra turns it into a rousing march in the orthodox key of
lat. The general plan of the whole movement is as follows:

I. Introduction.

II. Opening tutti or ritornello, containing all the themes.

III. First solo, entering quietly with a chromatic scale, and
·ning the whole opening ritornello into a vast exposition of a 'first'
·d 'second' subject: with such devices as the modulations just
·ntioned.

IV. Close of the exposition by resumption of last stages of the
·ornello, in the key of the 'second subject'. By a device first intro-
·ced by Beethoven in his Violin Concerto, the end of the ritornello
·ow diverted into a remote new key. Here in due course the piano-
·te again enters with its quiet chromatic scale. (No concerto that
·asts a modern or Mendelssohnian 'emancipation from the con-
·ntional classical ritornello' can achieve such impressive entries
·the solo part.)

V. Development, dealing entirely with Ex. 1. The pianoforte
·rt is, for all its beautiful colouring, at first no more than an
·companiment to the whispered dialogue in which the orchestra
·scusses Ex. 1, chiefly from the point of view of the turn which I
·ve marked with the letter (*a*). By degrees, the rhythmic figure
·arked (*b*) becomes more insistent, till it arouses the full orchestra,
·d sets the pianoforte off into a furious passage of octaves, de-
·nding in dialogue with the strings, while a solitary bassoon keeps
·e rhythm (*b*) mysteriously threading its way in the bass. I have
·lled these octaves 'furious', but must take the opportunity of
·inting out that the modern pianistic martellato effect is utterly
·eless here. Not only could Beethoven's pianoforte not produce
· but no first-rate composer has ever wished for anything remotely
·e it; and I for my part do not believe that Liszt himself, who
·culcated it, ever really did it as it is understood nowadays. He
·ay have *looked* as if he were committing all manner of awe-inspiring
·anistic crimes, but he had acquired a perfect touch at too early an
·e for any superb gestures to damage it. (The best evidence is
·at he sat immobile as a rock, but that his long arms caused him
· sit on a high stool and make his chords seem to fall from a great
·ight.) At all events, what Beethoven wants here is the fury of a
·il-storm; and you can see daylight through hail-storms, and hear

the bassoon through the right sort of octaves in this passage. (
the other hand there is no fury in the fall of a ton of coals.

The curtain of hail is lifted away into blue sky, and we find ot
selves in the very key in which the development started. The ca
closing theme of the ritornello reappears; and in the bass the tu
(*a*) of Ex. 1 moves in slow steps up through distant keys to t
threshold of home; and the quiet excitement becomes breathl
until at last a crescendo leads to—

VI. The introduction, followed by the recapitulation of II. T
modulations at the 'second subject' become still more wond
ful, the key being now one of those 'contradictory keys' (C sha
minor and D flat) of which such subtle dramatic use is made at
similar point in the Eroica Symphony.

VII. The Coda. The saddest chapter in the story of the concer
is the classical custom of leaving all but the orchestral win
up of the coda blank, and trusting to a display of the solo-playe
powers of improvization to fill up the blank with a cadenza. He
Beethoven has, for the first time, forbidden extemporization, a
written out in full a coda that begins like a cadenza, but so
settles down to what turns out to be a final glorified recapitu
tion of the whole ritornello, from the entry of Ex. 2 onwar
Gradually the orchestra joins in, beginning with the horns, un
the full band is in dialogue with the pianoforte. At last we he
a chromatic scale. It was of this passage that Schumann said th
'Beethoven's chromatic scales are not like other people's'. I
wonder! This quiet scale and the following trills have now bor
the Atlas burden of the whole mighty structure for the third time
first, at the outset of the first solo; then at the outset of the develo
ment; and now, leading unswervingly to the glorious close.

The slow movement needs no quotation. It is in B major, tl
first remote modulation in the first movement, and it has tv
themes—the serene, devout melody of the muted violins (it is a mi
print in the band-parts if the lower strings are muted); and tl
meditative theme with which the pianoforte enters and moves in
a rather remote key on the shaded side (D major) of the harmon
Here the pianoforte seems to be settling down in a cadence with
trill, but the trill rises and rises until it breaks over into the ton
key again. Thus the pianoforte comes to deliver its ornament
version of the main theme. As its close fades into a cloud of wa
light, three wind instruments, led by the flute, give out the who
theme again, the pianoforte accompanying with the wavy figu
which the admiration of Berlioz has made familiar to all studen
of orchestration. At last the waves die down, and nothing is le
but a cold grey octave. This sinks a semitone, and becom
glowing. As it continues, the pianoforte whispers a strange ne

heme with a mysterious rhythm and, finding itself already in flat, after a moment's hovering, plunges into the finale.

Ex. 3.

No further quotations are necessary for the enjoyment of this most spacious and triumphant of concerto rondos. Lovers of Schumann's *Carnaval* will easily recognize in the second part of Beethoven's main theme a phrase that enlisted in Schumann's army of Davidites marching against the Philistines. Equally obvious is the great part played by the rhythmic figure ♩♪♩ ♪♩ from its first formal appearance as part of the orchestral group of themes to its final mysterious domination in the person of the drum.

What gives this rondo its chief impressiveness is the immense breadth of its middle episode, in which the main theme has three separate escapades, firstly fortissimo in C major (a bright key in this connexion), secondly piano in A flat (a sober key), and thirdly pianissimo (breaking into forte) in E major, a remote key. The subsequent exciting return, where the violins remind us of what the pianoforte said at the end of the slow movement, will not escape notice. The drum passage at the end reveals the sublime depths from which all these outbursts of hilarity spring.

## CIV. VIOLIN CONCERTO IN D MAJOR, OP. 61

1 *Allegro ma non troppo*. 2 *Larghetto, leading to* 3 RONDO.

The autograph of Beethoven's Violin Concerto is a lesson in the correct attitude of a composer towards a player. It was written for a virtuoso of the name of Clement, and is inscribed to him with a vile pun on his 'clemency' towards the poor composer. The score assigns four staves to the violin solo, in order to leave room for alterations; and in many places all the four staves have been filled. The violinist whose criticism Beethoven took so much pains to meet produced (or, as he perhaps called it, 'created') the concerto under conditions of his own making that were not considered unusual in those days. The first movement was played in the first part of the programme, the slow movement and the finale in the second part. Among the items which took place between these

divisions was a sonata of Clement's own composing, to be playe
on one string with the violin upside down. Clement survived th
performance for many years, and as an old man was seen by
young violinist of very different calibre, who became perhaps a
inseparably identified with the Beethoven concerto as any playe
can be identified with a great work. Joachim's cadenzas earn th
right to be treated as integral parts of the composition, instea
of as necessary evils. I heard them from him only in an abbre
viated form; but he included the full version in one of his las
publications, the volume of concertos in his Violin School; and i
is interesting to note that in this form the cadenza to the first move
ment still contains a certain famous chromatic scale in octave
which made a tremendous impression when he played the concert
in London as a boy of twelve, though the cadenza as a whole i
very much more important than the already extraordinarily rip
achievement of his boyhood. I believe that in its full form it date
from the same period as his Hungarian Concerto, where, by th
way, the same chromatic scale occurs.

Beethoven's Violin Concerto is gigantic, one of the most spaciou
concertos ever written, but so quiet that when it was a novelty mos
people complained quite as much of its insignificance as of it
length. All its most famous strokes of genius are not only mys
teriously quiet, but mysterious in radiantly happy surroundings
The whole gigantic scheme is serene. The only two definitely
pathetic passages, the G minor episode in the development of the
first movement, and the G minor episode in the finale, are (in spite
of the immense solemnity of the horns and the trumpets in the
first instance) in a childlike vein, and show how Beethoven in hi
ripest middle period had far more command of Mozart's specia
resources than he possessed in those of his early works which
imitate Mozart. One might be inclined to say off-hand that the
most mysterious stroke of genius in the whole work is the famous
opening with five strokes of the drum which introduces the pecu
liarly radiant first subject on the wood-wind; but in truth there is
still more mystery in the astounding D sharp which follows the
second strain, for which reason I quote the whole first paragraph.

Ex. I.

In Beethoven's first sketches he thought of the D sharp as E flat, a distinction which, unnoticed on tempered instruments, is really important here. E flat means something harmonically clearer, but the point about the D sharp is that it indeed is D sharp, though Beethoven leaves it unharmonized and carefully avoids letting it move in the direction which would explain it away. We shall see the explanation in one of the later phrases. The remaining themes I quote as they occur in the opening tutti. First there is the important scale theme—

Ex. 2.

which the solo violin is eventually to work out as a transition theme. The orchestra, however, does not as yet think of it in that light, but makes it lead quietly to an unexpected crash in a foreign key.

Ex. 3.

This energetic outburst leads more or less in the manner of a symphonic transition to the second subject, but, as is usual in classical concertos, leads to it in the tonic, so that there has been no radical change of key. The second subject, given in the characteristically radiant colouring Beethoven extracts from the wood-wind throughout this work, is, as given by the orchestra, accompanied by that all-pervading rhythmic figure which the drums announced at the outset.

Ex. 4.

Broad as this melody is, it becomes still broader as the strings take
it up softly with a flowing triplet accompaniment in the minor.
This leads eventually to a smiling phrase in the major in which the
mysterious D sharp of Ex. 1 is now explained away.

Ex. 5.

Out of this arises a crescendo which brings the full orchestra to the
last and in some ways the grandest of this great procession of
themes.

Ex. 6.

Suddenly the orchestra dies away in the basses, as if warned of
the advent of its master, and the solo violin arises in one of the
most spacious introductory passages to be found in any concerto.
This entry is quite unforgettable; which is well, because it recurs
in a very subtly dramatic way. The solo violin, with the aid of the
orchestra, now proceeds to work out the whole procession of
themes *seriatim*. Ex. 2 becomes a symphonic passage of transition, leading with great breadth to the dominant of A major, and
there preparing for the second subject. (Ex. 3 is held over for
another purpose.) The second subject (Ex. 4) enters in the clarinets,
while the violin trills on the dominant until it is ready to take up
its second phrase. One of the most significant subtleties in the
structure of the whole work is that, under the guidance of the solo
violin, the second subject is no longer accompanied by the rhythmic
figure of the drums.

Mr. Cecil Forsyth, in his book *Orchestration*, remarking on the
difference between the tone-colour of a number of orchestral violins
in unison and that of a solo violin, says very truly that

in a violin concerto it undoubtedly gives the soloist a somewhat greater
chance of 'standing out' from the string ensemble, though, on occasion
the repetition of a simple solo phrase by the orchestral violins has had an
almost comic effect, as if they were saying 'this is how it ought really
to sound'.

The Beethoven concerto is a sublime object-lesson on this point,
inasmuch as that contingency never happens. Here, for instance,
the solo violin takes up the theme from the clarinets, and gives it
in a region to which the orchestral violins do not happen to mount.
(In the recapitulation Beethoven gives it an extreme height and

brings it down to normal regions with an impressive swoop
(essentially the gesture of a solo player.) Now comes the expanded
counterstatement in the minor. This is, indeed, entrusted to the
orchestral violins, and a wonderful background they make with their
melody to the ornamental figures of the solo violin, which does not
take up the melody until we reach Ex. 5, where it has the A sharps
(as they have now become) and some ornamentations of its own.
After this has been expanded to a brilliant conclusion, the orchestral
strings have Ex. 6 very quietly; and here again the solo violin,
instead of competing with them in sustained melody, soars aloft in
vast ramifications of ornament, while the great melody which was
originally so short and terse expands in rising sequences. A climax
is reached, and the solo violin broadens out on the basis of harmonies forming a cadence, which appears to be ending in the
conventional shake that in practically every one of Mozart's
concertos ushers in the re-entry of the orchestra. But below this
shake the rhythmic drum figure appears with the most mysterious
modulations that have yet occurred.

Ex. 7.

Above this profound harmonic cloud the shake rises, and eventually
gathers itself into a rush downwards and upwards over a long
penultimate chord, leading to the re-entry of the orchestra. And
now the orchestra bursts in with the crashing theme (Ex. 3)
which, it will be remembered, began in a foreign key, and accordingly now begins in F. With a sublimity which certain lewd
fellows of the baser sort would reduce by cuts, the orchestra
calmly proceeds with the whole of the original tutti from this
point onwards. Hence we have once more the whole second
subject, this time with its drum-taps in the violins, followed by its
expanded counterstatement in the minor. As if to emphasize the
spaciousness of all this repetition, this counterstatement is given
fortissimo, and continues unabridged through the appearance of
Example 5, still fortissimo. Here, however, there is a sudden twist
in the harmony which produces one of those dramatic consequences
that are true only when the ground has been thus thoroughly

prepared. The rest of the tutti finds itself diverted into the key of C major, a key utterly paradoxical in relation to the D major of the concerto. Accordingly in C major the last theme (Ex. 6) enters, still fortissimo, until, as at the end of the opening tutti, there is a sudden hush; and in this paradoxical key of C major the solo violin mounts upwards with its immense introductory passage. Just when it ought to be closing into the first theme, it pauses on a solitary expectant note. A vast distance below it the basses enter, and suddenly we are in B minor beginning a development of the first subject. The fourth bar of the theme is passed through several keys, always accompanied by the drum figure, until at last both it and the drum figure diminish to quavers, bringing us to a very deliberate settling down in G minor. And here, accompanied by no theme except the drum figure (given in succession by the horns and the bassoons, and lastly by the trumpets and drums), the violin has an entirely new cantabile in a vein of the tenderest pathos. With the entry of the trumpets and drums the key of D minor is reached, and the phrases of the violin become shorter and more and more wistful, while the trumpets and drums turn their rhythmic figure into a solemn steady tread. At last even this ceases; and there is nothing but a holding-note of breathless anticipation as the solo violin mounts upwards in chromatic arpeggios, until the rhythmic figure reasserts itself in different parts of the orchestra, which suddenly bursts out in full and gives the whole first sentence in the tonic, fortissimo. It continues triumphantly with the transition theme (Ex. 2), which the violin takes up and now carries through some new harmonic regions in such a way as finally to settle down upon its preparations for the second subject. From this point the recapitulation is quite regular, until the re-entry of the orchestra with its crashing theme in a foreign key (Ex. 3). This last orchestral tutti leads to the cadenza. Many a clever cadenza occupying the place of a symphonic coda has ruined the work into which its virtuoso perpetrator had introduced it; but Joachim's cadenzas are the work of a classical composer, and they combine the extempore quality, which the cadenza ought to have *ex hypothesi*, with the structural features which its position in a symphonic design demands. Joachim begins his cadenza with the rhythmic drum figure; continues with the transition theme (Ex. 3), and contrives to make a very effective development of the second subject in the triplet rhythm of the accompaniment, which the solo violin had given to it while the orchestra was playing it in the minor. This treatment secures it against any effect of forestalling its quiet appearance after the cadenza, on the third and fourth strings of the instrument when the orchestra re-enters. The sublime calm of the first movement of the concerto reaches its serenest height when the last theme (Ex. 6) is given out quietly by the bassoon, and is answered in its highest regions by the solo violin, bringing the gigantic movement to an end in five bars of a terse crescendo.

In the slow movement we have one of the three cases of sublime inaction achieved by Beethoven, and by no one else except in certain lyrics and masterpieces of choral music. The other two cases are the slow movements of the Sonata Appassionata and the Trio in B flat, op. 97. The form is that of a theme with variations; and in the present instance the theme, in spite of the rich modulations between its third and sixth bars, is practically a single strain, with a characteristic expansion produced by echoing its last two bars.

Ex. 8.

There are other differences between this movement and the two other examples I have mentioned; but the point in all three cases is that a strict set of variations, confined to a melody with none but its own local modulations, and with no change from major to minor and no change of time, constitutes a scheme in which there is no action; or, at all events, which is in so dreamlike a state of repose that it is impossible to bring the movement to any conclusion except that of a dramatic interruption. Wit or humour might explain it away, but the more natural style of such inaction is sublime, and only in songs or choral music can solemn things of this kind be brought to a natural end. Beethoven in his later instrumental works, notably the last quartets, was able to design complete slow movements in this mood by means of certain devices, which are equivalent to just enough action to allow the design to complete itself. In other words, he found that a set of variations on a slow and solemn theme could, without radically or dramatically changing its rhythm, develop the kind of energy that would enable him to construct a coda. At present this was not his intention, and the whole point of this slow movement is that it cannot end. The theme, with its touching broken rhythms and its rich local modulations, is given out by the muted strings. Then the solo violin enters with a dreamlike accompaniment to the theme in the wind instruments. This constitutes a complete variation. In a second variation the solo violin continues the accompaniment with an increasingly florid movement, while the theme is heard in a lower octave. Then the full orchestra (as reduced and muted throughout the slow

movement) restates the theme very simply but with the fulles
possible tone and harmony. This constitutes the third variation
And now occurs something unique in the history of musical form
The violin re-enters on the last chord with some dreamy arab-
esques, and without the slightest change of key settles down to ar
entire new melody, a single broad phrase beginning as follows—

Ex. 9.

which slowly comes to the final trill of a long-drawn cadence. This
trill behaves like all the cadential trills in this concerto; that is
to say, instead of ending conventionally, it mounts aloft and leaves
us awhile in doubt about what is going to happen. And what
does happen is true to the nature of dreams, for the main theme re-
enters, and we listen in peace to a fourth variation as if nothing had
interrupted the normal course of the form. Yet the interruption is
not without its results; for with the last bar of this variation another
and still calmer new theme appears, connected with the main theme
only by the rhythmic figure in the horns.

Ex. 10.

This new theme leads back to the other one (Ex. 9) with still
more serene colouring. Then again Ex. 10 sets the rhythm
swinging in its own impressively final way, until at last, as the
violin slowly mounts aloft, fragments of the main theme (Ex. 8)
are heard in the muted horns and strings, while the violin in
extreme heights dreams of the figure of the first variation. Nothing
can be really final in a movement so ethereal and so static as this
larghetto has been from the outset: there is only one way to prove
that the vision is true, and that is to awaken in the light of common
day and enjoy that light with the utmost vigour and zest. Accordingly the orchestra breaks in with a purposely conventional modulation to the dominant of D. The violin extemporizes a cadenza and
plunges into a finale, beginning with one of those drastic rondo
themes with which Beethoven loves to shock the superior person
(or would if he had time to think of him).

Ex. 11.

With all its light-heartedness and comparative simplicity of form,
the finale is the truthful outcome of its sublime antecedents. To

mplain that it is not the finest movement in the concerto is
make the mistake exposed a considerable time ago by Plato,
hen he derided the argument that 'since purple is the most
autiful colour, and the eyes the most beautiful feature, therefore
every statue the eyes ought to be painted purple'. In no art-form
it so constantly a mistake to expect the last part to be the 'finest'
in the concerto form. To find the *right* finale to a scheme so
btle and delicate as that of a classical concerto is of itself a
owning stroke of genius. And there is no finale which more boldly
d accurately gives the range, so to speak, of the whole, than this
ost naïvely humorous of rondos. Besides its first theme, we
ust quote the transition theme with the pendulous introductory
tes from which witticisms are to arise on its later occurrences
g. the only two pizzicato notes for the solo violin in the whole
ncerto)—

Ex. 12.

e main theme of the first episode or second subject in dialogue
tween the violin and the orchestra—

Ex. 13.

d the pathetic childlike second episode with its fully formed
elody in two parts, each of which is repeated by the bassoon—

Ex. 14.

s in many of Beethoven's finales, the main form of the move-
ent is carried through with a certain economy of development,
order to throw into relief the full proportions of his coda,
hich in some cases is as long as the whole of the rest of the
ovement. In the present case the main form, though simple,
kes up a good deal of room; but the coda, even if we did not
low for the cadenza which Beethoven has left to the player to
xtemporize, is considerably larger than any other section of the
ovement. It begins by working the most surprising of all the
iracles Beethoven produces from the cadential trill, which in this
ase actually modulates to A flat, the most remote of all possible
eys from D. Naturally it is only through a very wide and remark-

able sequence of harmonies that the figures of the first ther
can work their way back to the tonic. This done, there is
delightful dialogue on the first theme between the oboe and t
violin, and a glorious final climax, in which the violin shows
command of the whole orchestra by being able to silence the full
and most irrepressible outbursts again and again with its lig
arpeggios and scales.

## CV. TRIPLE CONCERTO FOR PIANOFORTE, VIOLIN, AND VIOLONCELLO, OP. 56

1 *Allegro.* 2 *Largo, leading to* 3 RONDO: *alla Polacca.*

Once or twice in the middle of Beethoven's career we meet wi
what is usually described as a reversion to an earlier style. Th
description generally means that certain works make a less powerf
and less definite impression on us than others. A close study a
a sympathetic hearing of such works is a valuable experience n
obtainable from greater things. Without the Triple Concerto Bee
hoven could not have achieved the Pianoforte Concertos in G a
E flat, nor the Violin Concerto. It is in some sense a study f
these works; and if it were not by Beethoven, but by sor
mysterious composer who had written nothing else and who ha
the romantic good fortune to die before it came to performanc
the very people who most blame Beethoven for writing below h
full powers would be the first to acclaim it as the work of a st
greater composer. Let us take it on its own terms, and see wh
it can tell us.

None of Beethoven's three previous concertos had satisfied hi
as to the treatment of the opening orchestral ritornello. In t
first two he had allowed the orchestra to develop themes a
sequences in a rather discursive way; in the third (in C minor)
had frankly begun like the exposition of a symphony, and ha
allowed the orchestra to change its mind abruptly just after th
impression had been irrevocably conveyed. He is now going
solve the real problem of stating the vast procession of themes
the orchestra in such a way as to prevent any group from seemi
to mark a separate development of dramatic action. If the pr
cession can thus be kept, so to speak, on one plane, then the so
instrument or instruments can produce the grandest dramatic effec
by spacing all this material out and adding their own material
as to build up a gigantic sonata form, with a second group in
suitable foreign key. But the opening tutti, in maintaining its pr
cessional movement, must also have its own dramatic characte
and must arouse in more than a negative way some expectatio

at the orchestral crowd is going to be addressed and dominated
~y an individual.

The true solution of an art problem is often first achieved on
~e largest possible scale.  Beethoven thoroughly enjoyed spacing
~t this first solution of his mature form of concerto on the huge
~ale required by three solo instruments, of which the pianoforte
~ill generally demand its separate statement of each theme, and the
~olin and 'cello (as a pair) their own statement.  The dimensions of
~arly everything except the opening tutti in this work are thus at
~ast twice those of any normal concerto, even on Beethoven's scale.
~oreover, he is so profoundly interested in the elements of trio-
~riting against an orchestral background, that his pianoforte part
~ very light, and his violoncello has, in virtue of its opportunities
~d position, quite the lion's share of the ensemble.  Lastly, the
~aterial both of ornaments and themes is severely simple.  Players
~d conductors who are not satisfied with art for art's sake, put
~ this more shortly and say that the work is dull.  Beethoven
~nnot be thus lightly dismissed, even in a work which is a
~epping-stone to greater things.  Sometimes, as in the second
~bject of the finale, its themes descend to dryness.  Throughout
~is extraordinarily severe; and it demands from performers and
~steners the fullest recognition of the grand manner in every detail.
The statement of the opening theme pianissimo in the basses—

Ex. 1.

one of those mysterious simplicities peculiar to great works.  If the
~mposer were Cherubini, every history of music would refer to it as
~och-making; and indeed the continuation is in its severe formality
~t unlike what Cherubini might have made it.  The ensuing cre-
~endo is in Beethoven's grand style, but not beyond lesser powers
~ invention.  I quote its climax for reasons which will appear later.

Ex. 2

Suddenly the unapproachable Beethoven shows himself ve
quietly in the calm entry of what is afterwards to become t
second subject.

Ex. 3.

Formal as this theme appears, it gives us that Greek combinatio
of simplicity and subtlety which is the highest quality in art.
appears here in G major, but under circumstances which make
impossible for the ear to take that key seriously. We simply acce
it as the dominant of C, and are not surprised when the them
continues in that key. A beautiful purple patch—

Ex. 4.

asserts for a moment a note of romantic solemnity, but leads
another tonic-and-dominant tributary theme in the same no
chalant marching rhythm as Ex. 3.

Ex. 5.

Then there is a formal and emphatic process of 'presenting arm
in G major, which again cannot possibly be taken as an establish
key. There is something mysterious in the way in which th
passage lets fall an unharmonized cadence figure; but it seems qui
natural that, this being so, the cadence figure should go a ste
farther and end emphatically in C.

Ex. 6.

Evidently we are waiting for something or somebody.
    The violoncello enters quietly with Ex. 1 as the main theme; t
violin answers it in the dominant; and the two move back to t
tonic with great breadth, gracefully ushering in the pianofort
which, with its third statement, rounds off the theme in tr
dialogue with proportionate brilliance and climax. The orchest
then surprises us by bursting in with a new military march.

Ex. 7.

The solo trio takes this up calmly, and proceeds to shed an unexpected light upon the whole past and future of the movement by modulating towards a key of which no hint has been given, the key of A, the submediant. The preparations for this are laid out on a huge scale; and we have the full power of Beethoven revealed in the radiant effect of the entry of Ex. 3 as second subject in A major. The violoncello and the violin have divided its two phrases between them; and the orchestra begins vigorously with a counter-statement, which, however, the solo trio instantly catches up as a variation, carrying it through the purple patch shown in Ex. 4. The variation now develops on a large scale, and comes to a deliberate close in A minor. Or rather, just as it is going to do so, the violin and the 'cello rush in with an energetic new theme.

Ex. 8.

f marcato.

The first four bars of this they turn into an expanded variation, and then they join the pianoforte in a vigorous counterstatement, presenting it in yet another variation, and expanding and delaying the close in the grandest style. Indeed, the close is interrupted by a sudden *piano*, and the approach and building up of the characteristic trill is an intense pianissimo unsurpassed even by the closely similar passages in the Violin Concerto. The orchestra bursts in with the new transition theme (Ex. 7), in the unexpected key of F major. From this it passes back to A minor, in which key it concludes matters with the passage of 'presenting arms' at the end of the opening tutti. And now is revealed the mystery of the unharmonized cadence which this otherwise formal passage let fall (Ex. 6). That cadence is made once more to swing round to A major, while the violoncello embroiders a beautiful cantabile upon it and passes straight on to an immense restatement of the opening theme in A major. The solo trio works this out at complete leisure as at the outset, as if there were no such things as modulating developments to trouble about. But when at last the trio chooses, it has no difficulty in starting the development with a sudden plunge into B flat. Indeed the trio seems rather to have been storing energy for this very purpose, and pursues a simple and direct course of dialogue in staccato triplets, while the wood-wind accompany with the quaver figure of Ex. 1. Soon the dominant of C is reached; the violoncello and the violin, joined in due course by the

pianoforte, call for the recapitulation in an expressive cantabile
followed by provocative references to Ex. 1 in a diminuendo that
reaches an exciting pianissimo, until suddenly the anticipatory
scales gather up strength and bring back the orchestra with the
first theme in full harmony and full scoring.

In the recapitulation Beethoven shows an appreciation of a point
established by Mozart, in that he follows this time the course of the
original tutti, breaking the fortissimo so that the solo trio can
participate in Ex. 2, which is now so developed as to lead to the
solo transition material on the dominant of C. This brings the
second subject with all its solo accessories into C major; and fresh
light is shed upon the vigorous new solo theme, Ex. 8, by the fact
that after the first four bars it is continued throughout in the major.
In due course the orchestra bursts out again with Ex. 7 in the key of
A flat. This is so worked as to lead easily back to C; and we are
now surprised by a huge symphonic coda in which the solo trio
calmly takes up a phrase which has not been heard since the
opening tutti (Ex. 5), and follows it up by making something very
brilliant and full of colour out of the passage of 'presenting arms'
(Ex. 6). This broadens out and makes, for the last time, one of
Beethoven's characteristic pianissimo climaxes, which settles down
to a beautiful cantabile for the solo trio, while the orchestra has
fragments of the main theme in the bass. Then the orchestra
wakes up (*più allegro*) pulling the figure of that theme into a livelier
form; and so the huge movement comes to a brilliant end.

It is doubtful whether a large architectural design can be combined with a severe study in pure colour, if the themes are such as
to attract attention to themselves. Beethoven's Triple Concerto
is rather like Mozart's writings for wind-band, in which Mozart
actually goes the length of avoiding any theme which is not
purely a formula. In no case of this type will any sensible person
suppose that the composer's invention is at fault. It may be significant that the great composer does not often restrict himself to
problems of the kind. He leaves it to pedagogues like Reicha to
turn out by the hundred perfect solutions of such a problem, for
example, as that of writing for five wind instruments that by no
human possibility can blend. But when a composer of Beethoven's
or Mozart's calibre does give us solutions to an extraordinary art-
problem, it is well to listen with some idea of the points at issue.

The indiscretion of Beethoven's Triple Concerto consists in combining a problem that makes for dryness of matter with a problem
that makes for exceptional length.

The slow movement foreshadows that of the E flat Concerto in
the dark and solemn tone colour of its opening melody with the
muted violins.

Ex. 9.

he melody is severely reserved; though here, as elsewhere in
he by-ways of Beethoven's art, it would have become famous for
s warmth and breadth if it had been ascribed to Cherubini.
After the fourth bar the violoncello lifts the whole continuation
o a higher octave. As the melody comes to its close the piano-
orte enters with a florid accompaniment, and the whole is restated,
he first four bars being given by the wood-wind, and the rest
ontinued by the violin and violoncello in the heights. The result-
ng impression is that of a very large opening indeed; and this
npression is strengthened by the broadly dramatic sequel which
wings slowly round to the dominant of C, whereupon the solo trio
roceeds to make preparations in an intense pianissimo. What it is
reparing for turns out to be not a central episode but the finale.

The style of the Polonaise was not uncommon for rondos and
nales in Beethoven's time (an example may be found in the slow
novement of one of Mozart's pianoforte sonatas); but Beethoven
as left us only three polonaises, one in the middle of the Serenade
io, op. 8, one a solitary pianoforte piece, op. 89, dedicated to the
'sarina, and the finale of this concerto. None of these shows any
f the formidable temper of Chopin's Polonaises; nor is it over-
ressed or in any other way similar to the polonaises of Spohr
nd Weber, who, when they write a *polacca brillante*—which is the
nly kind they ever do write—are inclined to make a very smart-
ociety person of it indeed. Otherwise all three of Beethoven's
olonaises are eminently aristocratic and charmingly feminine.
he genius and romance of the main theme lie in its exquisite
nodulation to E major and back again, for which reason I quote
n bars.

Ex. 10.

Violoncello.

Violin.

here is a crowd of orchestral and transitional accessories which
ill turn up at the end of the movement in the coda. They and
ne very formal second subject do not require quotation; but the
stener should look out for the characteristic way in which the
econd subject lands on its subdominant and thereon seems to

evaporate, until the chord flutters down among the three sol‹
players as a tonic chord and so leads back to the first theme. Th‹
second episode fills the middle of the movement with two contrasted
themes which no one but Beethoven could have written. Agains‹
the athletic energy of the first—

Ex. 11.

we have a note of reproachful pathos in the second.

Ex. 12.

*espressivo.*

This leads to a very dramatic passage of preparation on the domi‹
nant of C; and when the placid main theme returns it is accom‹
panied by one of the most Beethovenish of thunderous trills in th‹
pianoforte. A full recapitulation of the first episode ensues, whic‹
in due course evaporates on the subdominant chord. This chord
the solo trio now turns into something rather more mysterious
which instead of leading to the first theme, delights us by driftin‹
into Ex. 12. This leads melodiously back to the dominant of C, bu‹
instead of a thunderous trill we have a more matter-of-fact pause o‹
anticipation. Then the first theme astonishes us by trotting awa‹
at a brisk pace in duple time—

Ex. 13.
Solo variation.

a version which, after due statement and following up, the orchestr‹
transforms into the following—

Ex. 14.
Orchestral variation.

The orchestra stops abruptly on a 6/4 chord; whereupon the sol‹
trio executes a written-out cadenza accompanied with occasiona‹
chords on the orchestra, and suddenly dropping into a pianissimo a‹
its climax. The final trill swells out and fades away; and then th‹
full beauty of Beethoven's design is revealed in the fact that instea‹
of ending brilliantly in this double-quick tempo, the polonais‹

heme returns in its original rhythm, broken up into dialogue for
he solo trio, punctuated by acclaiming chords from the orchestra,
nd finally settling down in calm triumph to the unquoted accessory
hemes before the transition. These rise to an end the brilliance of
rhich lies in its formal and ceremonial fitness.


# CHOPIN

### CVI.  PIANOFORTE CONCERTO IN F MINOR, OP. 21

1 *Maestoso.* 2 *Larghetto.* 3 *Allegro vivace.*

Chopin's F minor Concerto, op. 21, is really earlier than that in
C minor, which is numbered op. 11. Both works belong to the
eriod of his triumphs as the young Polish pianoforte virtuoso
whose opus 2 (Variations for pianoforte with orchestra) was greeted
y Schumann with the expression, 'Hats off, gentlemen; a genius!'
t was necessary for Chopin to compose works with orchestral
ccompaniment in order to assert his position as a composer; other-
rise the public, which is not easily persuaded that an artist can
ccomplish anything besides the first object that happens to have
ttracted attention, might have regarded him as a mere pianist.
As it was, excellent pianoforte composers like Moscheles remained
o the end of their days convinced that their own musicianship was
nore solid than Chopin's. To demonstrate the sense in which they
vere right is a theoretic possibility. But it is not interesting.
   There is some interest in the fact that Schumann's enthusiastic
ecognition of Chopin's genius was elicited by just the works in
vhich he is hampered by forms for which his training had given
im no help. Some critics would go farther, and say that he had
ut little talent for the sonata style; but no judge of composition
vould say this of Chopin's Violoncello Sonata, nor can any serious
ritic explain away the masterly and terse first movement and
cherzo of the B flat minor Sonata. The concertos need more
ndulgence. The first movement of the E minor is built on a
uicidal plan which Chopin's adored master, Elssner, must have
t least approved if not actually taught, since it is to be found
n two earlier works and can hardly be conceived to have resulted
rom natural instinct. The F minor Concerto, though not a
owerfully organized work, has no fatal flaw; and its style is
he perfection of ornament. The chief subject of orthodox objec-
ion has been its orchestration; but nowadays we can take a
impler view of this matter. Klindworth, a very masterly and
nasterful pianist with an excellent all-round musicianship, could
ever contemplate a line of standard pianoforte music without
howing how much better it might have been arranged. When he

had tidied up Chopin's pianoforte technique he turned his atten
tion to Chopin's orchestration. This he found thin, and so it is
We may frankly concede that Chopin knew nothing about th
orchestra—at least, not much more than Sir Michael Costa. Bu
Klindworth seems to infer that the only alternative to thin is thick
At all events he reorchestrated the F minor Concerto really ver
cleverly, in the style of a full-swell organ, with a beautiful balanc
of tone. In order to penetrate this, even the tidied-up solo par
had to be rewritten in a heavier style. Klindworth duly points th
out, and remarks that those purists who wish to confine themselve
to Chopin's original pianoforte part must accordingly abstain fron
using the improved orchestration. In other words, Chopin'
orchestration, except for a solitary and unnecessary trombon
part (not a note of which requires replacing), and a few rectifiabl
slips, is an unpretentious and correct accompaniment to hi
pianoforte-writing. We may be grateful to Klindworth for takin
so much trouble to demonstrate this.

Chopin begins with an orthodox opening tutti. The quiet firs
theme—

Ex. 1.

is followed by an accessory used in the development.

Ex. 2.

Bassi 8va.

The second subject, though (as in Beethoven's C minor Con
certo) it appears in its destined complementary key instead of i
the tonic—

Ex. 3.

does not, in the manner of its entry, unduly forestall the broade
statement it is to receive later from the pianoforte. Altogethe
Chopin shows far too fine a gift for design in this opening tutti t
justify the prevalent custom of cutting it short. The impatien
dramatic entry of the pianoforte needs all the delay Chopin ha
given before it.

One other theme must be quoted, a passage in C minor, whic

key Chopin (striking out on unusual lines first found in Beethoven's Coriolanus Overture) adds to the scheme of his second subject.

Ex. 4.

&c.

In the development the orchestra accompanies the pianoforte with figures from Ex. 1 and Ex. 2. After a certain amount of dramatic expectation, the first subject returns in F minor. But the pianoforte promptly changes the topic and brings back the second subject not in the tonic, but in its old complementary key, a singular but not unsuccessful experiment in form. Chopin may have had in mind certain rare procedures in Mozart. The continuation is expanded in a different harmonic direction, which brings Ex. 4 in F minor, so that from this point Chopin is able to work up to a final climax. The short closing tutti alludes to Ex. 2 and the opening theme.

Schumann's enthusiasm for the slow movement, voiced through the persons of his imaginary Florestan and Eusebius, was boundless. I quote the main theme, divested of its ornaments. The listener will thus gain a clearer notion of Chopin's art than can be given by the sight of a mass of detail, which only long practice can bring into shape as intelligible phrases.

Ex. 5.    8va.................................................................... loco.

The unornamented portion stands out in relief as a haunting refrain.

Ex. 6.
     8ves....................................

&c.

The middle episode is a dramatic recitative, accompanied by an orchestral tremolo with pizzicato double-basses. This is as fine a piece of instrumentation as Berlioz could have chosen to quote in his famous treatise. In the final return of the main theme Ex. 5 is more elaborately adorned than ever. Ex. 6 remains in its perfect simplicity, but a bassoon imitates it at the second bar, continuing in counterpoint of an adroit simplicity worthy of Bach or Mozart. The movement ends with the same passage that served as its short

orchestral introduction.  Like the romance of the E minor Concerto
it is a masterpiece in a form and a mood which neither Chopin nor
any other composer reproduced later.

The finale is a delightful example of the long ramble through
picturesque musical scenery, first straight up a range of keys and
then straight down again, which Chopin, for reasons unknown to
history, called a rondo.  I quote the main theme—

Ex. 7.

an orchestral accessory—

Ex. 8.

the first item of the surrounding scenery—

Ex. 9.

and the important mazurka-like main second subject, accompanied
*col legno* (i.e. with strings played with the wood of the bow), an
effect rather in vogue in the concertos of Chopin's young days.
The respectable Hummel uses it, and Chopin revered him.

Ex. 10.
*Scherzando.*

This, when Chopin is comfortably home again in F major, is
reduced to a horn-call inscribed *Cor de Signal*; upon which invita-
tion the pianoforte perorates with fairy-like brilliancies, for the
most part new, alluding only at the last moment to one of the
sequels of Ex. 10.

# JOACHIM

## CVII.  HUNGARIAN CONCERTO FOR VIOLIN WITH ORCHESTRA

1 *Allegro un poco maestoso.*  2 ROMANZE.  *Andante.*  3 *Allegro con spirito.*

The Hungarian Concerto illustrates nearly, but not quite, every
aspect of Joachim's music.  To the violinist it is a complete revelation of what Joachim's playing must have been when his physical
powers were at their height.  To students of composition and of
musical history it is one of the most important documents of the
middle of the nineteenth century.  It is the second of three con-

certos that stand in direct line of descent, and that each cost their composer great efforts concerning fundamental matters of musical form. Joachim's model is Beethoven's Pianoforte Concerto in C minor, the work in which, without as yet perfectly solving his problem, Beethoven realized that his first and second concertos had misconceived the purpose of the long opening tutti. In the Hungarian Concerto Joachim begins by following Beethoven's C minor Concerto in organizing his first tutti on purely symphonic lines which give no hint that the work is going to submit to the dominance of a solo instrument at all. But Joachim finds a simpler way to explain the entry of the solo violin than the drastic stroke with which Beethoven diverted the course of his C minor tutti. He evidently did not trust himself to take Beethoven's later works as models: indeed to the end of his life he always had a smile of pity for the inexperienced composer who will not learn from any Beethoven earlier than the last quartets. And so the Hungarian Concerto accepts, as a definite principle, the element of conflict between symphony and concerto in the first movement. Within a few years of his meeting with Joachim, Brahms took up this problem with drastic power, and forced its extremest terms into a chemically indissoluble combination.

The process was accompanied, like many chemical experiments, with formidable eruptions of light and heat. Beethoven's Ninth Symphony and Wagner's *Tannhäuser* did not cost their creators greater agonies than Brahms's D minor Concerto. Joachim helped with advice and criticism at every stage of its growth, from its beginnings as a symphony drafted in an arrangement for two pianofortes, to its final perfection. When it was ready for orchestration, Joachim's relation to Brahms was practically that of master to pupil. In the handling of form Brahms was from the outset a bold and resourceful inventor who needed Joachim's criticism only as the painter needs to see his work reversed in a mirror. But in orchestration he was not only inexperienced but actually untaught. Moreover, orchestration had already come to be regarded as the special province of the progressive party in musical politics. Brilliant scoring was like brilliant playing; it was suspected of having a taint of virtuosity. Brahms would probably have worked out his own salvation even if he had not found a friend who believed in him. But in Joachim he found not only a believer, but a composer whose qualities were exactly fitted to complete his education. Joachim's artistic outlook was already becoming highly conservative, but his alienation from Liszt was a revolt, not a prejudice. At the outset Joachim had been as ready to revolutionize musical traditions as any of the groups who gathered round Liszt at Weimar. His objection to Liszt's compositions was based on no

orthodoxies as to musical form, but was as fundamental and insur-
mountable as Wagner's objection to Meyerbeer. But he was in no
danger of letting himself and Brahms miss the means to classical
ideals because other composers used these means to purposes he
did not approve. On his own instrument he was as great a player
as Liszt; and Wagner alone had a greater command of orchestration. This estimate of Joachim's orchestration will surprise those
who have never heard or read his scores, or whose judgement is
at the mercy of ready-made effects such as harp-glissandos and
prominent celesta passages, or, to use Brahms's gibe, 'Tam-tam
*divisi.*' All competent judges of orchestration will agree with
Stanford in regarding Joachim's mastery of this art as on a level
with his mastery of the violin. Nothing more fortunate could
have happened to Brahms than that his most whole-hearted admirer
should possess not only an exceptionally fastidious ear, but also
the most highly developed technique for satisfying that ear in
composition as well as in playing.

And so the two composers worked together. Their motto was
'*Frei aber einsam*', and its initials, F, A, E, form several themes in
Brahms's early works. They invert into the notes G sharp, E, A,
which may be read in a mixture of German and sol-fa terms, as
Gis-e-la, the name of Joachim's beloved Gisela von Arnim,
afterwards Gisela Grimm. Brahms pulled his mighty D minor
Concerto into shape with the united strength of his own impulse
and Joachim's advice. The orchestration did not get beyond the
first page before Joachim showed Brahms that its whole basis of
orchestral tone-production was wrong. Brahms was quick to
learn, and it is no exaggeration to say that he learnt orchestration
from Joachim. It would be a mistake to seek in the first two movements of his D minor Concerto for the influence of Joachim in
matters of form and dramatic content. But Brahms's finale clearly
shows the influence of the finale of the Hungarian Concerto. Both,
indeed, are closely modelled on that of Beethoven's C minor
Concerto; but it is from Joachim that Brahms has derived the
main points in which his form differs from Beethoven's.

The great length of the Hungarian Concerto results mainly from
the composer's determination to achieve clearness. Joachim told me
that soon after he had finished the concerto he thought a certain
passage too long; but that when he recast it the result came out
longer. Few are the young composers who have escaped damage
from well-meaning advice to shorten for shortness' sake. Horace
knew better, and so did Joachim and Brahms. If a young composer
is not a mere epigrammatist, he needs space in which to move
freely. By the time he is nearer sixty than fifty he may be trusted
to calculate rightly the force of the half-statement and to express

it the experience of a life-time. But when we advise young artists
move like old ones, we tell them not only to ape a sententiousness
at is unnatural to them, but actually to say things which they do
ot believe. The young Joachim believed everything which Beet-
oven uttered in his last works; but the Hungarian Concerto
presented Joachim's experience at twenty-three, not Beethoven's
: fifty-six. The young Joachim's experience was extraordinarily
ch, and he had had enough of his own efforts at what I have heard
im call 'psychological' music, such as his unpublished overture to
*emetrius*. The form of the classical concerto gave him exactly the
pportunity he needed both to find himself and to learn how to
elp Brahms. Both to him and to Brahms the principal danger of
eir reaction against Liszt was that their music, in aiming at
nsistency, might become schematic. With Brahms one security
gainst that danger was his constant preoccupation with the setting
f words on a basis consistently lyric instead of loosely declamatory.
e never accepted the dogma that sustained melody was contrary
the true declamation of words; and his instrumental melodies
l show the freedom which comes only to composers who are
customed to handle poetry. Joachim also made a deep study of
e art of song. But the concerto form gave him his freedom on a
rger scale. The first effect of his reaction against Liszt was to
ake him diffident about the more improvisatorial features of
usical art-forms. Thus, both he and Brahms were eminently
apable of designing an impressive or mysterious introduction.
ut the tendencies of progressive music in the 'fifties were all
r works consisting of introductions to introductions to introduc-
ons, without any prospect of a clear answer to the question which
eethoven put to a famous *improvisatore* after twenty minutes of
timulated expectancy: 'When will you begin?' And so Joachim
nd Brahms formed the habit of always beginning at once; and the
w examples of an introduction in Brahms's works make us in-
lined to regret that he did not more often take the risk of rousing
xpectation.

Now it is a fundamental necessity of concerto form that it should
ave large spaces of discursive interlude for the solo instrument.
oachim's character made any frivolity in such interludes unthink-
ble; his enormous powers as a violinist gave him freedom to
levelop the full resources of his instrument, and he had an in-
xhaustible inventiveness in ornamentation, inspired by instincts
kin to those of Bach and Beethoven. Accordingly his own classical
onservatism set him free in the spacious interludes which are as
ecessary to the concerto as parks to large towns and lungs to the
uman frame. The Hungarian Concerto thus became a composi-
ion from which Brahms was proud to learn. The forms, in their

general aspect, are four-square and youthfully weighty in the
completeness. To ask for compression would be to fall into tl
commonest of donnish errors. It is obvious that these large forn
lay an enormous burden on the function of ornamental detail th
is to fill them out. But herein Joachim's mastery is neither youthf
nor middle-aged; it is absolute. Nowhere outside Bach and the la
works of Beethoven is there to be found any such ornamentation
that of Joachim's violin works. There are plenty of good schoo
and formulas in this matter; but with Joachim, as with Bach ar
Beethoven, the ornaments are only in small part formulas, and a
mostly individual inventions as pregnant as any theme. Brahn
himself never attempts such a style. Still less does it come with
the imagination of the mere virtuoso player. Virtuoso ornament:
tion, even when it is as good as Liszt's, consists in knacks which,
more difficult than harp-glissandos, are hardly more intellectu;
The ornaments of the Hungarian Concerto (quite apart from tl
Hungarian formulas which I purposely refrain from quoting
the musical examples) are like Bach's. Play them slowly and yc
will find them to be living melodies with real harmonic meaning

One by-product of this style is that Joachim's violin-writing
almost always, even in his smaller works, extraordinarily difficu
He had a large hand, and extensions were easy to him which gi\
great trouble to most players. He retained his left-hand techniqu
in full efficiency to his last days, long after he had given up playin
works that depended on staccato bowing. The Hungarian Concer
shows, especially in the finale, that in his physical prime his bo\
arm was as wonderful as his left-hand. Above all, the concert
shows that he had the greatest of all technical gifts: the stayin
power without which Beethoven's Violin Concerto is inaccessibl
to players who think nothing of its individual passages. Beethove
writes no such difficulties as turn up in every passage in th
Hungarian Concerto; but he demands the same kind of stayin
power. The difficulties of a big piece of music cannot be measure
by the mere fact that its passages correspond to exercises of suc
and such a grade. Violinists, for example, usually defer the practic
of harmonics in double-stops until they have mastered mo1
necessary things. There are no double-stop harmonics in th
Hungarian Concerto. But pieces that have room for such follie
are easier to play, though they may be harder to practise at firs
Most violinists will probably agree that the Hungarian Concert
is the most difficult work ever written for the violin. Its difficultie
all have the double quality of being the work of a compose
who could play them, and of being the most straightforward an
economical expression of his thought.

The concerto opens with the following grave theme, typicall

Hungarian in its minor mode with raised fourth, and also in its later cadences.

Ex. 1.

The orchestra works this up in a broad symphonic exposition which soon comes to a grand forte modulating deliberately to F major, where a second group begins with a theme rhythmically derived from Ex. 1, but continuing in a vein of its own.

Ex. 2.

An important new theme is given to the oboe, an instrument which it suits to perfection, though it afterwards comes with new meaning from the solo violin.

Ex. 3.

Then with an impatient gesture—

Ex. 4.

The orchestra seems about to rouse itself to action; but with subtle dramatic purpose it soon comes to a series of dying cadences in F; and the solo violin makes its entry in a way not to be found in any other concerto. It begins quite quietly on its middle strings with dreamy meditation over the dying cadences, which have moved back to the home-dominant; but it soon gathers energy and in due course reaches a climax from which it descends to take up the first theme.

And now Joachim shows a freedom and truth of form that place him far above any epigonoi of the classics. The violin immediately follows Ex. 1 by Ex. 3 in tragic D minor harmony, and thence proceeds to a new theme which is to have the function of leading to the second group in F major.

Ex. 5.

The solo exposition has thus entirely avoided the effect of
transcription of the opening tutti, and by this very freedom weld
the whole movement into a more highly organized unity.  Othe
unorthodoxies are to follow; but at present the transition leads t
a quite regular reproduction of the whole second group (Exx.
and 4) suitably expanded in terms of the solo violin.  After thi
the orchestra bursts in with the first forte of the opening tutti i
F minor.  This leads to a sustained development of Ex. 2 passin
through several keys with beautiful changes of orchestral tone
This is another unorthodox feature, which gives the orchestr
more freedom than the normal scheme would allow.  But her
again the purpose is classical in its dramatic truth.  The abrup
entry of the solo violin with a new counterpoint to Ex. 2—

Ex. 6.

reveals itself as the explanation of the previous development an
lays the foundation for the coda.  The violin takes the rest of th
development into its own control, making energetic use of Ex
5.  In a few decisive steps it leads to the home-tonic and so to th
recapitulation, of which solemn warning is given by the whol
orchestra playing pianissimo below the climax of the violin passages

In accordance with Mozart's principles the recapitulation follow
rather the course of the opening tutti than that of the first solo
One of the most ingenious details is the passage of chromati
octaves with which the violin accompanies a quiet version of th
first forte.  Joachim himself compared this to a neighing horse.  I
is not the only striking feature in a recapitulation admirably fre
from anything like mechanical stiffness.

The coda is largely occupied by a cadenza, beginning, like th
usual extemporized cadenzas, with the violin alone, but joined a
intervals by a flute and an oboe, each of which intervenes witl
Ex. 6.  Thus the cadenza sums up the development.  When th
orchestra re-enters, the violin once more gives Ex. 3 in the tragi
D minor of its first solo; and then rounds off the whole structur
with Ex. 5.

After a meditative introduction the slow movement (entitle
*Romanze*) begins with the following theme—

Ex. 7.

The second part of this melody is worthy to rank, like Matthev
Arnold's 'touchstones of poetry,' among those things in grea

usic which we may keep in mind as standards of beauty.  I quote
e whole strain:

Ex. 8.

The typically Hungarian figure of its cadence becomes the main
ure of a square-cut but agitated middle section in E minor.
hen this is completed, a short passage leads to the return of
xx. 7 and 8 in the violoncellos accompanied by a most gorgeous
namental counterpoint in the solo violin.

The cadence-figure of Ex. 8 is used in fresh ways in the quiet
da, which also resumes the features of the introduction.

The finale begins by taking up the last notes of the *Romanze* in
e full orchestra as a call to action.  After some dramatic question-
gs the orchestra settles down to dance-rhythm over which the
olin plays a theme in perpetual motion.  (Note again the Hun-
rian minor scale with its sharp fourth.)

Ex. 9.

This is worked out as a rondo on the largest possible scale.  The
ansition passages are again admirably free and unexpected in
eir digressions and in the deftness of their returnings.  Their
fluence on the finale of Brahms's D minor Concerto has already
en mentioned.  A detailed analysis of the whole movement
ould be well worth the trouble of writing or even of reading it;
d experienced composers will not underrate the difficulty of
venting and developing a *perpetuum mobile* theme.  Such stiff-
ss as may be imputed to Joachim's phrase-rhythms disappears
the finale.  The other main themes are: the first episode—

Ex. 10.

III                                I

the middle episode—

Ex. 11.

and the entirely unexpected new presto theme of the triumpha[nt]
coda.

Ex. 12.

Presto.

The drastic simplicity of such themes is deceptive: there[ is]
drama behind and around them.

# BRAHMS

## CVIII.  PIANOFORTE CONCERTO IN D MINOR, OP. 15

### 1 *Maestoso*.  2 *Adagio*.  3 *Allegro non troppo*.

With this work the genius of Brahms shook itself free alike fro[m]
formalism and vagueness.  Not even Beethoven's Ninth Sympho[ny]
cost its composer more titanic struggles, and few works of art c[an]
have undergone stranger transformations.  It began as a sketch f[or]
a symphony, written for convenience as an arrangement for tw[o]
pianofortes to be scored later on for orchestra.  Brilliant pianofor[te]
writing, however, had an irrepressible tendency to break in on th[e]
one hand, while on the other hand the most important themes we[re]
clearly orchestral in conception.

The final result was inevitably a classical concerto, but one [of]
unprecedented tragic power.  There is no vestige of immaturity [or]
inconsistency in the style and form.  Everything that happens [in]
this gigantic work is as much a *locus classicus* as anything in the la[st]
two pianoforte concertos and the Violin Concerto of Beethove[n.]
The storm of disapproval which greeted its first performance [at]
Leipzig had origins of partisan opposition as disgraceful as the ro[w]
organized by the Jockey Club of Paris when Wagner produce[d]
*Tannhäuser* there.  But all this tale of storm and stress must b[e]
mentioned in order to guard ourselves against letting it at this tim[e]
of day lead us to think that what is still unfamiliar in the work

nature. Brahms attained maturity in it at every point; and
ther in performance nor in listening can we afford to shirk its
iculties as if they were crudities with no artistic justification.

The first danger of misconception rises at the beginning. It is
sible and natural to play so powerful an opening with a highly
ctive and orchestral-sounding fortissimo on the pianoforte; and
hms undoubtedly at first thought that this fact would represent
real orchestral possibilities. When Joachim (who, at the time,
far more orchestral experience) saw his first attempt to score
opening he burst out laughing; and the scoring as we now
w it shows (like many other important works of Brahms at this
iod) the result of Joachim's advice. What is not always under-
od by conductors is that the opening now does not represent
ortissimo at all. Nothing could be shallower than the criticism
t it is now, what it was at first, an unsuccessful attempt to
re pianoforte music for an orchestra. Brahms, whether on
chim's direct advice or on his own initiative, has abandoned all
ort to force the tone and has reduced his orchestra to a sound of
ant menace, growing thunderously nearer whenever the har-
ny changes. All that is needed in performance is to attend to
markings as they stand in the score, instead of deserving the
me, wrongly imputed to the composer, of remaining under the
l of the pianoforte. I do not claim that the scoring is fool-proof.
The first theme of the opening tutti is one of the mightiest
erances since Beethoven's Ninth Symphony.

climax subsides into a mournful cantabile, accompanied by its
quitous main figure (a).

In three slow swoops of wheeling flight this rises to a remote k
in which appears a new theme destined later to form part of
second subject.

Ex. 3.

In spite of the foreign key this has not been introduced in an und
symphonic manner, and we have not lost the sense of introduct
style which the opening tutti of a concerto should have. Hence
abruptly dramatic return to the main key and main theme is w
timed. With tragic irony the tutti rises to a note of triumph.

Ex. 4.

This dies away pathetically, and the pianoforte enters with
bravura display, but with a touching theme worthy of Bac
ariosos in the *Matthew Passion*.

Ex. 5.

From this the pianoforte drifts into a passionate development
Ex. 1 (beginning with the trills at the 8th bar), and passes on
Ex. 2, which it carries into the orthodox 'complementary key' of
there to give out Ex. 3 as the beginning of the second subject. A
now it asserts the function of the solo player in developing dran
tically on symphonic lines, and introduces an entirely new cantal
in a vein of noble consolation.

Ex. 6.

This continues with an impassioned development of Ex. 4 int
long flowing paragraph. Brilliant and sonorous as is the pianofo

iting, it has none of the habits or ambitions of virtuoso display,
t the paragraph dies away in gentle pathos, and the orchestra
ncludes the matter with an elegiac epilogue on Ex. 3.

The development starts unexpectedly with a fierce note of
umph (from Ex. 4) on the pianoforte. This turns out to be but
ragic plunge into developments of Ex. 1, which assumes more
nsformations than can be quoted here. But they will not prove
fficult to follow. First, however, Ex. 2 appears in the basses,
d modulates grandly into distant keys, as if there to seek Ex. 3.
iite unexpected is the change of mood in Ex. 3, when the piano-
rte bursts out with it angrily in 'diminution'.

Ex. 7.

This, combining with figure (a) of Ex. 1, becomes quite light-
arted in a graceful passage which eventually moves to the domi-
nt of D, thereby preparing for the return to the main theme.
he recapitulation begins with one of the grandest surprises
music since Beethoven. The orchestra has crashed on to its
iison D; the drums are rolling, and this time it is the pianoforte
at will deliver the theme. It does so; but instead of taking it on
e dark chord of B flat, it blazes out on the chord of E major
ominant of A minor). The rest follows in normal position. Magni-
ent new harmonic vistas are revealed when the orchestra, after
irsting out with the pathetic solo-theme (Ex. 5) in high rage,
odulates with it to E minor, and again to F sharp minor, where
e pianoforte resumes it, leading to the recapitulation of Ex. 3 in
at key with exquisite new ornamentation. A slight change in the
llowing harmonic conduct brings the rest, the recapitulation,
om Ex. 6, into the tonic D major; and there is no further change
til the final dying away of Ex. 4, which descends to the drums.

From this the pianoforte rouses itself to the tragic issues of the
da. No cry of triumph, such as that which began the develop-
ent, breaks in here. The pianoforte takes up Ex. 7, beginning
iietly and proceeding in a short crescendo till it calls forth the
chestra, with Ex. 1, this time on the chord of D major with an
fect of tragic irony. The stormy antecedents of Ex. 4, as at the
d of the opening tutti, are worked up to a passionate conclusion
the movement.

It is known that the tragic mood of this first movement was
spired by the catastrophe of Schumann's illness, on the terrible
iy when he threw himself into the Rhine. The slow move-
ent is a Requiem for Schumann; and that is why in one of

the sketches for it Brahms inscribed its quiet devout theme as
*Benedictus*; a fact that gave rise to an erroneous impression that
at first intended it for a choral work.

Ex. 8.
Be - - - ne-dic - tus qui ve - nit in    no-mi-ne Do - mi - ni

The phrasing throughout the movement is very broad and fre
The pianoforte enters with a kind of meditation on the main them
without binding itself to follow the lines of the whole melody mo
than allusively. In a quiet dialogue with the orchestra it modula
to B minor, where a spacious middle episode alternates two them
(a long 8-bar paragraph and a short phrase) in binary form.

Ex. 9.

Ex. 10.

The return to the main theme is effected by one of Brahms
master-strokes of harmonic poise (Mendelssohn was the discover
of the device, which is emphatically not a mannerism). The medit
tive pianoforte development of the theme now rises to a grai
climax, and the ensuing dialogue dies away into a simple b
exquisitely poetic cadenza, after which the orchestra concludes wi
its *Benedictus* in a line of austere beauty. The entry of the drur
(silent throughout the rest of the movement) completes the soler
nity of the last chords.

The rondo of Beethoven's C minor Concerto has had an extr
ordinarily strong influence on the form of two concerto final
powerfully independent in their styles. One of these is the finale
Joachim's Hungarian Concerto, a great work which, if it will nev
be widely popular, will also ever remain one of the major events
the history of the form. The other is the finale of this concert
There is a superior prejudice to the effect that an orthodox rono
cannot be an adequate finale to a work with so tragic a first mov
ment; but this is not borne out by the immense energy of Brahms
main theme (Ex. 11), with its impassioned second part which aris
from its 7th and 8th bars and modulates with romantic depth in
C sharp minor, to return in a kind of cadenza evidently modell
on Beethoven's procedure in the C minor Concerto.

Ex. 11.

Nor is there any loss of symphonic power in the immensely broad transition and in the gorgeous paragraphs of the second subject, from which I quote the beginnings of two themes.

Ex. 12.

Ex. 13.

The spacious returns to the main theme are again modelled on Beethoven's C minor Concerto; and so, in spite of its greater richness of phrasing and variation, is the middle episode—

Ex. 14.

including its development in a fugue—

Ex. 15.

in which Brahms shows himself a contrapuntist of the calibre of Bach and the lightness of Mozart. The main theme (Ex. 11) also enters into combination with this fugue subject, which is moreover treated by augmentation (i.e. given in notes of twice the length) and by diminution.

In due course the rondo theme returns again in D minor, and now the movement strikes out on independent lines. The normal recapitulation is represented by an abridgement of the calm theme of Ex. 12 in a towering passion in D minor, and the coda grows

grandly and slowly into triumph by a development of Ex. 14 in D
major, leading through a pastoral passage on Ex. 11 to a great final
stretto on its first bars, the pianoforte becoming an integral part of
the symphonic orchestra, with complete maintenance of its own
independence.

## CIX. PIANOFORTE CONCERTO IN B FLAT MAJOR, OP. 83

1 *Allegro non troppo.*  2 *Allegro appassionato.*  3 *Andante.*
4 *Allegretto grazioso.*

Of all existing concertos in the classical form this is the largest. It
is true that the first movement is shorter than either that of Beethoven's E flat Concerto or that of his Violin Concerto; shorter also
than that of Brahms's own first concerto. But in almost every
classical concerto the first movement is as large or larger than the
slow movement and finale taken together, and there is no scherzo.
Here, in his B flat Concerto, Brahms has followed the first movement by a fiery, almost tragic allegro which, though anything but
a joke, more than fills the place of a symphonic scherzo: the slow
movement is the largest in any concerto since Beethoven's C minor;
while the finale, with all its lightness of touch, is a rondo of the
most spacious design. We thus have the three normal movements
of the classical concerto at their fullest and richest, with the
addition of a fourth member on the same scale.

This stormy extra allegro appassionato rather puzzled Brahms's
friends at first. Like Beethoven, he was apt to answer questions
according to the insight shown by the questioner; and so, when he
was asked why he inserted that movement, he said, 'Well, you see
the first movement is so harmless' (*simpel*).

Perhaps the music itself may give us more light.

The first movement, in spite of appearances, does *not* (with due
respect to the text-books) 'abolish the conventional opening tutti'.
It simply begins with an introductory statement of the first theme
in dialogue between a horn, the pianoforte, and the wood-wind.

Ex. 1.

Then the pianoforte bursts out alone with an energetic figure, and follows it with an impassioned and melodious cadenza preparing the way for the orchestra, which begins the 'conventional opening tutti' or (as it is better called) ritornello with a triumphant version of Ex. 1, passing rapidly on to a review of several themes. One of these—

Ex. 2.

*mp espress.*

with its vigorous sequels, the pianoforte will later on show to be the principal part of the second subject. Here it is given in D minor, a key not used in the rest of the movement, and concludes with a majestic short cadence-theme fortissimo for full orchestra, derived from the figures (*a*) (*b*) and (*c*) of Ex. 1.

From this foreign key the pianoforte brings us back to the tonic in three powerful chords (figure (*a*) of Ex. 1), and then proceeds to broad and leisurely discussion of the first theme in dialogue with the orchestra. By degrees the design reveals itself as the real sonata-form exposition of first subject and transition to second subject; that symphonic exposition for which all that we have hitherto had is but an introductory pageant. Several new themes and derivatives appear, and the drift is steadily towards F major or minor, the normal key for the second subject. One important new theme needs quotation—

Ex. 3.

for the quiet rhythmic figure (*d*), here marked with brackets, underlies the whole of the development-section. At present it leads up a long straight avenue to the second subject itself (Ex. 2). It was easy to see that there was passion therein when we heard it in the orchestra; and the usual experience in concertos is that the orchestra can deliver with massive force what the solo-player can make subtle and delicate with eloquence and ornamentation. But here Brahms surprises us: there is ornamentation indeed, but the orchestral version of the second subject was mild compared with the version given by the pianoforte. To the continuation a new theme is added (which clever speculators may, if they choose, derive from figures (*a*) and (*b*)—Brahms will not care), and a furious climax is reached, figure (*a*) booming in the bass beneath cataracts of trills, until at last the pent-up orchestra bursts through with the

fortissimo cadence-theme that closed the ritornello. (Yes—'you
see, the first movement is so harmless.')

The orchestra continues with an angry allusion to Ex. 2; at last
there is a high wail from the clarinets, and, answering from the
darkness, the horn gives out the first theme (Ex. 1) sadly in D
minor. The pianoforte carries on the dialogue as at the beginning
of the work. When it reaches the energetic continuation which
it formerly had as an introductory solo, the orchestra takes the lead.
(This device, of giving to the orchestra what formerly belonged to
the solo, is another of Brahms's new resources; hitherto it had
always been the solo that borrowed from the orchestra; and the
composers who 'abolish the ritornello' have done less than nothing
towards this other side of the balance.)

Soon the key shifts to an immense distance (B minor), and we
are in the full swing of the development. This now settles down to
a witty dialogue on the rhythmic figure (d) from Ex. 3. The smooth
melody that binds Ex. 3 together does not appear here, the fore-
ground being occupied by a quite new theme given to the pianoforte. But in the background you will find the steps shown in
Ex. 3 systematically carried out in sequence through many rich
modulations, all of which, however, group round and revert to
B minor, their starting-point. The details crowd closer, and the
action, which started in comedy, becomes serious. At last the
figure (a) of the first subject crashes in, and, while smoky arpeggios
rise in the pianoforte, that figure and its continuation (c) move
grandly from key to key, the bass slowly creeping upward, until a
solemn calm is attained on a harmony still very distant from the
tonic. Nevertheless this harmony yields easily to the dominant
of B flat, our tonic, and in sails the first subject on the horn taken
up, as in the introduction, by the pianoforte.

The recapitulation, thus dramatically brought about, represents
the first subject only by its first two phrases, and passes thence
immediately to Ex. 3 in (or rather, *about*) the tonic. From this
point all is exactly reproduced in the tonic, until we reach the furious
cascade of shakes which revealed the 'harmless' character of this
gigantic movement. Here a momentary deviation into a foreign
key gives a point of departure for the coda. The tonic is restored
with a sudden plunge into extreme darkness. Out of subdued
mutterings the first theme again arises and hovers, while the air
seems full of whisperings and the beating of mighty wings. Suddenly the sunlight breaks through, and the movement ends with
a triumphant summary, in broad melodious flow, of those topics
arising from the main theme that were left unaccounted for in the
exposition and recapitulation.

The second movement, a scherzo in form if not in mood, is no less powerful than the first; and if it were a finale instead of being (as it obviously is by nature as well as position) a middle movement, we might be in two minds about calling it tragic, in spite of its jubilant central episode (or trio) and its elemental enjoyment of its own rage. Of its three principal themes the first two—

Ex. 4.

*Allegro appassionato.*

Ex. 5.

*p tranquillo e dolce.*

are presented like a first and second subject in a terse sonata-form exposition. This exposition is repeated. Then a development ensues; but we are surprised to find it soon veering round to the tonic (D minor), where, after a tremendous orchestral climax, there enters a jubilant new theme in the tonic major—

Ex. 6.

*largamente.*

which, with an important sequel, has much the effect of a trio. After this trio has thus been grafted on to the development, we naturally have no mere da capo of the scherzo, but a free sonata-like recapitulation of its materials (Exx. 4 and 5) in the tonic. Then there is a tremendous coda. Brahms has blended the solo and the orchestra on quite new principles, with perfect freedom and adequate scope for both, in this unique movement.

If there ever could be any doubt as to the purpose of that stormy second movement, the first notes of the andante should settle it. The key is B flat, the key of the first movement, and its emotion is a reaction after a storm, not after a triumph. Thus both in harmony and mood it would be fatally misplaced immediately after the first movement. After the second its emotional fitness is perfect, and is enhanced by the harmonic value of its being in the tonic of the whole work. It gives this slow movement a strangely poetic feeling of finality, though the slow tempo and lyric style make it obviously unlikely that it can really be the end. The first movement had its storms; the second movement was all storm, and here we are not only enjoying a calm, but safe at home again.

The orchestra begins with a broad melody for a solo violoncello.

Later on an oboe joins the violoncello in dialogue; and in the last two bars the pianoforte enters with a new figure (*b*) and delivers a free monologue suggested by the first two bars of the theme (see especially figure (*a*)).

(*b*) continued in bass.

No composer has ever surpassed Brahms in the art of making a closely-woven passage seem as if it was extemporized whereas it really carries the communicating threads of a whole vast organization. Compare the slow movement of the Violin Concerto.

The time of storms and anxieties is not yet past: the orchestra breaks in with much agitation, and the pianoforte transforms the calm figures of its first solo (Ex. 8) into matter for a very impassioned dialogue with the orchestra. This is worked out on a large scale and with an energy which goes far to make this slow movement as difficult as the finales of ordinary concertos. At last, however, it comes to a mournful end in the tonic minor; there is sudden modulation, and then, in F sharp major and in slower tempo, an entirely new melody rises. The pianoforte is accompanied by two clarinets. The melody consists of few notes spaced out like the first stars that penetrate the sky at sunset. When the strings join in, the calm is as deep as the ocean that we have witnessed in the storms of this huge piece of music. To crown all, the solo violoncello enters, still in F sharp major, with the main theme. A slight digression at the end of the first phrase brings the

continuation round into the tonic, B flat; and then the rest of the
movement is simply a recapitulation of its orchestral opening with
the addition of an ornamental pianoforte part, until the original
entry of the pianoforte is reached (first two bars of Ex. 8). To this
the pianoforte and violoncello add a close, with a simple chain of
shakes, a slow arpeggio, and soft final chords.

And now we have the finale. What tremendous triumph shall it
express? Brahms's answer is such as only the greatest of artists can
find; there are no adequate words for it (there never are for any art
that is not itself words—and then there are only its own words).
But it is, perhaps, not misleading to say here, as so often of
Beethoven's finales, something like this: 'We have done our work
—let the children play in the world which our work has made safer
and happier for them.'

There are no trumpets and drums in this finale. Neither are
there any storms. There is abundance of young energy and grace,
and there is all that greatness of design which, as Mozart and the
Greeks have proved, is unfailingly sublime, whatever the ostensible
range of the subject. Here the emotional reaction is so convincing
that, with all the 'roaring cataracts of nonsense' that were poured
out on the subject of Brahms's concertos when they were new, it
has, as far as I know, never been suggested that this finale was too
light-hearted for the rest of the work. In the same way it has never
been suggested by even the most sacerdotal Wagnerians that *Die
Meistersinger* is in any way a slighter work than *Tristan*. Such cases
are really well worth noting for the light which they throw on the
relation between the 'subject' of a work of art and the emotions
which the art itself calls forth.

I will leave this great and childlike finale to call forth the right
emotions without further analysis in words; but the listener may
perhaps find some use in a specially full budget of quotations, as
there is a very large number of themes. I therefore subjoin the six
principal ones in the order in which they occur, marking, as usual,
with letters those figures which are used in derivative themes.

Ex. 9.

First Theme.

Ex. 10.

Second strain of First Theme.

Ex. 11.

First Episode or 'Second Subject' I.

Ex. 12.

First Episode continued, II.

Ex. 13.

First Episode continued, III.

Ex. 14.

From middle Episode, or Development.

*simile.*

Ex. 14 alternates with meditations on Ex. 10, which eventually returns in the tonic without waiting for the main theme.

## CX. VIOLIN CONCERTO IN D MAJOR, OP. 77

1 *Allegro non troppo.* 2 *Adagio.* 3 *Allegro giocoso, ma non troppo vivace.*

This work is of the same period as Brahms's Second Symphony in the same key. It is his second work in concerto form, the first being the gigantic D minor Pianoforte Concerto, op. 15. Mr. Huberman summarizes a whole essay on the aesthetics of this and of all concertos in the following correction of a famous epigram of Bülow's. Bülow said that Max Bruch had written a concerto *for* the violin and Brahms a concerto *against* the violin. Mr. Huberman says that 'Brahms's concerto is neither *against* the violin, nor *for* violin *with* orchestra; but it is a concerto *for* violin *against* orchestra—and the violin wins'. One of my earliest recollections of a great musical scholar, A. J. Hipkins, is his delight at discovering that the etymology and musical history of the words 'concertanto' and 'concerto' originate in 'certare', to strive.

I give, with slight changes, the analysis I wrote for the London concerts of the Meiningen Orchestra in 1902.

Brahms's opening tutti states all except one of the themes of the first and second subjects, with such terseness that the first three sound like a single theme, being, in fact, absolutely continuous.

Ex. 1.

Energetic as Ex. 3 is, in contrast to the quiet beginning, we are much surprised to find that in three more bars the whole orchestra crashes out in a grand fortissimo, with (a) in the bass, imitated by the treble, and treated in diminution. We may already realize that this is no symphony that we are hearing, but the true headlong single outpouring of manifold material by an orchestra, to be worked out by a solo instrument in classical concerto form. The outburst leads to the themes of the second subject, another series of three themes, all stated in the same continuous style. These are—

Ex. 4.

with its derivative—

Ex. 5.

and a mysterious variation thereof which must rank as an important separate theme, so much is it changed by the division of ( f ) among the instruments and the conjunction of a new figure (g).

Ex. 6.

This leads to an energetic cadence theme in the minor, beginning thus—

Ex. 7.

(h)

and followed by a running figure in semiquavers which may speak for itself. Suddenly the solo violin enters, with rolling drums and a solemn sustained tonic pedal on the deepest notes of the horns. The violin begins with a fiery transformation of the quiet first theme (Ex. 1 (a) (b) ) in the minor—

Ex. 8.

(a)

(b)                                                        &c.

while the string band throws in the strong rhythm ⌐ ♩ ♪ ♩. ♪ of Ex. 7 (h).

Soon, through the flaming arpeggios of the solo violin, we hear the original form of (a) in broad sequences of minor harmonies on the oboe, answered by clarinet, bassoon, and flute, always with the tonic pedal in horns and drum. Gradually the sweeping arpeggios of the violin become more gentle; until in a moment the flame burns softly and steadily, the harmony brightens to major, the tonic pedal gives place to a 6/4 chord, and the rhythm expands, as the orchestral colouring seems to drift away in clouds, leaving the pale tone of the string-band as the background to the solo violin that soars calmly into the quiet heights above, there to begin its song.

The solo restatement of Ex. 1 must be quoted, as the new quaver accompaniment (i) of the viola is very important.

Ex. 9.

(i)                                                        &c.

Between Exx. 1 and 2 the violin interpolates a meditative passage with that sublime calm which only the greatest artists have learnt to call their own. Ex. 2 is made to pass into the dominant. It will be heard in the violoncellos, with a wonderful counterpoint for the solo violin. Ex. 3 appears first in the deep basses and is then

peated in canon by the other strings, the solo violin having
another new and independent theme.

The second subject follows Ex. 3 in the orthodox dominant,
beginning with Exx. 4 and 5. When we reach figure (g) of Ex. 6
the violin turns it into a lovely new theme, beginning thus—

Ex. 10.

(g)    New theme.    &c.

This is worked out at some length, before we reach the rest of
Ex. 6, which we find at last much enhanced by the new contrast
just gained, and still more mysterious from being placed in a firm
position on the tonic instead of on a secondary chord as in the tutti.
The effect of the double-stops on the solo violin is unique.

Ex. 7 follows, and its continuation is expanded so as to bring the
exposition to a stormy close. The orchestra bursts in—with the
ritornello, as in all previous examples of concert-form? No;
Brahms hits on the grand idea of giving it that stormy transformation of (a) Ex. 8, with which the solo made its first sudden
entry.

As in Beethoven's Violin Concerto at the same point, the
orchestra modulates simply and broadly to C major, the key
that is most of all opposed to our tonic D. There it groups the
solo violin's additional theme in the second subject, Ex. 10, into
eight-bar phrases together with (f) as in Ex. 6. This closes in
C minor; and the solo violin re-enters with the following intensely
plaintive development of (f), a landmark in the musical experience
of many a Brahms-lover.

Ex. 11.

(f)    (f)    &c.

True to those principles of balance and variety which have led
the great classical concerto-writers to make their developments
decidedly episodic in character, Brahms not only dwells long on
this without change of key, but enriches it with an entirely new
counter-subject (x).

Ex. 12.
tranquillo.
(x)

(f)    &c.

III    K

After some time the violin awakens angrily to an energetic moo
and the orchestra takes up the new theme (x) and works it o
independently in a few stormy sequences, till suddenly there
a bright flash of trumpets. The solo violin re-enters in high ra;
with an extraordinary new figure on the dominant of D (our ma
key) as an accompaniment to the gigantic strides of the transiti
theme, Ex. 3 (e), which we hear in the bass. Soon, on a domina;
pedal, we find ourselves preparing for the return of the first subjec
in a storm of excitement. The solo violin has the powerful variatic
of (a) with which it made its first entry (Ex. 8), and the winds ha
that figure of accompaniment (i) which we saw in Ex. 9. T
rhythmic figure (h) ⸓ ⸓ ♪ ♩. ♪ also plays a prominent part in th
tremendous passage, which at last ends in the appearance of t
first subject in grand triumph on the full orchestra. The counte
point (i) is given to the violins in their most brilliant register, wh
the theme is trumpeted forth by all the wind-band.[1]

The violin re-enters with sublime calm, and we have Ex. 2 ;
placed as to lead to an exact recapitulation, in the tonic, of tl
whole of the rest of the solo exposition. An amazing new ligh
however, is thrown on the point at which the violin introduced i
own new theme, Ex. 10. The omission of one step in the sequenc
just before brings it unexpectedly into F sharp major, the brillia;
major mediant used by Beethoven in the Waldstein Sonata an
the Leonora overtures.

The return to D is easily managed without greatly enlarging th
ordinary course of the melody, and the rest of the recapitulatio
is again quite exact, until the fiery climax which is crowned by th
inrush of the orchestra.

And now, will the orchestra enter with Ex. 8 as it did at th
beginning of the development? Brahms has something in stor
which, in this context, is yet more grand. In the unexpected ne
key of B flat (admirably chosen, as it exactly counterbalances tha
startling change to F sharp in the middle of the recapitulation) w
have that splendid blaze of full orchestra which, in the openin

---

[1] Note how the trumpets themselves alter the first two bars in order t
avoid the note B, which is not in their natural scale. Brahms has th
modern trumpet, with a complete scale, at his disposal, but he detests an
use of the instrument that audibly contradicts its character as a 'natura
instrument whose scale is the harmonic series that exists in the very natur
of musical sound itself. Beethoven shows the same fastidious taste in th
finale of the Ninth Symphony, where in giving the great choral theme t
trumpets he distorts two bars in the second part to avoid a note which
though actually in the natural scale of the instrument, is so harmonize
as to sound as if it were not. Such subtleties are among the things which
even more than matters of noise or economy, distinguish the great com
poser's treatment of brass from the vulgar abuse of it.

utti, had followed Ex. 3 with the suddenness of a tropical sunrise.
This quickly returns to D major, and Brahms actually makes
the time-honoured pause on a 6/4 chord, and leaves it to the
player to furnish something like half of the coda in an unsupported,
quasi-extempore cadenza. Brahms could afford to risk this, since
he had dedicated this concerto to the player and composer of the
most ideally appropriate cadenzas that have been produced since
those grand inspirations that Beethoven extemporized (and so
signally failed to write down).[1]

The short conclusion, after the cadenza, begins with a quiet
resumption of the first theme with sublime harmonies, and a
development of the second figure (*b*) into sequences crowned by
some of the tenderest notes ever drawn from a violin. Faint
suggestions of the rhythm of Ex. 7, ♩ ♪ ♪♩, in the horns, are
answered by triplets in the solo violin, that recall, in a far-off way,
the triplets of Ex. 8, transformed into something infinitely touching
and gentle. Then, with astonishing speed, the air becomes full of
life and energy; the rhythm ♩ ♪ ♪♩ ♩ is insisted on sharply by
trumpets and drums; the pace quickens; the solo violin has an
extremely brilliant version of the counterpoint-figure (*i*), divided
between it and the wood-wind—

Ex. 13.

Flutes.

Solo violin.

and the grand movement is ended in triumph before we have
regained our breath.

The slow movement is very highly organized on a remarkably
broad melody; and the treatment, though thoroughly classical in
spirit, is in detail so unlike anything else that a little technical
knowledge is apt to be a misleading preparation for its enjoyment.

[1] The hypothesis of the concerto cadenza nevertheless implies that a
new cadenza may be produced on each occasion. The problem of cadenza-
writing is extremely interesting. In the case of the violin it is complicated by the fact that a composer writing (like Bach) for unaccompanied
violin invents themes that require no accompaniment; whereas the
cadenza-writer has to make the violin produce an unaccompanied coda-
like fantasia on themes that have been conceived as supported by harmonies which they need not have the power of implying in themselves.
I append my solution of Brahms's problem at the end of this essay. Two
points may be taken as essential to any cadenza for this concerto; namely,
the first bar and the final close, where any other plan than Joachim's
would be unthinkable. Elsewhere the possibilities, on the right general
principles, are incalculable.

The opening theme must be quoted at some length, as the whole
subsequent solo is best followed from it.

I number the bars of the melody for reference. The closing strain
of this great tune must also be indicated.

The strings make their entry with the initial chords (a), and the
solo violin appears with phrases that on a first impression seem to
be freely declamatory. If that was all that could be said, they
would not have the wonderful and touching effect that we experience in them. As a matter of fact the violin is giving us an
exact and systematically expanded variation of the whole opening
melody. I quote the three bars that correspond to those numbered
1 and 2 in Ex. 14.

With this hint we can follow the rest by fixing our attention on
Ex. 14, making two of its bars correspond with three or four of
the violin solo. When we come to figure (e), bars 9 and 10, there
is a sudden change to the key a semitone higher; one bar being
still systematically expanded into two. The time slackens; (e) is
given by 'diminution' (i.e. in semiquavers instead of quavers), and
in the extremely distant key of F sharp minor the violin begins an

mpassioned central episode. This consists of a highly ornate
nelody, containing two new figures (g) and (h)—

Ex. 17.

(e) diminished.

h), it will be seen, being accompanied by (e) diminished. As soon
s this has formed a regular eight-bar melody, it is given again in
n expanded counterstatement. (g) is assigned to the violoncellos
n a form which I give here, as it is important that it should not
scape notice.

Ex. 18.

(g) varied.

The counterstatement follows the lines of Ex. 16 on a larger scale
vith more and more elaborate ornamentation, especially as regards
gure (h), while the diminution of (e) is treated in splendid rising
nodulations in the accompaniment. Three bars of these modula-
ions bring us back to our tonic, F; the clouds drift away leaving
he violin singing peacefully in the blue vault, and the oboe returns
vith its world of melody. The violin, which now has a rich accom-
animent, interpolates, after the second bar, three bars of its
ugmentation, Ex. 16, after which the melody proceeds as at first,
ll we come to the twelfth bar. Here the violin gives us a new
evelopment of figure (b) in dialogue with the horn, crescendo.

Ex. 19.

Horn.

This comes to a climax, and as it dies away, we are thrilled to
ear the lovely codetta, Ex. 15, for the first and last time since its
riginal appearance. The initial chords (a) entering again on the
assoons and horns, followed by a beautiful closing change of har-
nony, round off this wonderful organization so perfectly that even
ie vast range of key and contrast through which we have been
arried cannot dispel the impression that the whole movement

is a single unbroken melody. Thus the reason why some critic
have thought it too slight is the very reason why it is gigantic.

The same inexhaustible variety and resource in unexpected alter
nations and correspondences in melodic grouping that we find in th
slow movement appear in the extremely spirited and humorou
finale. This is a rondo; like many of Beethoven's finales, rather ters
in its formal body, but with an enormous expansion in the coda.

The first theme is given by the solo violin—

Ex. 20.

*Allegro giocoso, ma non troppo vivace.*

in alternation with the full orchestra. The last figure (*c*) should b
specially noted. The tune has a second part on the same materia
which must be quoted independently here to facilitate referenc
later on.

Ex. 21.

This leads, with a short crescendo (listen to (*a*) in the basses), t
a resumption of Ex. 20 by the full orchestra, with a characteristi
tightening of the sequences of (*a*), bringing the cadence-figure (
into the tonic.

A transition passage founded on (*c*), first augmented and the
diminished, leads playfully by a devious path to a very stormy an
wayward second subject in the dominant. The scales that preced
it should be noted, but I need only quote the beginning of th
second subject itself.

Ex. 22.

ike many second subjects in Beethoven's finales, this soon shows
tendency to drift back from its key. It dwells on the chord of
sharp minor, till it overbalances itself and falls straight back
ito the first theme in the tonic as at the beginning. But the
rchestral counterstatement does not continue to recapitulate this
fter the third bar. Figure (*b*) is broken up into rising sequences,
id the violin enters with placid arpeggios in the quiet key of the
ibdominant, while (*a*) is worked out by the orchestra. The
iolin arpeggios merge into a graceful new theme in a totally
nexpected rhythm.

Ex. 23.

The arpeggios and figure (*a*) intervene for a moment, in their
wn 2/4 time in B major. The new 3/4 theme returns in E major,
key strongly opposed to our tonic, D, and then in C major, the
ne key that is still more opposed. Then the orchestra breaks up
nese new figures (*f*) and (*g*), giving (*g*) by augmentation, while the
iolin has expressive counterpoints, all in the key of G minor (in
ne major of which this episode began).

Suddenly the gentle theme is brushed impatiently away. We
ear an expanded version of the scale passages that led to the
econd subject, and the second subject itself inevitably follows in
he subdominant. And Brahms gives us a perfectly regular recapi-
ilation of it, as if this were quite a normal position for its
eappearance, instead of being a unique combination of two formal
eculiarities that had hitherto always stood alone; the appearance
n a foreign key, and the omission of the first subject. When he
omes to the point where it overbalanced itself on the chord of
sharp minor, now of course B minor, we naturally expect the
eturn of the long-lost first theme. Instead, we are surprised and
lelighted to hear its still more long-lost second part, Ex. 21. The
istener will readily appreciate its powerful effect in pulling the
vhole structure together. It has not been heard since the opening;
t reminds us of the first part of the theme, which was last heard
efore the paradoxical middle section, that so tersely combined
he qualities of a melodious and independent central episode with
hose of a solid piece of thematic development. Then we had the
inexpected recapitulation of the second subject in the sub-
lominant. Now we return, not to the tonic, which would not be
right enough to give relief immediately after so unusual an
xpanse of subdominant, but to the key of this second part. And

Brahms now expands it, making it cover other keys, such as the
dominant of F. And as he proceeds, we understand yet more.
That second part did originally lead to a final restatement of
the first theme, which of course now returns with greater force
than ever. It takes its fill of expansion and climax; and its closing
figure (*c*), augmented, becomes the text for a great accompanied
cadenza by the solo violin.

Ex. 24.

As the violin settles down to a trill that gradually becomes a chain
of modulations, we hear (*a*) in the strings; and when, after the
modulations, the tonic is re-established, the whole phrase (*a*) (*b*) is
heard in the basses (a fine point that should be watched for). Then
on a dominant pedal, the rhythm of (*a*) ♩ ♪♪♪ ♩ is, to borrow
Sir George Grove's happy phrase, *blown at the hearer*, in answer
to the sequences of the violin. We reach a climax and a pause.
Then the time quickens, to a stirring march rhythm, in which
we have a new version of the principal theme, with laughing
*gruppetti* on the wind instruments, and a lively tread of drums
and trumpets.

Ex. 25.

This rapidly rises to a climax, especially through the aid of its new
version of (*b*). No less suddenly does each successive climax (there
are several and short) give place to the following transformation of
the second subject (Ex. 22).

Ex. 26.

Vith a running fire of unexpected variations on (*a*) and (*b*), the
igantic work ends in a glory that is intensified by the sudden
lternations between *forte* and *piano* which, while they take our
·reath away, preserve the balance between solo and orchestra up
o the last moment.

Cadenza for Brahms's Violin Concerto by D. F. Tovey.

## CXI. CONCERTO FOR VIOLIN AND VIOLONCELLO, OP. 102

### 1 *Allegro.* 2 *Andante.* 3 *Allegro non troppo.*

An important work for an unfamiliar combination of instruments is always at a disadvantage; mainly for the reasons which make the combination unfamiliar. One *chinoiserie* by Ravel does not make an art-form of duets for violin and violoncello; and the sound of this combination of extremes is inherently strange without a middle part to bridge the gap. But the strangeness is not an absurdity, such as the combination of a violin and a double-bass would be. It is, when properly handled, a powerful stimulus to the musical imagination alike of listeners, players, and

composers. When Brahms brought the resources of his ripe
experience to the handling of this combination together with a
orchestra in the last of his orchestral works, the novelty for man
years completely puzzled even those critics who took an offici
attitude of apostleship towards his music. The explanation of th
difficulty is simple enough. Brahms did not make the new wor
a systematic display of the charms of the new combination, bu
simply expressed some of his most powerful and dramatic idea
for all the world as if the combination of instruments was perfect
familiar. His critics and his admirers had, in short, to deal wit
Brahms's most powerful ideas as well as with the unfamiliar con
bination, and it is pathetic to see the struggles of such a critic a
Hanslick with this excursion beyond the lines laid down by hi
in his apostleship. The most familiar features of Brahms's way o
developing themes, as for instance in the middle of the finale, wher
the phrases of the heroic middle episode are in their restatemen
dramatically interrupted by echoes through which the solo instru
ments are heard with their own ornamentation, similar devices i
the middle of the slow movement, and the terseness of the slo
movement as a whole—these and other equally normal feature
impressed Brahms's friends as well as his hostile critics just as
they were technical immaturities. There is no other explanatio
for this than the fact that everybody expected in a modern doubl
concerto to hear as much of the violoncello as if there were n
violin, and as much of both as if there were no orchestra. In th
meantime Brahms did as Mozart and Beethoven always did—h
treated his orchestra symphonically. Accordingly the orthodo
complaint became, first, that the solo parts were enormousl
difficult; secondly, that it was impossible to hear them; and thirdly
that there was not nearly enough of them. As for the pathos an
the poetry of the work, all this general disappointment made it ou
of the question to speculate whether such qualities existed at al

It is to be hoped that at this distance of time there may be les
difficulty in taking the work as it really comes. Any one who ha
made a study of musical first impressions in general and of con
certos in particular, knows at once that the complaints describe
above are illusions. If the work is of a loosely-knit texture, th
composer can thicken his score almost with impunity. For instance
the Dvořák Violoncello Concerto (over which Hausmann on hi
last visit to Brahms found him boiling with generous admiration
is, on a moderate computation, twice as heavily orchestrated a
this, the most difficult of Brahms's concertos; and the truth is tha
Brahms's thickest accompaniments in this Double Concerto are
written with scrupulous economy, whereas Dvořák's are alarmingly
reckless. But with a loosely-knit work many points may escape the

stener without much damage to the sequel. In works such as this
f Brahms, every theme and every inner part has its results in later
hapters of the story. Therefore it is as well for us to have a good
umber of quotations for our present analysis.

The dominance of the solo violin, the still greater dominance of
ne violoncello, and finally, the wonderful solidity of harmony and
ide compass of the united couple, are demonstrated in the intro-
uction. First the orchestra throws out a challenge in the shape
f the figures of the first subject on the dominant (that is to say,
ne threshold of the key).

Ex. 1.

he last three notes of the orchestral phrase are instantly taken up
y the violoncello, entirely unaccompanied, in a most impassioned
ind of recitative. Then the wood-wind enter gently in the major
ith the first phrase of the second subject, one of Brahms's
nderest themes.

Ex. 2.

his time the solo violin takes up the last three notes, at first
editatively. It is soon joined by the violoncello and works up to
climax of extraordinary fullness of harmony, ending in an uprush
f scales and chords which leads to the entry of the whole orchestra
ith the first subject launched full on the tonic into the course of
mighty concerto ritornello.

Ex. 3.

rahms proceeds simply and broadly, but in a style which does not
ake any confusion between the lines of a concerto and those of
symphony, though he boldly strikes out into a foreign key in
reparation for his second subject. The passage of preparation

with its fierce syncopations is the most impassioned theme in th
whole work.

Ex. 4.

And when the theme of the second subject bursts out in F majo
(a different key from that for which it is destined in the solo), it con
tinues in a storm of passion.  No worse mistake in interpretatio
could be made than for this orchestral version to be treated in th
style of the solo.  Again I must quote the theme as it occurs here
on account of its continuation.

Ex. 5.

Very soon it has passed back to A minor with abrupt questioning
and a new theme bursts out which will be heard again in the coda.

Ex. 6.
8va..........................................................................

With this the orchestra comes to its conclusion, and the violoncell
impetuously enters with a new development of the first theme—

Ex. 7.                                                                    (a 2)
    (a 1)

answered after four bars by the violin.  (Always it will be found tha
the original first bar of Ex. 1 ($a^1$) is answered sooner or later b
the second bar ($a^2$) whatever new developments have happene
in between.)  The two instruments develop this idea rapidly an
passionately to a climax in which they discuss the second phrase o
Ex. 3 (those very striking minims in its fifth bar), and after thi

ney settle down to a spacious and entirely new transition theme
a dialogue.

Ex. 8.

tarting with the utmost energy and drifting towards the orthodox
ey of the second subject (C major), this yields to a melting mood;
nd the preparation of the second subject, with the figures of the
rst theme tenderly reiterated in the oboe and flute through the
nterlacing arpeggios of the solo instruments, broken by an im-
ressive silence in the middle, would be the most pathetic passage
n the concerto, but for the fact it leads to the still more pathetic
xpanded version of the second subject announced by the violoncello and eventually taken up by the violin. I know no more power-
ul instance of the dramatic possibilities of concerto form than the
ay in which this melody changes its character according as it is
tated in the ritornello or expanded in the solo. Suddenly how-
ver it breaks into a stormy passage, leading to what in the ritornello
ppeared to be the transition theme (Ex. 4). The violin and
ioloncello have but to state the first two bars of this (which they
o with extraordinary fullness of sound) for the whole orchestra to
urst in at the same height of passion as it had reached in the ritor-
ello; and it comes to an even greater climax, being under the stress
f plunging into a somewhat distant key for the development. In
he midst of the storm the two solo instruments enter together with
he first theme, and proceed to work out the figure of triplet
rotchets which characterizes its third bar. This becomes a mys-
erious figure at twice the pace with a characteristic change of
ccent in the wood-wind.

Ex. 9.

I may mention, as a sample of the intelligence which is sometimes
rought to bear upon the interpretation of Brahms, that at a per-
ormance by a good foreign orchestra, I found that some one had
orrected this 'discrepancy' of rhythm in the band-parts!) Soon the
yncopated theme reappears in a pathetic calm in the orchestra,
hile the solo instruments weave round it a network of trills.
efore long the calm becomes a stiff breeze, and the breeze a
orm, through which the first theme cries out angrily in the
ood-wind. Suddenly the storm ceases, and the syncopations of

Ex. 4 soar upwards in the violoncello and violin through remo
modulations in a pathetic passage, which the most disappointe
detractors of this work on its first appearance admitted to b
sublime. We are on the threshold of the tonic, and the violi
and violoncello come back to the uprush of scales and chord
(the chords now alternating with the orchestra) with which the
ended the introduction.

And so the recapitulation now begins in the tonic in the orchestr
just as the big ritornello did. Its second sentence, however, is de
livered by the solo players, and leads straight to the solo transitic
theme of Ex. 8. Slight changes in the course of the harmonic
keep the music in the key of A. There is the same pathetic passag
of preparation, with its impressive bar of silence. Then the ex
panded version of the second subject is given out high up by th
violin, the violoncello having a new flowing accompaniment. I
due course the fatal syncopated theme evokes the stormy orchestr
which now carries the latter part of the ritornello to its greate
climax. This owes much of its power to the fact that its last them
(Ex. 6, which has not been heard since its first appearance) is no
combined with the figures of the first subject (Ex. 1). This bring
the violin and violoncello back upon the scene in tragic passic
with the same statement as that of their first entry after th
ritornello. There is something extraordinarily sonorous in the
appearance here in octaves, and still more in their boldly coalescir
in unison as the passion yields to a tragic calm with a rita
dando. From this they rouse themselves with the syncopated figur
(Ex. 4), and the tragedy is consummated by the transformatic
of the second subject itself into a final outburst of indignatio
the theme being given in pizzicato chords in the minor, while th
solo instruments emphasize the bass of the harmony by a storm
figure of their own. With a final allusion to their transition them
(Ex. 8) the solo instruments bring down the full orchestra upon th
last chords.

The slow movement begins with a signal of two notes on th
horns answered in the upper part of the scale and in a high octav
by the wood-wind. On the four notes thus delivered, the so
violin and violoncello immediately build one of the broadest ar
most swinging melodies ever written.

Ex. 10.

This is worked out as a complete tune in two parts with repeat
The second part is peculiarly gorgeous in its deep harmonies, ar

ts climax is heightened on repetition. Then without further
.evelopment or pause the middle episode enters in the somewhat
emote key of F. It begins with a very quiet melody for the wood-
/ind scored with a highly-seasoned reedy tone.

Ex. 11.

he violin and violoncello answer this with a new theme in rather
/istful dialogue which modulates richly.

Ex. 12.

'hen the reedy theme (Ex. 11) returns unaccompanied, with semi-
[uaver movement by the solo instruments, and expanded by very
haracteristic echoes of the last two notes of each phrase in pizzi-
ato chords. A quite short but far-reaching passage moves in a few
teps through remote keys, when suddenly the first two notes of
he introductory signal are heard in the trumpets. The solo instru-
nents respond to them, and in a notoriously difficult but very
najestic passage float down again to the whole first melody, which
n repetition they expand in a simple but surprising way which
/ill not escape notice. When the great melody has come to an end,
here is a short and peaceful coda in which the two middle themes
Exx. 11 and 12) are heard simultaneously. As this reaches an
xquisite dying fall, the figures of the first theme come surging
·ack again until the solo instruments rise up on to the answer to
he opening signal (that is to say, the second bar of Ex. 10), to
/hich the trumpets reply quietly with the first bar; and so, with
he majestic and difficult returning passage on the tonic chord, the
low movement ends in a golden glow.

From the point of view of first impressions, the finale of this
louble concerto commits the most deadly crime possible to a great
/ork—it shows a sense of humour. Let us admit this, and let
us accept the still more serious fact that the first theme is playful,
/hich is not always the same thing as humorous. This does not
·revent it from giving rise at the end of the movement to one of the
nost pathetic passages in the whole work. Apart from the humour
nd the unusual combination of instruments, the chief difficulty
n contemporary appreciation of the finale arose from the fact that,
ike the slow movement, it is very terse, and therefore failed to
mpress the listeners of the 'eighties and 'nineties with the true

breadth of its proportions. (It is an odd thing that the critics who
are loudest in their denunciations of unnecessary length are always
the first to grumble that a terse statement is inadequate.) The form
of this broadly designed but short finale is the clearest of rondo-
types. In Ex. 13 I give the first phrase, calling attention to the
figure I have marked (a), for the sake of its extraordinary consequences in the coda.

Ex. 13.

The first episode or second subject is a full-toned aspiring melody—

Ex. 14.

the rhythm of which expands in a remarkable way in its counter
statement, compelling Brahms temporarily to change his time to 3/4
and 4/4, until he abruptly breaks it off and leads back to the first
theme. This now gets no farther than its first phrase, after which
it is playfully laughed into evanescence until nothing is left
but rhythmic fragments amid a silence. Suddenly out of these
rhythmic fragments arises a fiercely triumphant new theme in a key
compounded of F major and D minor with a preponderance of
D minor.

Ex. 15.

With the aid of an angry alternating second part, which I do not
quote, this leads to a counterstatement by the orchestra, interrupted by characteristic echoes of the last two notes of its phrases.
(These echoes form the only discoverable ground for the allegation
that the structure of this very spacious middle episode is disjointed.
As a matter of fact, the device is one of those bold simplicities
which give the scale of design, and secure that it shall continue
to surprise by its breadth and flow long after we have known the

hole work by heart.) Then follows a calm swinging tune in
major given by the wood-wind, with a delicate accompaniment
rising arpeggios in the solo instruments derived from those
hoes.

Ex. 16.

he solo instruments work it up vigorously on their own account,
l it leads to a gorgeously bright and soft version of Ex. 16 in D
ajor with the syncopations smoothed away. Then Ex. 15 bursts in
ain. Its angry sequel is now used to lead us back to the tonic, and
e rondo theme (Ex. 13) re-enters in due course, followed by all
accessories. This now goes through a wide range of key before
ighting upon the second subject (Ex. 14) triumphant in the tonic
ajor. The second subject now leads immediately to the coda,
hich is in the major throughout. It begins in a slower tempo
ith a calm version of the first theme (Ex. 13), from the third bar
which arises a most touching stream of melody in dialogue
tween voices of different octaves outlined in arpeggios by the solo
struments.

Ex. 17.

is the privilege of works in sonata form that they can, without
eakening or falsifying tragic issues, bring their finales to a happy
ding. The tragedy of the first movement has been told without
nching, but told within the quarter of an hour which contains
mphonic movements on a large scale. Within that quarter of an
ur we have not time to see enough of the world in which such
agedies take place; and we are allowed to see its glorious melodies,
humours, and its capacities for happiness, in the other move-
ents. And so the whole concerto leads up to the wonderful
nderness of this last page which finally breaks into joyful triumph,
d brings the great work to an end.

# DVOŘÁK

## CXII. VIOLONCELLO CONCERTO IN B MINOR, OP. 104

1 *Allegro.* 2 *Adagio ma non troppo.* 3 FINALE: *Allegro moderato.*

The superstition still survives in some quarters that Brahm
because of his own consciousness of supreme mastery and fastidio
taste in form, must have been a pedantic critic of composers who
style was less disciplined. It still passes for orthodox criticism
compare Brahms and Dvořák as composers of opposite school
The historic facts are that Brahms and Joachim were the two fir
to recognize and acclaim the genius of Dvořák. This does n
mean that either of them pledged himself to regard all Dvořák
output as worthy of him, and still less does it imply that eith
thought his most popular works his best. Among friends Brahm
could be generously indiscreet, and at this time of day there can
no harm in publishing one of his indiscretions, which was told to n
by Hausmann. On perhaps the last occasion on which Hausman
called upon Brahms in Vienna he found him reading a score th
had just been sent him. Brahms, before he would talk of anythir
else, must first give vent to his grumble: 'Why on earth didn't
know that one could write a violoncello concerto like this? If
had only known, I would have written one long ago!' This is
the more remarkable as Brahms had in fact given the violoncel
the lion's share in one of his most recent and greatest works, t
Double Concerto for violin and 'cello, op. 102; a work which, th
violently abused by all the critics, is now coming into its own. T
Violoncello Concerto of Dvořák is not without its composer's mo
amiable weaknesses; nor is it possible to say that all the weak poin
are, as in some other great works by Dvořák and Schubert, sugge
tive of new types of form. But it is permissible to plead that t
weaknesses do not matter. Both the slow movement and the fina
relapse into Charles the Second's apologies for being such a u
conscionable time in dying; but it is impossible to grudge the
their time, and as a matter of fact none of the three movements
the concerto is of unreasonable length. Dvořák developed in l
later works a curious habit of planting his harmonies firmly on
the tonic of whatever key he had drifted into, and giving there
a series of short phrases, each of which comes in the manner of
afterthought suggested by the one before. There are not mai
forms of instrumental music where this kind of construction
dramatically effective; but it has its claims where the style c
inspire affection, and it goes far towards explaining itself when t

...eans of expression is a solo instrument to which a large orchestra
...ppears to be listening with rapt attention.

...In the first movement there is no feeling of diffuseness or
...edundancy, though the construction is by no means close-knit.
...)vořák is, as throughout the work, peculiarly full of invention;
...nd, to begin with, he abandons the modern position adopted by
...im in his comparatively slight and sketchy violin concerto, and
...ates the main themes of the movement in a full-sized classical
...rchestral tutti. He even goes so far as to put the second subject
...ito its own foreign key; a device which Beethoven in his C minor
...Concerto contradicted at the very moment of suggesting it, because
... makes the opening tutti too like the beginning of a symphony.
... quote the two main themes of the first subject and the second
...ibject as they occur in the opening tutti.

Ex. 1.

Ex. 2.

...he second subject is one of the most beautiful passages ever
...vritten for the horn. I purposely quote more than its first phrase,
...s its highest merit lies in the simple originality of the continuation.
...n the opening tutti this leads to a naïvely perfunctory new theme
...or the full orchestra which I do not quote. It gets Dvořák out of
...he difficulty of concluding a tutti which might otherwise just as
...vell have done for the exposition of a symphony; and we need not
...rouble ourselves about its unpolished manners, since, having
...lone its duty and declined in a dramatic diminuendo, it is never
...ieard again. Then the violoncello enters, quasi improvisando, and
...iours out an inexhaustible flow of splendid developments of the
...irst theme, leading (in dialogue with the orchestra, on lines quite
...lifferent from those of the opening tutti, but equally naturally) to
...he second subject. The second subject is now followed by a large
...ariety of new accessory themes with some very rich changes of

key, and eventually comes to a climax, upon which the orchestra
re-enters grandioso and begins the development with a dramatic
transformation of the first theme, modulating to the distant key
of A flat minor ( = G sharp minor). In this key the violoncello
re-enters and, instead of carrying the development through further
wanderings of key, settles down to a sustained episode in which
the figure of the first theme is worked out in a cantabile. Soon the
violoncello takes to a rippling arpeggio figure, while the cantabile
is carried on by wind instruments. This drifts easily towards
minor, and thus we feel that we are returning, perhaps unexpectedly soon, to the tonic. The entry of a drum with an impressive
low roll is dramatically ominous, and the violoncello swiftly rushes
to the crisis. The event paradoxically justifies the shortness of its
preparation and the suddenness of its accomplishment, for the
theme which enters in the tonic is not the first subject but the
second subject, triumphant in the full orchestra. Dvořák has, to
put the matter briefly, brought this great loosely-knit first movement within surprisingly moderate dimensions by 'short-circuiting'
its development and recapitulation. The success is brilliant, both
in form and in dramatic expression; and the total impression left
by the movement is unequivocally that of a masterpiece, whatever
theorists may say.

The slow movement has either two themes or five or six, according as you choose to single out any of the numerous afterthoughts
tacked on to each of its sentences. I compromise by indicating its
material in two composite quotations, one from the quiet main theme
and the other from the tragic central episode.

In both groups of material there is the persistent tendency to come
time after time to a close on the tonic, as I mentioned at the outset.
This is accentuated when the violoncello in the recapitulation turns
the first theme into a sort of cadenza in dialogue with the orchestra,
where every phrase is so explicitly of the nature of an ending that
it is not easy to separate the coda from the rest of the design. The
listener will be materially helped in his appreciation of the whole
by the following quotation. It shows that the extremely quiet
passage which follows the quasi-extempore recapitulation of the
theme is really a transformation of the stormy first phrase of the
middle episode (Ex. 4).

Ex. 5.

We shall do justice to such a piece of music if we imagine that
its habit of perpetually closing in the tonic is merely a weakness.
It is obviously essential to the point of the music; nor is the point
really difficult to appreciate when every moment is an outstanding
example of euphony.

The finale, a short-circuited rondo, begins with a dramatic
marching introduction for the orchestra, foreshadowing the main
theme, the gist of which is then given out by the violoncello.

Ex. 6.

From the large number of other themes I quote the transition with
its continuation for the violoncello (which continuation elsewhere
brings about a return to the tonic)—

Ex. 7.

and (overleaf) the theme of the first episode, which never recurs—

with the first theme of the second episode in rather slower time—

which eventually surprises us by short-circuiting the whole
structure (compare the similar case in the first movement) and
appearing on a solo violin in the tonic major. Here, then, Dvořák
settles down to another glorious series of epilogues in a steady pro-
gression of picturesqueness and calm. Eventually, in quite a slow
tempo, the ghost of the first movement (Ex. 1) appears seraphically
in the clarinets. But at last the orchestra rouses itself. The trombones give out the figure of the rondo theme (Ex. 6) in solemn big
notes; and, after all, the work ends allegro vivo in high spirits.


# ELGAR

## CXIII. VIOLIN CONCERTO IN B MINOR, OP. 61

### 1 *Allegro.* 2 *Andante.* 3 *Allegro molto.*

Elgar's Violin Concerto, like the *Enigma Variations*, and probably
like many other of its composer's finest inspirations, is a character
study. This is attested by its dedication to some one unnamed, in
the words prefaced in the score: '*Aquí está encerrada el alma de*
...(1910).'

Of all external subjects for music the illustration of human
character is the most purely musical; if indeed it can be an external
subject at all. Music either has character, or it is meaningless, and
the character either has human interest or none. We nourish our
interest in the characters of animals by describing them in human
terms; and if there is such a thing as 'cosmic emotion', it is
nourished by contrasting the vastness of the universe with the
insignificance of man, while at the same time we pride ourselves in
the fact that it is the human mind which recognizes the contrast.
The blank space which stands for the name of the person whose soul
is enshrined in this concerto shows that nothing is to be gained by
inquiring into the private affairs of Sir Edward Elgar and his friends.
The soul of the music is musical, and we need no further external
programme. My analysis, therefore, will have nothing but musical

cts to present to the listener. I give as nearly as possible a com-
lete list of the themes, a policy which saves many a difficult para-
raph of description. But the quotations, though numerous, are
ery short; and the listener will be grievously misled if he infers
rom this that the melodies represented by them are short. There
; in fact the same danger here as there is in the orthodox dis-
ussion of Wagnerian leitmotiv, and such famous examples of the
se of an all-pervading figure as the first movement of Beethoven's
: minor Symphony; the danger that the analysis may ignore the
owing paragraph in its fascinated study of the pregnant word.
Vhen such one-sided analysis is made a basis for the teaching of
omposition, the results may be paralysing or destructive; and
here are such things as compositions that have no flow and no real
oherence, because the composer has been deceived into believing
hat a composition can be built upwards from single figures,
logically' connected by a process which has little more logic in
t than a series of puns.

The following fifteen quotations are, then, no more than the first
vords or leading words of the paragraphs and the processes which
hey initiate. I quote them thus briefly, not because the melodies
re short, but because there are so many different long melodies
nd long processes based on the same figures that it is convenient to
quote their common factors. If this work were a Wagnerian opera,
1othing would be easier than to label one pair of bars the motive
of longing, and another the motive of ambition, and to imagine
hat the composer and the dramatist were both equally capable of
lesigning a dramatic scene by permutations and combinations of
;ome twenty such motives and titles, each consisting of six or seven
;uch highly significant notes that the initiated listener is miracu-
ously certain of their meaning. Such a doctrine would not be
vorth refuting, but for the fact that composers themselves have
>een misled by it. This concerto refutes it triumphantly. I have
heard it admired for the shortness of its themes, and I have heard
it blamed for its lack of broad melodies. The answer to the equally
mistaken admiration and blame is already to be found in the fact
that the first paragraph is an entirely straightforward matter containing three distinct and important themes.

Ex. 1.

Ex. 2.

Ex. 3.

Even so it is not quite complete, but closes into the next paragraph which works out, in broad melodious sequences of urgent character a new theme announced in a darker key.

Ex. 4.

The next theme is destined, later on, to express a serene calm—

Ex. 5.

but the modulations to which it here gives rise, lead quickly t an excited climax in an extremely remote key, with a new figure closely allied to Ex. 2.

Ex. 6.

This swings round in five bars back to B minor, where we have Ex. 4 in an inner part below new counterpoints, followed by a further development of Exx. 1 and 2. So far we have heard nothing of the solo violin. What we have been listening to is a fine modern example of the classical opening tutti of a concerto. These six themes have been welded together in a continuous flow of melody The changes of key, though more remote and more frequent than those of any older concerto, have all been changes possible in a flow of melody; they have not been events marked off from each other by dramatic action. The master who is to hold this large orchestra spell-bound, and set all these themes out on their various different planes, has not yet spoken. We have now reached the moment when the orchestra is eagerly awaiting him. The strings speak of him wistfully, as in the two bars represented by Ex. 1 Their sentence is finished for them by the master himself.

This entry of the solo violin realizes in a new way the true relation between the solo and the orchestra in the classical concerto form. After a short but broadly ruminating recitative, the violin passing through Ex. 2, discusses Ex. 4 with the orchestra. Then Ex. 3 (which, by the way, is obviously closely allied to Ex. 1) s developed through a wide range of keys as a rich transition passage, drifting slowly but surely, with the aid of its ally Ex. 6, to G major. In this key Ex. 5 now blossoms out as a broadly lyric second subject. After this has been given free expression we are surprised for a moment by the appearance of Ex. 1 in its original key, a phenomenon which, however, does not mean a return to the tonic, inasmuch as one of the subtleties of the opening tutti was that its first chords were ambiguous in key. Thus the oracle proves its tragic infallibility, for the key turns out to be F sharp minor, the dominant minor. Ex. 4 is worked up, with various derivatives from Ex. 1, and a new counterpoint from the solo violin, to a great climax in which Ex. 3 also plays its part; until at last the full orchestra crashes in with an impassioned tutti beginning with Ex. 4 and passing through remote keys with a still more impassioned development of what was once the calm lyric strain of Ex. 5. Ex. 1 joins powerfully in the stormy dialogue and soon brings the development round to the original key.

Suddenly the storm subsides, and the solo violin re-enters, completing the half-spoken word of the orchestra as on its first entry, but with a quite new meaning, while muted horns murmur the rhythm of the first bar of Ex. 4. The effect is quite clearly that of a return to a recapitulation; and what now follows has all the manner thereof. In actual fact it is very free. The main theme of the second subject (Ex. 5), for instance, appears almost at once below the meditative florid figures of the solo violin, and executes some beautiful remote modulations before the violin resumes the transition themes, Exx. 4, 3, and their accessories. It then appears again in sequences that recall its tentative appearance in the opening tutti; and when at last it settles down to a real feeling of recapitulation its key is not the tonic, but D major. This establishes the same balance of keys that Schubert has in his Unfinished Symphony; but as the original course of Elgar's second subject swerved from G major to the dominant F sharp minor, it now has to take a different direction to swing round from D major to B minor, the main key. This it effects with more sombre dramatic force than before; the entry of the brass being particularly impressive where the violin resumes the discussion of Ex. 4 in B minor. From this point the coda grafts itself on to the recapitulation, and, with the impetuous intervention of Ex. 2, brings the movement to its impassioned end with the first theme, Ex. 1, and its variant, Ex. 3.

The slow movement is in the extremely remote key of B flat. There is something quaint in the fact that two modern violin concertos which are almost at opposite poles of artistic outlook should both be in B minor, and both have this exceptional key relationship

in their slow movements. Of Saint-Saëns's third Violin Concerto
it may be said without offence that it is all publicity, whereas
Elgar's Violin Concerto is one of the most intimate works of this
century. In most respects the comparison between the two works
sheds little light on either of them, but it is interesting to compare
the most obvious single feature in the slow movement of each.
Everybody who remembers the slow movement of Saint-Saëns'
B minor Violin Concerto instantly thinks of the passage where the
violin plays arpeggios in harmonics two octaves above a clarinet.
Everybody who remembers the slow movement of the Elgar Violin
Concerto thinks of the way in which the orchestra first states eight
bars of naïve melody, whereupon the solo violin enters with an
equally naïve counterpoint *as an inner part*.

Ex. 7.

Soon the violin leads the orchestra into remote regions; and new
themes appear—

Ex. 8.

Ex. 9.

which rise to a climax in D flat.

Ex. 10.

In this key the first theme (Ex. 7 with its counterpoint) is resumed,
and leads through Ex. 8 to a broad new theme in D natural—

Ex. 11.

&c.

This, though it sets out very firmly in D, does not remain there long,
but fetches a compass quickly back to B flat, where, with the

return to the main theme, we also have other themes freely recapitulated in their order. The last words are said by the orchestra with Ex. 10 pianissimo, answered by the violin with Ex. 9.

The finale is very rhapsodical and dramatic. Its outstanding features are an opening in which the solo violin seems to be playing a kind of prelude on a figure of rising turns. This requires no quotation until an inner part of the orchestra interpolates a theme which afterwards becomes important.

Ex. 12.

(a)

This appears to be a determining point, inasmuch as it brings the harmony to the crisis of closing in the key of B minor, which all this improvisatorial opening is intended to establish. It is obviously right that after the slow movement in the remote key of B flat, the main key of the work should be specially emphasized. This impression once clearly conveyed, the harmony, after all, swerves boldly aside, and in D major there enters the most prominent theme in the finale.

Ex. 13.

sf

Other themes that are used with a sense of being transitional material are Ex. 12 (soon taken up with majestic passion by the whole orchestra) and a combination of it with new figures—

Ex. 14.

b    c    a

foreshadowing the second subject itself.

Ex. 15.

3

Out of these materials the scheme of exposition and recapitulation is easy to follow, and soon runs its course. It accordingly lands us in B major; and now, in what is formally speaking the coda of the work, comes the real series of events for which all this is a prelude. The second theme of the slow movement, Ex. 6, enters in B major

adapted to the tempo of the finale, and is brought by both the solo
violin and the orchestra through a wide range of key to a climax
over which the themes proper to the finale (Exx. 13 and 12) return
in full vigour.

Suddenly the music dies away into the minor, and the themes
of the first movement reappear slowly and mysteriously (Exx. 1,
4, and 5) in the cadenza, which has become famous as one of
the most original dialogues between a solo instrument and an
orchestra that have ever been imagined. The device of the 'pizzicato
tremolo', which Elgar has invented in this passage, ought hence
forth to be a matter of common knowledge in orchestral music.
There is nothing like it for filmy harmonious transparency and
mystery; and it is one of the simplest things in the world. But we
wrong this cadenza if we ascribe its aesthetic value to an orchestral
effect. The priceless thing is to find such devices invented in the
service of music which enshrines a soul. It is not a sensational
effect; and those who have heard of it by reputation and expect to
be startled by it will be disappointed. It is simply a common-sense
solution of the problem of providing an exquisitely faint harmony
that will keep entirely in the background on any notes required.
After the cadenza, the introduction to the finale is resumed and
leads to a brilliant coda in which Exx. 8, 15, and 3 conclude the
work in triumph.


# ARTHUR SOMERVELL

## CXIV.   VIOLIN CONCERTO IN G MINOR

### 1 *Allegro moderato*. 2 *Adagio*. 3 *Allegro giocoso*.

There will never be too many violin concertos in the world. They
are immensely difficult to write, even on post-classical or experimental lines; and while violinists clamour for additions to their
repertoire, they find more difficulty in learning new concertos than
in keeping their classical repertoire up to the demands of their
engagements. Accordingly a new concerto will have a better
chance if its design is a light post-classical framework for the display
of the violin than if it is either on full-sized classical lines or experimental in the latest phases of revolution. Nevertheless, some living
composers are so fond of music that the full-sized classical form of
concerto still gives them a greater stimulus to musical invention than
any other; and so Sir Edward Elgar designed his Violin Concerto
with a broad opening tutti and a full exploitation of the consequences thereof. And now Sir Arthur Somervell does likewise.
The two works resemble the classics no more than they resemble
each other. They agree with the classics and with each other in

eing individuals, in owing their form to their matter, and (a third
ay of saying the same thing) in being the work of masters
ho know their own minds and are not diverted from saying what
ey mean by any consideration as to whether 'one can do this
owadays'.

The Somervell Violin Concerto is easy to follow, and is in fact so
uch less complex than the Elgar that the comparison between the
vo cannot possibly illuminate either of them. Unfortunately the
omparison is quite certain to be made by most people who know
at both works are violin concertos and both are by contemporary
nglishmen. Accordingly, let the possibility of comparison here
e mentioned as a subject hereafter under taboo. The Elgar Con-
erto is obviously the more difficult to understand and to play.
he Somervell Concerto will, like most of its author's works, attract
e listener at once, and will not present him with anything
vidently difficult to understand. The wise listener will, neverthe-
ss, refrain from concluding that what he appreciates on a first
earing comprises the whole work in all its dimensions and
nplications; nor will he be worried by that most destructive of
rejudices, the belief that what pleases immediately must always
e wrong somehow. This belief has never been shared by great
asters. They know that bad works may be 'best sellers'; but they
ave no conviction that good works may not; and their own criteria
re far too humdrum to impress as profound criticism. The highest
raise ever given by one great composer to another was Haydn's
ft-quoted assertion to Leopold Mozart; but usually only the
nimportant half of it is quoted. 'I assure you', said Haydn, 'that
our son is the greatest musician I have ever seen or heard of.'
ery generous and superlative, but not so pregnant as the con-
nuation: 'he has taste and the most thorough knowledge of
omposition'.

And now let us all devote what taste and knowledge of composi-
ion we possess to the enjoyment of a violin concerto by a composer
ho has abundance of melodious and rhythmic invention, and
hose technical resources are all devoted to making his music clear.
his end he attains so thoroughly that probably few listeners will
ealize how free his rhythms are, and how impossible it is to pre-
ict what turn the end of a phrase will take. I purposely quote
he themes only as far as the first square section: the continua-
ions are always inevitable when we have heard them, but never
redictable. The harmonic style is in keeping with the themes
nd rhythms; the treatment of the minor mode is tinged with the
Doric and Aeolian of English and kindred folk-song, while the key-
ystem of the whole work is by no means tied down to classical
recedent.

The opening tutti begins with the following main theme—

Ex. 1.

The figure (*a*) of the first bar is used in several other themes, as late quotations will show. In the rhythm ♩ ♪♩ ♪ | ♩ it pervad the next theme (unquoted), which makes a deliberate symphon transition to the complementary key (B flat) in which the secon group of themes is to be cast. The procedure is that of Joachim Hungarian Concerto, a modification of Beethoven's in his C min Concerto, but less symphonic than either. Beethoven's C min tutti was so thoroughly symphonic that when his second grou began in its complementary key Beethoven found himself compelle to shift it back to the tonic before the pianoforte could enter at al and then the pianoforte had no chance of diverging from a stri recapitulation of the tutti up to that shifting point. Joachim foun it possible to let his second group die away before the orchestra ha gone far into it; and so his solo arose out of it quietly but drama tically, and there was no difficulty in continuing with freedo throughout. Somervell's tutti has contrived, somehow, to kee its processional and preludial aspect throughout in spite of i apparently symphonic form. The orchestra gives out the tw main themes of the second group. Of these the first is a fir example of a long and close-knit musical sentence. I am strong tempted to quote the whole 18 bars (closing into a 19th as first the next theme), but the listener may learn more by finding out f himself what comes of the simple-seeming first 4-bar clause.

Ex. 2.

As the melody approaches its close it makes use of figure (*a*) i smooth rhythm. That figure then takes an entirely different for in the energetic next theme.

Ex. 3.

The above three quotations show that this opening tutti has

ll events this difference from its classical models, that its material
hows three radically different time-measures instead of only one.
There is, nevertheless, a common denominator implied, however it
may yield here and there to rubato. The half-bar of Ex. 1 is the
ame size as that of Ex. 2, and as one-third of the bar of Ex. 3.

The orchestra disposes of Ex. 3 in 18 bars, which die away in
vident anticipation of something dramatic. And the solo violin
nters with a solemn meditation in recitative, alluding to figure (*a*),
nd punctuated by pizzicato chords which descend in chromatic
teps from D (the dominant) to the tonic G. The pizzicato chords
ettle into a swinging accompaniment to Ex. 1, and the solo violin
roceeds to translate the whole opening tutti into its own language.
But it cannot confine itself to the lines laid down by the orchestra;
: must have a new transition theme, though (*a*) is still latent.

This leads through one or two new incidents to a regular solo
ersion of the whole second group (Exx. 2 and 3); to which the
iolin adds a serene closing-theme made of figure (*a*).

A horn repeats this while the solo adorns it with arpeggios. Then
he orchestra intervenes and starts the development in B flat minor.
There is no trace of the classical procedure which is to reproduce,
with or without some new modulation, a substantial portion of the
pening tutti; the orchestra and violin plunge at once into a
iscursive development of figure (*a*) in dialogue and in various
orms new and old, seldom giving more than the first $3\frac{1}{2}$ bars of the
heme as in Ex. 1, but producing several contrasted episodes from
t. Eventually the second group (Ex. 2) intervenes in C major and
noves towards E minor. The solo violin alludes to its opening
adenza, and the orchestra, apropos of figure (*b*), enters with a
hort crescendo that lands unexpectedly in the tonic major, G.

Hereupon the recapitulation begins, with a triumphant transla-
ion of Ex. 1 into the major mode. The solo violin diverts the
ontinuation to its own purposes and leads to Ex. 4 in E minor, from
vhich point the recapitulation becomes exact. The end of Ex. 5

leads to the cadenza. This, though on different lines from thos
of the first entry of the solo, somewhat recalls that entry by it
ruminative recitative style and its development of figure (a)
During its course the muted strings of the orchestra enter with a
augmentation of Ex. 2, while the solo violin breaks into arpeggios
The cadenza, however, extends beyond this incident and lead
eventually to a serene coda devoted to Ex. 1 in the major mode
But at last the tone changes and the theme returns to its origina
heroic mood, in which the movement ends.

The slow movement (in E flat) begins with a 4-bar phrase fo
low-pitched wind, anticipating and closing into the main theme
This is given out by the solo violin in a big paragraph with subtl
rhythm, involving in two places a two-beat bar of two beats instea
of three. I give the first six bars, which overlap with the longe
continuation initiated by the entry of the horn.

Ex. 6.

At the end of the theme a transition-passage leads to a middl
section in the bright key of G major. Its main theme begins i
dominant harmony, thus—

Ex. 7.

and is continued with an allied theme, also hovering on a half
close—

Ex. 8.

which is used separately later on.

The return to the main key and theme is effected in twice tw
bars of such masterly poetic power that I must quote them. The
arise out of the tonic chord on which the solo violin has at las
succeeded in resolving the persistent dominant of its themes
And so the main theme returns, as it were, in mid-stride

Ex. 9.

The recapitulation is terse, and on to it is grafted a peaceful coda beginning with Ex. 7, alluding, in cadence, to Ex. 6, and ending with a tonic pedal below an expanded version of the procedure shown in Ex. 9.

The finale is a joyous rondo on lines differing from classical precedent in certain matters of key-relation which need not worry the listener. The quotation of its main themes is all that is needed.

*Rondo theme.*

Ex. 10.

The second strain of this theme is on a contrasted figure. There is also a new transition theme arising out of the close, and leading to—

*First Episode*, or Second Group.

Ex. 11.

Starting in the orthodox dominant, this soon goes to remoter regions, such as F major, a thoroughly unorthodox key, from which, however, the return to G (and to Ex. 11) is effected with insolent ease, the orchestra seeming to stretch itself in a slow yawn while the solo violin blows smoke-rings.

*Second Episode.*

Ex. 12.

The supertonic, A minor, is a key which, though closely related to the tonic, is never chosen by classical composers for cardinal features of form. The present unorthodoxy is partly a natural result of the previous unorthodoxy of F major, and for the rest it forms the right base of operations for the subsequent adventures that take us through various other keys and surprise us with incidents like the tutti outburst of Ex. 11, in B major. This outburst eventually shortens the normal course of the finale considerably, for when next the main theme (Ex. 10) returns (on a trumpet) there is no need for another explicit recapitulation of the whole first episode (Ex. 11) in the tonic, but it can be dealt with allusively together with all the other themes, including the unquoted transition theme, in a spacious perorative coda.

# CXV–CXXXV. VARIATIONS AND CONCERTOS
## WITHOUT RITORNELLO
### JOACHIM
#### CXV.   VARIATIONS FOR VIOLIN WITH ORCHESTRA

Joachim's violin works are full of technical difficulties produced with unconscious ease by the masterly player handling his own instrument. But not a note is there for display. Joachim never wrote a bar that did not aim instinctively for clearness and completeness in the presentation of true musical ideas. It has been well said by Moser that Joachim's playing and teaching inculcated 'the utmost simplicity together with the utmost presence of mind (*Besonnenheit*)'. In his compositions the *Besonnenheit* has an immense field for exercise. All his compositions are early works, and they show a richness of invention which needs all the organizing power that a composer's technique and experience can give. Joachim's early musical ideas and ideals might easily have occupied him as a composer for the rest of his life, had they not found easier and more direct expression in his playing of the classics. I once ventured to ask him how it came that he ceased to compose, and this was substantially the explanation he gave me, adding thereto: 'and then, you see, there was Brahms'. Nothing in the history of music is more delightful than the early passages in the careers of Brahms and Joachim in which the two composers kept up a regular correspondence in the exchange of compositions and mutual criticism. At the outset of this intercourse Joachim was by far the more experienced master of the two, especially in the handling of the orchestra. In spite of one or two obstinately conservative habits in the treatment of trumpets, Joachim's orchestral scores are remarkably rich and free; nor does it seem to make much difference whether the orchestra is acting as an accompaniment to his solo violin or is independent, as in his Overtures to *Hamlet* and to a comedy by Gozzi. Popularity his works never sought, and virtuoso players will not find in them opportunities of display comparable to their difficulty. This greatest of players will always be a composers' composer. Thus the interest of his works will grow with the passage of time; for it depends on ideas that stand on their own musical merits without regard to fashion.

The Variations for violin and orchestra are a culminative growth from the following short melody, which is announced by the wood-wind after a ruminating introduction by the violin.

Ex. 1.

In the 1st variation the violin restates the theme an octave lower. The 2nd, 3rd, 4th, and 5th variations embroider it with increasingly rapid rhythms. In the 6th variation the melody is in a lively hunts-man's rhythm for the horns and bassoons, while the violin has dashing scales and arpeggios. The 7th variation springs vigorously along in anapaests.

In the 8th variation the violin throws down the gauntlet to the orchestra, being left entirely to itself with a uniform series of chords. The 9th variation repeats this with the full orchestra. It is a bold plan and completely successful. It is as if the spirit of the violin had evoked the orchestra. We can appreciate the point if we consider how fatal it would have been to change the order of these two variations.

The 10th variation gives a new and melancholy melody on the
fourth string of the violin over the harmonies of the theme, and
the 11th variation changes to the major, the violin floating seraphically over the high wood-wind in an even flow of crotchets.
This is repeated in the 12th variation by the whole orchestra very
softly over a rustling accompaniment.

Variation 13 (*poco animato*) is in a syncopated figure in double
stops. In variation 14 this is repeated by the wood-wind, while the
violin has a peaceful flowing accompaniment.

Variation 15, twice as slow, is a stream of expressive florid melody.

Variation 16, almost twice as fast again, slides smoothly along
in a flow of quavers for the orchestra in dialogue between the
strings and wind, while the violin weaves gossamer threads over
its three upper strings.

In variation 17 the violin sings a lively hunting chorus, in which
it rivals the horns of the orchestra.

Again, in variation 18, the full orchestra takes up the challenge.
This variation expands into a coda which returns to the minor
mode and leads to the finale, a lively movement on the following
new theme—

Ex. 2.

*Allegro marcato.*

which combines, as shown by the lower stave, with a diminution
of the original theme. This combination is worked up with several
cognate ideas into a brilliant kind of rondo, and the work ends in
triumph in the major.

# CÉSAR FRANCK

## CXVI. VARIATIONS SYMPHONIQUES FOR PIANOFORTE
### WITH ORCHESTRA

No two art-forms in instrumental music can be much more unlike
each other than the two kinds of variation-work represented by
Elgar and César Franck. The Elgar Variations are a series of
tone-pictures each asserting its own completeness and its contrast
with its neighbours, but, with only three exceptions, all very
closely confined to their theme. The Franck Variations are a
single flowing series forming little more than an episode placed

between an introduction about half as long and a finale more than twice as long. The introduction and finale are on a totally different theme from that of the variations, this variation theme being only hinted at in the introduction and being only brought in as a bass counterpoint in two passages in the finale. Of regular variations there are only six, all flowing without change of tempo out of their theme, which is not a long one. In fact the work is a finely and freely organized fantasia with an important episode in variation-form. All the habits of César Franck's style contribute here to the happiest results. He is before all things a master of the extempore manner. This is a very different thing from being a composer who extemporizes on paper. Except in the hands of a master whose experience is so vast that it has become forgotten in the depths of instinct, the process of extemporizing on paper is disastrous, being too slow for spontaneity and too quick for self-criticism. The memory (on which musical form depends) is in a false position, and drugs itself with mechanical copying of recapitulatory passages in the required keys, instead of developing the healthy imagination which vividly realizes the effect a passage will have when it re-appears in the recapitulation.

The improvisatorial manner of Franck is a very different thing; it is a genuine love of portraying the growth of ideas. His introduc-tions and connecting links are vast and ruminating; but Franck does not fall into the error of making them lead only to each other: they lead very surely to the ideas they aim at. The ideas themselves are epigrammatic, like most good things in the French language; and there is no danger of their being lost in the ruminating pro-fundities which surround them. As for the moods and contrasts, with all their subtlety nothing can be clearer. The manner is always openly dramatic without ever descending to theatrical makeshifts. Franck has been compared to Bruckner, the sym-phonic composer whom the Wagnerian party of the 'seventies hoisted into the position which they loudly denied to Brahms. It seems a pity that Teutonic patriotism forbade them to discover Franck while they were about it. Franck and Bruckner certainly have in common the completest unworldliness, combined with a style which is dramatic in gesture and range, but constitu-tionally incapable of adapting itself to the theatre. Otherwise, to compare the two composers is unilluminating: it is difficult to exaggerate the clumsiness of Bruckner and the deftness of Franck.

The introduction to these Symphonic Variations states with dramatic roughness a figure (a) which is dimly suggestive of part of the variation theme. The pianoforte, however, answers with something really much more important, figure (b).

Ex. 1.

These two themes are worked up in dialogue in Franck's delightful ruminating style, together with another idea which I do not quote. Soon the time changes to 3/4, and the strings (pizzicato, with staccato wind over a roll of kettledrums) give out two phrases of the variation theme as it is going to be. The pianoforte, however intervenes with a sustained and impassioned speech on the theme of figure (*b*). Then the orchestra re-enters, and the dialogue is resumed in ominously dramatic tones. After a fierce climax it calms down, and at last the pianoforte is free to give out the variation theme in the shape of the following quiet melody, much on the lines of that of the middle movement of Franck's Symphony.

Ex. 2.

The first variation is in dialogue (figure by figure) between pianoforte and orchestra. In the second variation the violoncellos have the theme. The third is in flowing movement for the pianoforte accompanied by pizzicato chords for strings, the winds gradually joining in melodically. The fourth variation takes the theme fortissimo, passing through various keys, in terms of figure (*a*) in Ex. 1. It expands dramatically and leads to a softer but not less lively fifth variation in the same rhythm in D major, with an easily galloping pianoforte accompaniment. This fifth variation (if it is rightly so counted) dies away into the original key (F sharp minor) before it is complete; and the sixth variation sails in slowly in F sharp major. A beautiful meandering counterpoint ripples throughout the pianoforte part while the theme, in the violoncellos, forms the bass for the first eight bars (you can follow it from Ex. 2). The rest is given by the wind instruments.

Then the mode changes to minor, and slowly, below the flowing arpeggios of the pianoforte, the violoncellos spell out a wonderful dream on the theme of Ex. 1, figure (*b*). There is no more thought now of variations: the rest of the work is concerned with building up a brilliant finale on this other theme. The dreaming passage which leads to this finale is obviously the most poetic part of this very poetic work. The finale itself is quite reckless in its innocent gaiety. It represents the variation theme only by its first two notes (*a*); and the other theme (*b*) is too happy to be shocked at its transformation into a dance-tune.

Ex. 3.

Later on the variation-theme appears to the extent of a clear eight-bar phrase as the bass of one of the episodes in the dance.

Ex. 4.
Pianoforte.

There is, shortly after this, one hint of dramatic darkness, which gives way to a brief pianoforte passage of peacefully flowing meditation; but soon the lively tempo returns and the work dances cheerfully away to its happy end.

# ARTHUR SOMERVELL

## CXVII. 'NORMANDY': SYMPHONIC VARIATIONS FOR PIANOFORTE WITH ORCHESTRA

The title of this work refers to its theme, a folk-song sung at the present day by the peasants of Varangeville. The notion of 'symphonic variations' may perhaps also indicate something a little more definite than the mere general importance of the orchestra in their design: certainly it means more than Schumann meant by *Études Symphoniques*. Sir Hubert Parry's Symphonic Variations are strict variations on a short theme, but grouped in four great sections in tempi corresponding suggestively to the first movement, slow movement, scherzo, and finale of a symphony.

Sir Arthur Somervell's variations are, after the first two formal counterstatements of his 'Norman' theme, free fantasias which cannot possibly be numbered off into single variations. The theme, for that matter, is not a closed melody but rather a thing that returns into itself. But these free fantasias have a very obvious resemblance to the four movements of a symphony; though on this view we must regard the three opening statements of the theme, with the following cadenza and allegro, as an introduction beginning the main movement at the alla breve time, including its important 3/2 section as a middle part, and calling the later group of variations in 4/4 time either a return to the introduction or the first part of the slow movement. All these questions, however, are of less importance than the natural flow and inexhaustible variety of the whole work, which (in times when the motto of musical fashion is *omne absurdum pro magnifico*) are perhaps not so justly appreciated as the opposite qualities would be revered. At present, when a living composer says anything which can readily be understood there is a real danger that the arbiters of musical fashion will assume first that they have understood all that he has said, and secondly that he has said nothing. Neither progress nor permanence in the fine arts has ever been secured by arbiters of fashion: it is even doubtful whether they have been hindered by them. When a work of art says a great deal, even the most favourable fashions can popularize only a fraction of its meaning. And as Ruskin pointed out in one of his clearest and most accurate passages, it is really the loose and obscure writer that is least misunderstood: the clear and accurate writer is always taken up in mid-sentence by the careless reader who thinks he agrees with him.

We have here to deal with a clear and spontaneous work of art so highly organized that its form is free, and so full of point that its clearness does not exhaust its meaning at a single hearing.

After a short and solemnly dramatic introduction, into which the figures of the theme are introduced by the brass instruments intervening softly in a remote key, the pianoforte states the theme in full, each of the two strophes being repeated by the orchestra

Ex. 1.

The oboe then takes up the theme, which thereafter bursts out in the full orchestra, coming at last to a pause which gives occasion for a cadenza for the pianoforte. Then, in a quick flowing tempo (allegro), the pianoforte begins a free development from figure (*d*) of Ex. 1, and continues, in dialogue with the orchestra, by an impassioned discussion of the three notes comprised in figure (*b*)—the most important and variously treated figure in the work. In spite of the interest of this whole passage it does not advance beyond an introductory manner; the slow tempo returns, with the mood of the original theme; and the figure (*e*), from its close, droops away in dreamy modulations; when suddenly a new movement (molto allegro in 2/2 time) starts with a vigorous awakening.

Ex. 2.

Ex. 2 gives its introductory start, showing figure (*b*). The main new theme, beginning on the tonic, is only harmonically connected with 'Normandy', but when it shifts its key to B flat the orchestra surges up with figure (*d*), and then, in D minor, gets into dialogue with the pianoforte on a new version of (*b*). At the climax there is a pause, and with a change to 3/2 time the pianoforte, imitated by various single instruments, works out a sustained and melodious new development of (*b*).

Ex. 3.

The orchestra interpolates a sentence which puts figure (*d*) into a similar new light. The pianoforte then resumes its sustained treatment of (*b*) with a shifted accent and a more flowing accompaniment. Soon the inner parts of the orchestra get to work on the theme of the molto allegro. The hint is not taken at once; but eventually, after very remote modulations, the pianoforte asks suggestive questions, and the horn gives impressive warnings (figure (*a*), across the 3/2 time). The main theme of the molto allegro then swings back in such a way that the precise moment of the change back to 2/2 time is imperceptible. It continues on the

same lines as before, but coming to its climax in the tonic, which
gives it a distinct air of allusion to the form of a symphonic first
movement. Its final close plunges into a return to a slower tempo
exactly half its pace, and slightly suggestive of the mood of the
opening. What follows is in the manner of a sustained variation
of 'Normandy', chiefly in terms of figure (c). The pianoforte takes
it up serenely with a sudden change to the major mode; and this
change is followed up with increasingly intense calm and happiness. Here for the first time some development is made of the
last figure (f) of the theme. Then the note deepens, as the pianoforte recalls the rhythmic figure of (a) (which has been absent for
some time); and with a change of time a new section begins, which
that figure pervades in great solemnity, with masses of deep
harmony in the brass.

Ex. 4.  *Adagio.*

&c.

This is worked up with great breadth and swing twice to a solemn
climax and a not less solemn quiet close. When it has died away,
the drum turns the rhythmic figure of (a) into a lively introduction
to what may fitly be called a scherzo; of which the main theme is
as follows:

Ex. 5.

&c.

It alternates with a trio in which still more of the figures of 'Normandy' are neatly embodied, while the drum maintains the rhythm
of Ex. 5.

Ex. 6.

&c., till

Modulating widely, this trio leads back to Ex. 5 in a new key, from
which it easily swings back, not to its starting-point, E minor, but
to its second key, G major, and thus rushes straight on into the
finale. This begins in a very original way, with a series of wide

urling arpeggios ending in violent chords on the fourth beat of 4/4 bar. This explosive utterance conceals a ground bass—

Ex. 7.

*Allegro ma non troppo.*

Ground.

n which the first part of the finale proceeds. The eleven variations on this ground show great variety in their unity; with the fifth here is a change to triple time, to say nothing of the happy entrance of the major mode for this one variation; at the ninth the 4/4 time eturns, and the eleventh is a fierce climax. Meantime the figures of 'Normandy' have been very happily interwoven at various points bove the ground-bass, so that when the fury of the climax is spent nothing can be more natural than that the tune itself should, specially in its second part with figure (*c*), swing lustily in and tride from key to key with growing zest until the whole orchestra prings the work to a triumphant end.

# DOHNANYI

## XVIII. VARIATIONS ON A NURSERY SONG, FOR ORCHESTRA WITH PIANOFORTE, OP. 23

The composer has dedicated this work 'to the enjoyment of lovers of humour and to the annoyance of others'. And we know that the man who can write comedies as well as tragedies makes better and wiser tragedies than the man who is annoyed by comedy. There is nothing unreal or undignified in the artistic organization and emotional range of this work, which must rank high among the modern classics in one of the severest of art-forms.

The work begins very tragically, the brass being specially afflicted.

Ex. 1.

Through this 'symphony in Woe minor', a solemn canto fermo o
eight notes—

Ex. 2.

(with sharps and flats that come and go) looms large in the horns
The tragic introduction dies away—

Ex. 3.

—with a bang; and then the pianoforte enters with the theme—
which explains the solemn canto fermo. (Nothing will induce
me to quote it.) The string orchestra accompanies with delight
in harmonies that become increasingly learned as confidence i
gained; until at the last clause a bassoon bursts out with the vener
able ecstasy of the parent of the Jabberwock-slayer who 'chortled
in his joy'.

The first six variations follow the theme closely in combination
and dialogue with different groups; of which we may mention th
two-flutes-and-piccolo *versus* two-bassoons-and-contra-fagotto o
Var. 4; Var. 5, with its combination of pianoforte, harp, and bell
(the bells giving the theme in its form of canto fermo wit
the sharps and flats that come and go); and the astonishingl
ingenious Var. 6, an étude for pianoforte and wind instrument
without parallel in classical or modern orchestration.

Ex. 4.
Wood-wind.

Pianoforte.

With Var. 7, the theme blossoms out into a spirited Viennes
Waltz, developed at leisure.

Ex. 5.

Var. 8 is a March, glum but dogged. Into the guileless tonality of the underlying theme, the sharps and flats come and go with such freedom that the foundations of the key settle and heave with alarming irregularity.

Ex. 6.

*Alla marcia.*

The next variation is a scherzo full of grim surprises—

Ex. 7.

—such as the unison of the piccolo and contrafagotto with the canto fermo; and it culminates in a desperate recitative of the pianoforte which leads to Var. 10, a passacaglia, or solemn dance on a ground-bass—the ground-bass being our canto fermo in the minor mode. As the first of the eight notes of this canto fermo is the same as the last, its recurrences overlap the eight-bar rhythm by one note. Röntgen hit on the same device in the Waltz in his *Azzopardi Variations*, a *jeu d'esprit* I hope some day to describe.

Ex. 8.

The pace gradually increases until the whole orchestra finds itself wailing like the brass in the introduction (see Ex. 1), and at last the theme bursts out in the major (Var. 11) as a chorale. The harmonies, as usual, become more and more chromatic as the tune proceeds, drifting into the whole-tone scale of Deomnibussy (which is a more eclectic affair than that of Debussy). It dies down, and, after a dispute between the pianoforte and the wind as to what the key shall be, the finale breaks away in a merry fugue.

Ex. 9.

The subject and counter-subject of this fugue are just as happy
inverted as right side up, and after a brilliant climax the original
theme of childhood returns.  It is not surprising that its adventures
have taught it a new and elegant phrasing which it had not
possessed when it first appeared.  There is some little argument
over its last notes, but the contrafagotto agrees with the piccolo
as to how that should be settled, and the orchestra gathers itself
up and hastens to reach the end in time with the pianoforte's final
glissando.

# SPOHR

### CXIX.  SCENA CANTANTE FOR VIOLIN WITH ORCHESTRA

1 *Allegro molto, leading to* 2 *Adagio, leading to* 3 *Andante, introductory to*
4 *Allegro moderato.*

Spohr was one of the best of men; and he enjoyed an amiable self-
satisfaction which is one of the rarest rewards of virtue.  He was
never more satisfied than when he had invented a new art-form,
a feat which he accomplished with consummate ease, because with
him the new form required no change of matter.  Once upon a
time he gave a concert at Milan.  Fearing that the public there
would not appreciate a symphonic concerto, he had the brilliant
idea of writing a concerto in the style of an operatic scena.  His
delight at the success of this new art-form resembled that of a hen
which should have the intelligence to be pleased rather than
frightened when its clutch of supposititious ducklings took to
swimming.  Of course a concerto in operatic scena form is bound to
succeed; for the classical concerto form itself is a glorification of
aria form, and has in fact no other origin.  For the rest, Spohr's
experiment produced in later times the G minor Concerto of Max
Bruch, besides a host of kindred phenomena in the concertos of
Saint-Saëns and other adroit masters.

The opening Allegro requires no quotation, the orchestral
theme being a formal prelude (in A minor and a marching rhythm)
to a recitative by the violin.  This leads to an aria in F major, of
which Ex. 1—

Ex. 1.

is the first subject; Ex. 2—

Ex. 2.

he second subject; while the middle section, in remoter keys, is in
2/4 time—

Ex. 3.

Solo Violin.

and is a *locus classicus* for the power of a solo violin's fourth string
to penetrate a high-lying and elaborate accompaniment skilfully
devised for transparency.

Another recitative (andante) leads to the finale, a symphonically
developed movement (Spohr's fear of the Milan public has
vanished) with a theme unusually majestic for a concerto finale.

Ex. 4.

The second subject, however, shows the aristocratic composer's
most seductive frivolity—

Ex. 5.

and so does the indolent middle episode.

Ex. 6.

Schumann very wisely warned the superior person against supposing that Spohr's facility was a thing anyone could easily imitate.
One need not at this time of day hear enough of Spohr to find his
mannerisms cloying; but in his best concertos and violin duets
(which are really astonishing *tours de force* in sonorous handling
of small material resources) his mannerisms do not overdo themselves; and his sense of beauty is such as only an unhealthy taste
will despise.

III         N

# MENDELSSOHN

## CXX. VIOLIN CONCERTO IN E MINOR, OP. 64

1 *Allegro molto appassionato, leading to* 2 *Andante, leading to*
3 *Allegretto non troppo, leading to* 4 *Allegro molto vivace.*

How often do we hear the most remarkable stroke of genius in
this most popular of violin concertos? I had not heard it in 1921
when I wrote this analysis. The manners of British concert-goers
have improved since then; and even then my audience was not
offended at being told that a burst of applause between the first
movement and the andante obliterates a dramatic orchestral effect
and reduces the introductory bars of the andante to one of those
ugly misconstruings which produce the conviction (ascribed by
a Master of Balliol to the British schoolboy) that no nonsense is
too enormous to be a possible translation from a classical author.
I have never been able to make out why, when disaster overtakes
this connecting link, conductors do not adopt the only possible
remedy, which is simply to repeat the short final tutti, and so secure
that Mendelssohn's intention shall somehow be realized.

Mendelssohn is supposed to be the typical classicist in music;
that is to say, he is supposed to be the master of those who after
a classical period imitate the classical forms faithfully and skilfully.
As a matter of fact, the best works of Mendelssohn have all in
their respective ways been the starting-points of some musical
revolution. Mendelssohn may truthfully be said to have destroyed
the classical concerto form, inasmuch as his perennially beautiful
Violin Concerto and his two somewhat faded pianoforte concertos
revealed to all contemporary and later composers an easy way of
evading a problem which only Mozart and Beethoven could either
state or solve in terms of the highest art. In the Violin Concerto
Mendelssohn's inspiration is high and vigorous. He is not so much
evading a classical problem as producing a new if distinctly lighter
art-form. It is not unprofitable to speculate whether the pathetic
and tranquil second subject (Ex. 3) would not have gained in depth
and dramatic power if some hint of its melody had been given
with force and passion in the first energetic orchestral tutti. This
could very well have been managed with no notable increase in
length of that tutti, and would have instantly brought the first
movement into the lines of a genuine development of Beethoven's
concerto style, besides anticipating by some forty years Brahms'
re-discovery of the true function of the orchestra in a concerto.
But the possibility escaped Mendelssohn's notice, and was indeed
very unlikely to occur to a man who had twice before deliberately

suppressed the orchestral tutti, function and all, in his treatment of the concerto form. His Violin Concerto thus became the original type of the majority of modern concertos; and being, as it is, an original inspiration, it is far greater than any work that has ever followed its tradition. Again and again it turns up as a source of inspiration for later composers, many of whom would be horrified at the notion of confessing a debt to anything so old-fashioned. Yet I rather envy the enjoyment of any one who should hear the Mendelssohn concerto for the first time and find that, like *Hamlet*, it was full of quotations. This being so, I will leave the rest of my description to the most necessary of the quotations, viz. the first theme—

Ex. 1.

given out in full by the solo violin and worked up to a climax on which the orchestra breaks in; the transition theme—

Ex. 2.

given out by the orchestra and developed by the solo violin; and the second subject—

Ex. 3.

given out by the wood-wind above the famous long holding note which the violin supplies as bass. The usual procedure in concertos is for the brilliant passages of the solo player to culminate in a shake closing into the re-entry of the orchestra. Mendelssohn here makes his brilliant passages an accompaniment to the first theme. They do culminate in a shake; but, by one of Mendelssohn's wittiest inspirations, it is the orchestra that bursts out with the shake, which the violin answers with impassioned dialogue from the first theme. The development begins with the transition theme and comes to its climax in a remote key with one of those intensely quiet passages of slow return to the tonic which Mendelssohn

always executes with consummate mastery, and sometimes, as here
with the poetic power of a great composer. On to this passage i
grafted the cadenza which, both for its unusual position in the
movement and its extraordinary skill and effectiveness, constitutes
one of Mendelssohn's most famous strokes of genius. Here, as else
where in the concerto, Mendelssohn's example has been imitated
with disastrous consequences by less adroit composers, notably
in a once well-known and well-meaning violoncello sonata by
Rubinstein. You must not transplant Mendelssohn's cadenza
*totidem notis* into every place where you find it better than any
thing of your own invention.

Mendelssohn's cadenza is of extreme simplicity, which conceal
an almost Greek subtlety of fitness. It is thoroughly dramatic in
the way in which it prepares for the return to the opening theme
The orchestra softly brings the first subject into full swing as the
arpeggios of the violin settle to a rapid spin; and the recapitulation
follows an easy and effective course, omitting much and expanding
nothing, until the coda, which moves in faster tempo to a storm
end. But hush!—what is this that emerges from the last chord?

Ex. 4.

Solo Violin.

Few things in music are more essentially ugly than a vague and
meaningless introduction to a lyric melody, designed with the
avowed and sole aim of marking time 'till ready'. Of such intro
ductions this opening of Mendelssohn's andante has most unjustly
been made the prototype. It is no such thing, except when un
timely applause has made it begin with a nonsensical entry of the
bassoon on nothing in particular, followed by a few other fumbling
notes which can only drift from the unintelligible to the obvious
What Mendelssohn wrote and meant was one of his most romanti
changes of key and mood. And it is perfectly naïve: all the spuriou
imitations in the world will not rob it of its freshness.

The movement has true breadth and dignity. Its middl
episode, which I need not quote, achieves a real expression o
agitation and anxiety without the fussiness which Mendelssohn

was too often apt to express instead; and the serene coda is
of that childlike truth and simplicity which it is an insult to call
pretty.

The wistful little allegretto that connects the andante with the
finale is also quite an unspoilt child. The finale has perhaps been
the cause of some unpleasing perkinesses in ill-bred descendants—
but there is no doubt about its own good-breeding. Its first theme
I quote in its combination with a sedate new theme that first
appears in G major in later developments.

Ex. 5.

The second subject—

Ex. 6.

is undeniably 'cheeky'; but we can stand this from Mendelssohn
in this work—just as we can stand it from Rossini. I doubt
whether Mendelssohn was particularly tolerant of it in Rossini:
'cheekiness' is an aristocratic schoolboy term of reproach, and no
two schools can abide each other's 'cheek'. But all schools unite
in the detestation of an outsider's imitation of their own 'cheek';
and we can enjoy these indiscretions of Mendelssohn and Rossini
because the delinquents are not imitators, but complete if un-
scrupulous masters of the situation. And so this finale spins along
in high spirits, in which no one need be ashamed to share. It is not
in Schiller's world of Joy as attained by Beethoven—the world
where 'all men are brothers'; but if it cannot ignore the superior
person, it has every right to poke fun at him.

# SCHUMANN

## CXXI. PIANOFORTE CONCERTO IN A MINOR, OP. 54

1 *Allegro affetuoso.* 2 *Intermezzo: Andantino grazioso, leading to*
3 *Allegro vivace.*

There is a depth and a breadth in Schumann's lyric vein which already shows that it was no mistaken ambition that led him to turn from it to larger designs. His career was shortened and clouded by illness, but this concerto is one of at least a dozen large works which utterly refute the Wagnerian judgement of Schumann as a might-have-been. A work so eminently beautiful from beginning to end, so free, spacious, and balanced in form, and so rich and various in ideas, is more than proof that Schumann was justified in attempting any and every art-problem. It is a worthy monument to the sanity of art; and while it illuminates the tragic pathos of Schumann's later years, it is itself untouched.

The first movement, composed in 1841, had an independent existence for four years as a fantasia for pianoforte and orchestra. Thus, though it has all the essentials of a very big first movement in sonata form, it never professed to be the first movement of a classical concerto. The orchestra makes no attempt to muster its forces for its own full connected statement of the themes. At the climaxes it bursts out with a short triumphant passage in the manner of a ritornello; but for the most part it behaves very much as the strings behave in Schumann's quintet: though it has far more colour, and is, for all its reticence, much above Schumann's normal achievement in its purity and brightness of tone.

My first quotation gives the energetic introductory figure (*a*), which leads to the first theme, and is used once in the development.

Ex. 1.

After the pianoforte has answered the plaintive cantabile theme, the violins give a transition theme—

Ex. 2.

of which the figure (*c*) becomes very important later. The second
subject is made of a broad stream of impulsive melody derived
from (*b*) of the first theme—

Ex. 3.
Clarinet.

and using figure (*c*) in the course of its dialogue. Figure (*c*) also
forms the text of the triumphant ritornello with which the orchestra
bursts in at the climax. Then there is a dramatic change of key to
A flat, in which remote region the pianoforte gives out an altogether
new version of the first theme (*b*) in slow 6/4 time, in the tenderest
of dialogues with the orchestra. When this comes to its natural
close, the pianoforte breaks abruptly into the original tempo with
figure (*a*), and then proceeds to work up figure (*b*) in an impassioned stream of melody, joined by more and more of the orchestra
and driving irresistibly through a wide range of key until at last it
resigns itself in a solemn close into the main theme in the home tonic.

From this point the recapitulation follows its normal course,
until the point where the orchestra is to break in with its ritornello.
But here the pianoforte goes on playing through it, and soon breaks
its way into an unaccompanied cadenza. A triumphantly paradoxical feature of this very happy outburst of apparently extempore eloquence is that its themes happen to be entirely new until
at last figure (*b*) appears below a long trill. Then the threads, new
and old, are gathered together, and the orchestra re-enters with
figure (*b*) marching at the double, in 2/4 time. Much passion lies
suppressed in the gallant spirit of this march, which approaches,
makes its climax, and recedes into romantic distance, until at last
it flashes out in an abrupt end.

Whatever Schumann may have felt about this fantasia in 1841,
his instinct was true when in 1845 he recognized that it was only
the first movement of a larger work. The slow movement is of the
very centre of Schumann's most intimate and tender vein ; childlike in its gently playful opening—

Ex. 4.

while in its sustained, swinging second theme—

Ex. 5.

it attains a beauty and depth quite transcendent of any mere prettiness, though the whole concerto, like all Schumann's deepest music, is recklessly pretty.

Nothing can be more romantic than the coda, in which figure (*b*) of the first movement reappears and leads dramatically into the finale.

From the six or seven important themes of this glorious movement I select the first subject—

Ex. 6.

the second subject with its famous *deux-temps* rhythm—

Ex. 7.

&c.

the new theme which appears in the course of the rich development—

Ex. 8.

and the delightful surprise of another brilliant new theme which cheerfully begins the coda as soon as the recapitulation is over.

Ex. 9.

Never has a long and voluble peroration been more masterly in its proportions and more perfectly in character with the great whole which it crowns with so light a touch. Every note inspires affection, and only an inattentive critic can suspect the existence of weaknesses to condone. Fashion and musical party-politics have tried to play many games with Schumann's reputation, but works like this remain irresistible.

CXXII. VIOLONCELLO CONCERTO IN A MINOR, OP. 129

1 *Nicht zu schnell; leading to* 2 *Langsam; leading to* 3 *Sehr lebhaft.*

Schumann's Violoncello Concerto, long regarded as a thankless task, has been brought to light in the present day by consummate musicianship and sense of beauty on the part of a leader among those violoncellists who refuse to confine the possibilities of their instru-

ment to the obvious. The scoring of this concerto is no obstacle to
its performance, being remarkably free from the dangerous thickness of Schumann's usual orchestral style. In general his orchestral
sense is at its best in his accompanying of solos of all kinds. If
the violoncello seems, on a first hearing, to be at any disadvantage,
this is not because the accompaniment (*Begleitung des Orchesters*
is Schumann's own title) is heavy, but because the form shows
little or no disposition to expand. Terse exposition, short ruminating developments, and interludes all gathered up as quickly as
possible to the business of schematic recapitulation; every feature
indicates Schumann's growing dislike of anything that could be
called display. Still, the work was written before this dislike
merged into the morbid condition which ended in fatal illness. The
qualities of the violoncello are exactly those of the beloved enthusiastic dreamer whom we know as Schumann; and as a flow
of intimate melody the first two movements rank high in his art.
The finale, too, has its point. In the 'eighties Kensington used to
compare Browning with Brahms. The unavowed reason for this
profundity was that both begin with Br: the more conscious reason
was that both were considered obscure, manly, and rugged.
Brahms, who throughout his life spent as much pains in smoothing
his style as Browning took in winning and carrying off his bride,
would probably have not been flattered by the comparison had he
been more conscious of the existence of Kensington or of England.
But there is a real analogy between Schumann and Browning. Both
are the 'essentially manly' poets of people who innocently wallow
in sentiment: and when Schumann is nervous he is apt to develop
exactly Browning's habit of digging you in the ribs and illustrating
grave realities with some crack-jaw quadruple rhyme. And so we
may accept Schumann's finale as Browningesque.

The following list of themes will suffice for all purposes of
analysis.

Ex. 1 is a broad melody, announced, after three opening chords,
by the violoncello, and developed for thirty bars to a climax.

The orchestra enters with an impassioned new theme—

built up into a short tutti, into which the violoncello breaks with

ruminating phrases leading into C major. Here they grow into a
regular second group. From this one figure requires quotation, with
its simplification in the wood-wind, which becomes prominent in
many sequels.

The movement runs its course with all Schumann's quiet antithetic
rhetoric.

The development begins by introducing an agitated triplet
figure, traceable perhaps to a casual ornamental detail in previous
violoncello passages.

Later on the violoncello combines with Ex. 4 another figure (which
persons who pay super-tax on brains may derive from Ex. 5 by
'augmentation' without making the slightest difference to its
intelligibility).

This develops into one of the most thoughtful passages in the work,
and leads to the first theme (Ex. 1) in F sharp minor, soon broadly
moving to the tonic, A minor, where a full normal recapitulation
follows.

A short tutti (compare Ex. 5) leads to a sudden dramatic change
of key and tempo, and the slow movement which now follows
consists of a single lyrical melody in F major. No quotation
is required, but the listener should mark the exquisite moment
where the violoncello sings in slow double-stops—a triumph of
Schumann's instrumental imagination.

The orchestra alludes to Ex. 1, which the violoncello continues
in agitated recitative, combining it with topics from the slow move-

ment and other themes, until it breaks into the finale, with a bluff
reaction against sentiment.

Ex. 7.

'Cello.

Ex. 8.

Gentler utterances (especially the main figure of Ex. 1) contrive
nevertheless to work their way into the design; and the provocative
first theme itself strikes tender notes as a second subject, in spite
of gibes from the violas.

Ex. 9.

An ingenious cadenza, remarkable, like most of this concerto,
for its predilection for the lower strings of the violoncello, leads
to a rapid coda, in which keen listeners will detect an allusion
to Ex. 5. Ingenious as Schumann's cadenza is, there is good
classical precedent for letting the violoncellist produce something
not quite so gruff. Jacobi has written an excellent one, piously
in touch with Schumann's *Innigkeit* and efficacious in conciliating
us with the finale as a whole. Jacobi having thus broken the ice,
I confess to some hankering to try and write a cadenza myself; but
Schumann's shyness is very deterrent.

### CXXIII. INTRODUCTION AND ALLEGRO APPASSIONATO
### FOR PIANOFORTE WITH ORCHESTRA, OP. 92

I cannot account for the neglect of this work, which has always seemed to me to be one of Schumann's happiest and most inventive pieces. Even its orchestration is unusually successful, with little of the thickness and few of the risks of Schumann's orchestral writing.

The introduction, with its recklessly pretty romantic theme—

is really beautifully scored; and both the form and matter of the allegro appassionato are admirably dramatic and in perfect proportion. The Allegro starts in a towering temper in E minor—

suddenly yielding to a quieter but energetically rising theme starting in C.

This only establishes E minor more firmly, and a new theme sets the action of the drama fully in motion.

Another figure arises out of this, which I quote as it occurs later, on the dominant of C.

It leads to a second group preceded (as the example shows) by figure (b) from Ex. 1, which figure now becomes an important factor in the development.

Ex. 6.

The second group contains several more themes and is one of Schumann's finest specimens of the art of making flowing paragraphs. The way in which the aforesaid figure (*b*) insinuates itself into the texture is admirable; and so is the brilliant staccato theme (unquoted) which provokes the trumpets to assert the triplet figure of Ex. 2.

The development begins quietly with Ex. 3 on a chord of F, which promptly leads back to E minor, where Ex. 4 re-enters, soon to modulate further. Ex. 5 is taken up busily, but suddenly the theme of the introduction, Ex. 1, floats in above. With these threads a fine and dramatic development is built up, with none of the stiffness that may be imputed to many of Schumann's longer forms elsewhere. The return comes at the top of a grand climax, and the subtlety of the whole design is revealed by the fact that G major, the key of the introduction, proves to be that chosen for the recapitulation of the second subject, instead of E, the key of Ex. 2. The theme of the introduction again intervenes (in B flat, a soft and dark key in relation to G) at the beginning of the coda, the rest of which is greatly enlivened by a deliciously voluble new theme—

Ex. 7.

such as only the Schumann of the Quintet and the Pianoforte Concerto could invent.

## SAINT-SAËNS

### CXXIV. FOURTH CONCERTO FOR PIANOFORTE IN C MINOR, OP. 44

1 *Allegro moderato, leading to* 2 *Andante.* 3 *Allegro vivace, leading to* 4 *Andante, leading to* 5 *Allegro.*

Saint-Saëns's Fourth Pianoforte Concerto is, even more than the other adroit and brilliant essays of its composer in this form, on a plan which brings its various movements into a unity of themes without losing their individual character as types of movement.

In many respects it reminds us of his most ambitious orchestral
work, the Third Symphony, in which, stimulated by the desire to
commemorate Liszt, Saint-Saëns has still more closely followed
the general method of transforming themes *en masse* shown in
Liszt's *chef-d'œuvre*, the Faust Symphony.

But Saint-Saëns's Fourth Concerto is both more attractive in
theme and more terse in form than his Third Symphony. Yet the
forms, in spite of the terseness of the whole, are very broad.
Saint-Saëns here deals with quite symmetrical and complete
melodies, and treats them in a simple but resourceful variation-
form. The first movement starts at once with a broad symmetrical
melody in two parts, of which Ex. 1 is the opening.

Ex. 1.

&c.

Each half of this fine theme is given out by the strings, and repeated
by the pianoforte. Then follow two regular variations. In the first
variation the 'cellos have the theme as bass to the harmony, and
the pianoforte repeats the clauses with florid ornamentation.

In the second variation, the full orchestra gives out the clauses
forte; the repetitions give a syncopated version of the melody to
the wood-wind, while the pianoforte accompanies with arpeggios.
This leads to a climax, in which the pianoforte and the wood-wind
break into a new theme, which I quote, for convenience, not in the
form in which it occurs here, but in the compressed form in which
it later on appears as a scherzo theme.

Ex. 2.

At present it dies away into a cloudy close in the major, and leads
to an andante in A flat. After a long passage of dusky arpeggios a
chorale-tune emerges. [It is impossible not to be thrilled by Gustav
Doré.]

Ex. 3.

8va..........................................................

&c.

It takes shape in four symmetrical phrases, after which the pianoforte gives out a new theme.

Ex. 4.

&c.

This is very soon worked up by diminution (quavers instead of crotchets) and, after coming to a dramatic climax, leads to a triumphant re-statement of the chorale. After this, Ex. 4 is worked out again broadly to a quiet conclusion, with a romantic pianissimo cadenza. Thus this first of the two divisions into which Saint-Saëns has grouped the concerto has no resemblance whatever to any other concerto form, but is simply a broad exposition of the material for the whole work.

The second division of the work begins with Ex. 2 in its compressed form as the opening of a brilliant scherzo in C minor. Soon Ex. 1 follows in G minor the dominant, hurrying along in quavers. It soon moves excitedly to E flat major, in which an extremely lively second subject appears. It deserves to break the bank at Monte Carlo, being much stronger than its twin brother the once popular song of that exploit. [Sir Henry Hadow has remarked that the public of that period accepted the illustrator of the *Contes Drolatiques* as a great religious teacher. Compare Ex. 3.]

Ex. 5.

After some development with a few other accessories, the opening of the scherzo returns, and takes a somewhat different course, which, after the climax, dies away dramatically. Then the diminished form of Ex. 4 is worked out in a solemn and mysterious fugue in the original andante tempo, the first phrase of the chorale tune itself being once heard. There is an exciting crescendo; and the pianoforte, breaking into a cadenza, leads to the triumphant finale. This begins by taking the whole chorale tune in a lively triple-time.

Ex. 6.

Here again, as in the first movement, breadth and clearness is attained by quite simple repetitions of this square melody, with varieties of scoring. A diminished derivative—

Ex. 7.

leads to other developments and new accessories. One of these should be quoted (overleaf)—

No. 8.

for the sake of its brilliant combination with a transformation of Ex. 4, together with an inner part derived from the continuation of Ex. 6.

Ex. 9.

&c.

With these materials, the finale wends its easy way to a triumphant end.

*N.B. The remarks in [ ] are not addressed to concert audiences.*

### CXXV.  VIOLONCELLO CONCERTO IN A MINOR, OP. 33

1 *Allegro non troppo, leading to* 2 *Allegretto con moto, leading to*
3 *Tempo primo, leading to* 4 *Un peu moins vite.*

The worldly wisdom of Saint-Saëns is at its best and kindliest in this opusculum, which is pure and brilliant without putting on chastity as a garment, and without calling attention to its jewellery at a banquet of poor relations.

Here, for once, is a violoncello concerto in which the solo instrument displays every register throughout its compass without the slightest difficulty in penetrating the orchestral accompaniment. All the adroitness of Saint-Saëns is shown herein, and also in the compact form of the work, which, following Mendelssohn in abolishing all orchestral tuttis, except connecting links, goes further than Mendelssohn inasmuch as it relegates to the finale the function of the recapitulation in the first movement, and thus combines the effect of three movements with that of a single design.

The violoncello opens at full speed with a lively subject in cross-rhythms that evidently means business.

Ex. 1.

The second subject is a Schumannesque epigram, of which the tender mood is soon broken into by the business of Ex. 1.

Ex. 2.

An orchestral interlude on new material—

Ex. 3.

leads to a development that, instead of going to remote keys, returns to that of Ex. 2, which it expands, leading peacefully into B flat. (Saint-Saëns has often made effective use of keys a semitone apart, as here, A minor to B flat; the B minor Violin Concerto with its slow movement in B flat; the C-minor-D-flat pair in his Third Symphony; the C minor Violoncello Sonata, &c.)

The middle movement, a slow-movement scherzo, suggests a group of those little dancers supported on a tripod of bristles that move so prettily if you put them on the lid of a pianoforte and play.

Ex. 4.

The violoncello enters ruminatively—

Ex. 5.

and accompanies the dance with sustained melody, taking up its figures only at the end, to subside into Ex. 4 in deep bass: whereupon the orchestra brings back the business of Ex. 1 and leads to the finale.

This begins with a new melancholy tune (compare Ex. 5)—

Ex. 6.

which is followed by a bustling semiquaver theme which I do not quote.

There is a calm middle episode, giving the lower strings of the violoncello a welcome opportunity to sing.

Ex. 7.

After Ex. 6 returns, the design of the whole work is completed by further use of Ex. 1, and by the reappearance of Ex. 3 in A minor. Whereupon the violoncello triumphantly sings quite a new tune in A major. And so they lived happily ever after.

# MAX BRUCH

## CXXVI. VIOLIN CONCERTO IN G MINOR, OP. 26

1 PRELUDE: *Allegro moderato, leading to* 2 *Adagio*.
3 FINALE: *Allegro energico*.

When Max Bruch died at the age of 83, the news came to many as a revelation that he had lived so long. Though he never dominated the musical world as Spohr did in his own day, yet he was the type of artist universally accepted as a master, about whose works no controversy could arise because no doubt was possible as to their effectiveness and sincerity. Like Spohr, he achieved this mastery in all art-forms; and, unlike Spohr, he developed no irritating mannerisms. If it were possible to imagine a large work by Spohr in which there were no cloying chromatic harmonies, the idea would closely correspond with that of a masterpiece by Max Bruch. At present it seems the correct thing to say that his G minor Violin Concerto is his only surviving work; but the two other violin concertos (both in D minor) and the Scottish Fantasia need nothing but the attention of violinists to prove quite as grateful to performers as to the public. Moreover, I find myself entirely in agreement with the writer of the article in Grove's *Dictionary* who says that Bruch's greatest mastery lies in the treatment of chorus and orchestra; and I have not the slightest doubt that a revival of Bruch's *Odysseus* (which the writer regards as his most successful work), and perhaps still more of his last choral work, a Kyrie and Sanctus, which I heard in Berlin in 1907, would make a fresh and stirring impression on any audience that will listen naïvely to beautiful music for music's sake. Poorer things have survived from the enormous output of Spohr, simply because players periodically rediscover their effectiveness. Spohr and Mendelssohn were so completely idolized by a masterful majority of musicians in their own day that grave injustice was done to all music in which new and refractory elements were struggling for expression. The result was that kind of so-called classical period which should accurately be called pseudo-classical. The injustice of a pseudo-classical period produces with the swing of the pendulum another kind of injustice in the next generation. No art is then allowed to have any merit that does not consist almost exclusively of new and refractory elements nobly struggling

or expression. This does not repair the older injustice, it merely
ransfers it. Clever people tell us that you can train a poodle to
produce pseudo-classical art. If this is true, you have only to shave
our poodle hind part foremost and let its hair grow where formerly
t was shaven, and the very same poodle will produce art in which
efractory new elements are nobly struggling for expression. But
fter all, in the long run mastery tells.

The lot of a fastidious artist, conscious of mastery as a gift
ntrusted to him during a period of destruction, is not enviable;
or, perhaps, do the wisest of masters so regard their own personal
nastery or their own period. Brahms's mastery was so great that
t gave rise to furious controversy, but he knew how to extricate
imself from encounters with the shockable; and on the few occa-
ions when he encountered Max Bruch his disposition to tease
ppeared at its worst. Lovers of music ought, at this time of day,
o show more gratitude to those who devote themselves to making
beautiful things. It is not easy to write as beautifully as Max Bruch.
But', you will say, 'that does not go to the root of the matter:
perhaps the very reason why this beauty of yours bores us is that
ve see it is a mere matter of mastery over difficulty.' If you can
ee that in the case of Max Bruch, I give it up; but I find his case
quite different. It is really easy for Bruch to write beautifully, it
s in fact instinctive for him; and such instinct is a matter which
ll modern critics and psychologists will agree to rate very high.
Further, it is impossible to find in Max Bruch any lapses from
he standard of beauty which he thus instinctively sets himself.
I have only to call attention to the second subject of the rondo of
his concerto as a touchstone. There are several popular violin
concertos which now hold the field, and in all of them the second
subject of the rondo is a most regrettable incident, and is also the
most popular feature of the work. I forbear to name the instances
but it is surely significant that this most successful of Max Bruch's
works shows one of its noblest features just where some of its most
formidable rivals become vulgar.

The concerto is in three movements, only two of which are
complete. Instead of the formidable organization of a first movement in classical concerto-form with a great orchestral exposition
of themes afterwards to be fully developed in sonata-form by the
solo player, Bruch contents himself with a prelude in which the solo
violin enters into a solemn dramatic dialogue with the orchestra.
The themes do not require quotation, though soon after the main
key G minor has been established, a contrasted melody, quite
definite enough for a second subject, appears in the key of B flat.
In spite of this, however, the manner of the whole movement is
introductory; it is an introduction so broad that it tends to take a

definite shape; and we need not do it the injustice to imagine that i
was merely an abortive first movement. Thus its design is not cu
short but is completed when, after the violin has returned to G
minor, the orchestra comes storming in with a vigorous tutti, ir
which the gentle second theme has become an impassioned outburst in the minor. When this has run its course, it subsides inte
the opening phrases, and the declamation of the solo violin return:
in greater elaboration. Suddenly the orchestra bursts out ir
pathetic enthusiasm on the dominant of E flat, and leads to the
second movement, a fully developed slow movement in sonata-
form. I quote the three main themes; the first subject—

Ex. 1.

the all-important transition theme—

and the second subject as it appears in the bass below flori
counterpoint (unquoted) of the solo violin.

Ex. 3.

The exposition of the second subject ends with Ex. 2, which i:
always used to effect cardinal action in the piece. By way o:
development we have an expanded version of the first subject ir
G flat, followed by the transition theme, Ex. 2, in the same key
with a beautiful new melody above on the solo violin. By degree:
this works round to the tonic, E flat, with a crescendo; and now
occurs with the entry of the orchestra, a masterly and dramatic
stroke of form which I summarize in outline.

Ex. 4.

This shows how the first bar of Ex. 2 is taken up by one orchestral group after the other, until the second subject enters grandly below and so carries us out on the full tide of its recapitulation. The coda is grafted very simply and naturally on to this and brings the movement to a peaceful end.

The finale begins in the key of the slow movement with an excited crescendo anticipating the figure of its main theme and swinging round to G major. It works out a broad and transparent scheme with the aid of its lively first subject—

Ex. 5.

and its bold and noble second subject.

Ex. 6.

There is no lack of rich accessory themes, but they can be appreciated without quotation. Max Bruch's First Violin Concerto thoroughly deserves the great success it has always had. Nobody who can appreciate it will believe for a moment that its composer has written nothing else worthy of the like success.

## C. V. STANFORD

### CXXVII. CLARINET CONCERTO, IN ONE MOVEMENT, OP. 80

This work, composed in 1902, presents a masterly solution of the problem of a modern clarinet concerto. Although it is described as in one movement, it contains, like the Violoncello Concerto of Saint-Säens in the same key, all the essentials of three closely connected movements; a first movement, a slow movement, and a finale. Of these three the slow movement is a complete design. The first movement and the finale complete each other, and surround the slow movement with their own symmetry. The character of the clarinet is revealed in its full range, including that earliest of its functions which the classical treatment of the instrument has relegated to obscurity, its military tones. These are indeed idealized as chivalry, but they provide plenty of contrast to the more feminine accents, to the dramatic ecstasies and sweetnesses of this most resourceful of wind instruments. Most of the themes throughout the work are derived from two figures which I first give in their common formulas.

The first theme starts at once vigorously in the full orchestra and is promptly challenged by the clarinet.

My quotations show by the letters (*a*) and (*b*) how far the themes may be referred to the two formulas given in Ex. 1. Before the key changes another theme requires quotation, part of its purport being to combine with figure (*a*).

Soon after this, a highly organized transition is made to another key, and the clarinet gives out a second subject where you see figure (*b*) brought into daylight.

This is broadly developed and brought to a peaceful end. Then the orchestra re-enters as if to develop the first theme, but the idea of a normal development is carried just far enough to assert itself duly and the clarinet guides the course of events into the slow movement. This begins with what may well pass for a beautiful Irish melody, being, as it is, pure Stanford.

Ex. 5.
*Andante con moto.*

Nothing could be more convincing than the naïve way in which the clarinet takes this tune up, expanding it by echoes. (Those who know their way about the orchestra could tell mythologists that the real end of the story of Echo and Narcissus was that Echo's soul passed into the clarinet.) The middle of this slow movement, beginning with an impassioned outburst on the clarinet with its most dashing arpeggios, leads to the following second subject.

Ex. 6.

From this a straightforward return is made to the first theme (Ex. 5), which, after a certain amount of dramatic expansion, is allowed to bring the movement to a peaceful close.

Hereupon the orchestra re-enters with the interrupted middle tutti of the first movement as if to continue its development. The wind instruments, however, turn figure (*b*) into one of the themes of the finale in 2/4 time.

Ex. 7.

Soon the clarinet enters in its fighting mood, with the following derivative of figure (*a*).

Ex. 8.

It works this up with some other figures including Ex. 3 and the
following—

Ex. 9.

(a)                                                          &c.

and in a surprisingly short time enough has been said to suggest
that we are listening at the same moment to an independent finale
and to a recapitulation of the second subject of the first movement.
At all events the 2/4 version of that subject sails in happily on the
violins, while the clarinet is warbling Ex. 9 in the tonic major;
and it is not long before the design is grandly crowned on an
altogether broader scale by the reappearance of the theme of the
slow movement (Ex. 5); thus revealing the calm depths which
underlie the brilliance of the happy end.


# ELGAR

### CXXVIII. VIOLONCELLO CONCERTO IN E MINOR, OP. 85

1 *Adagio, introductory to Moderato, leading to* 2 *Allegro molto.*
3 *Adagio, leading to* 4 *a recitative, leading to*
5 *Allegro ma non troppo.*

Although the musical language of this work is unaffectedly classical,
its forms are unlike those of any other concerto; conspicuously
unlike, for instance, the elaborate classical design of Elgar's Violin
Concerto.  The Violoncello Concerto is a fairy-tale, full, like all
Elgar's larger works, of meditative and intimate passages; full also
of humour, which, in the second movement and finale, rises nearer
to the surface than Elgar usually permits.  Though the work is
highly organized, an elaborate analysis is not necessary so long as
enough themes are quoted.  Lucidity is the aim and the achievement of its form and style; not the thin mundane lucidity of a
Saint-Saëns concerto, nor yet the arrogant lucidity of the epigrammatist who has not got over his famous discovery of the stupidity
of most people.

*Mutatis mutandis*, this violoncello concerto well represents its
composer's Schumannesque mood.  This term will seem grotesque
to those numerous musicians to whom orchestration is the *sine
qua non* of musical thought; but Schumann's helplessness in that
category rather reveals than conceals the shyness that goes with such
intimate moods.  The shyness is, however, just as compatible with
consummate mastery of the orchestra; and indeed Elgar's orchestration is as unworldly as it is masterly.  In the Violoncello Concerto

the orchestra is throughout concentrated on the special task of throwing into relief a solo instrument which normally lies below the surface of the harmony. Brilliant orchestration is thus out of the question; but there is no lack of subtle and beautiful tone-colour, inexhaustibly varied within narrow limits and by the simplest means.

After a short recitative-like introduction by the violoncello—

the first movement begins with an indolent sequential theme, announced unharmonized by the violas—

and repeated by the violoncello. The movement is not in sonata form, but is a simple lyric design with a middle section in 12/8 time. This is introduced by the following theme—

which then blossoms out into the major mode thus—

There is a free recapitulation of the main section (Ex. 2). Then, after a momentary allusion to the introduction (Ex. 1), the second movement, a lively scherzo in G major, begins tentatively with the following figure:

This soon gathers speed and seems about to work itself out, with a few other themes, as a free sonata-form movement, with a second subject beginning in the remote key of E flat, which, however, it soon abandons.

Ex. 6.     *largamente a tempo.*

Having produced just enough effect of development to take us beyond lyric forms, the impish little movement scurries back to its G major and vanishes with the detonation of a burst bubble.

The serene slow movement, in B flat (the Ultima Thule from E minor, the key of the concerto), is a single broad melody. For future reference I number its first two phrases separately.

Ex. 7.
*Adagio.*

Ex. 8.

&c.

The movement ends on the dominant, with its first phrase (as in Ex. 7), and thus leads into the introduction to the finale. This introduction begins in B flat minor, with an adumbration of the future main theme, which is turned by the violoncello into a recitative not unlike that at the beginning of the concerto. The finale then begins, in full swing.

Ex. 9.

It is a free rondo, with a mischievous second subject, slightly suggestive of dignity at the mercy of a banana-skin.

Ex. 10.
*allargando.*     *a tempo.*
*f dolce.*    *p*    *f*    *sf*

The movement is spaciously developed on a large scale, with many and varied episodes. A complete surprise awaits us towards the end in a new slow theme of romantically abstruse harmony and full of pathos.

The metre, already new, changes to 3/4, where yet another fresh theme—

rises to a climax of passion, thence to subside into the second strain of the slow movement (Ex. 8), and from that to the opening of the concerto (Ex. 1). Then the main theme of the finale works up tersely to a spirited and abrupt end.

# DELIUS

### CXXIX. VIOLIN CONCERTO

In the art of to-day, there is no more intimate note than that of the later works of Delius. He was never a sensational composer; and the large orchestra and brilliant technique of his early works never displayed any tendency incompatible with the almost oriental depth of meditation which he has attained in recent works such as the Violin Concerto and the Double Concerto.

It would be a mistake to infer, from the shortness and number of the themes here quoted, that the Violin Concerto is either a disjointed or a complicated work. It is, on the contrary, so continuous a stream of ruminating melody that the shortness of the quotable themes is really, as with Wagner's Leitmotivs, a symptom of the length of the paragraphs; while, on the other hand, the course of Delius's work is subtle only (and a very important 'only') in its emotional reactions, and extremely simple in plan. The themes follow in a natural sequence of discourse, with no more complex link than might be supplied by the clause 'and that reminds me': until a point is reached at which it is agreeable to recapitulate some of them from the opening. The classical key-system is only occasionally alluded to, and most of the harmonic phenomena depend on regarding chords of all degrees of artificiality as direct tone-sensations, unanalysable as the taste of a peach, with none of the classical sense of their individual notes as coming from given directions in order to 'resolve' on explanatory notes.

In Delius's art, even more than in Debussy's and Cyril Scott's, the instrumental tone-colour of every chord is quite as important as the actual notes. For the most part the tone-colours are exquisitely soft and mellow; and even when Ex. 3 finds itself forced to the extreme high notes of the trumpet, there is a technical mastery in the scoring which ensures that with first-rate playing the effect is glowing rather than shrill.

The function of the solo violin is to sing and to decorate; chiefly to decorate. The difficulty of its part arises entirely from the almost complete absence of familiar harmonies and intervals, and at no point is the difficulty connected with technical display.

After two introductory bars for the strings, the solo violin pours out the three following themes in a wayward stream of meditation.

To these may be added a majestic outburst of the brass.

The middle section (if one may use the term of such unsectional music) is in a slower time, and comprises two important cantabile themes.

Ex. 6.

A short cadenza leads to a recapitulation of the first four themes with a change in the direction of key. Very unexpectedly a quaint new section, in a naïve dancing rhythm, creates a diversion from the ruminating mood of the whole.

Ex. 7.

*Allegretto.*

It alternates, however, with a variation of Ex. 5 in the following form.

Ex. 8.

Finally the figures of Ex. 1 conclude the work on a chord once known to theorists as the 'added 6th'—one of the very few names in musical theory that fit the facts.

Ex. 9.

For more reasons than concern theorists we might well regard this music as an example of the Lydian mode, as Milton would describe it—

> And ever against eating cares
> Lap me in soft Lydian airs,
> Such as the melting soul may pierce . . .

# RICHARD STRAUSS

## CXXX. PARERGON TO THE 'SINFONIA DOMESTICA', FOR PIANOFORTE WITH ORCHESTRA, OP. 73

The relation between this work and the 'Sinfonia Domestica' is, apart from a few allusions to fine details of melodic figure, based on the all-pervading presence of a theme which in the 'Sinfonia' represented the Baby. The 'Sinfonia Domestica' is one of Strauss's largest symphonic poems, and represents a day in the life of himself, his wife, and his infant son. The son is now a doctor in a learned profession and has edited his father's profoundly interesting correspondence with his operatic coadjutor, the dramatist Hofmannsthal. Paul Wittgenstein, for whom the Parergon was composed, probably knows any number of delightful and witty inner meanings in every detail of the work; but great artists, even when they give their works domestic titles, do not really invite us to examine any of their private affairs except those, most private of all, which they reveal by simply expressing universals without speaking in abstractions. Let us listen to this Parergon as to a piece of music, so that we may learn what Strauss wishes to tell us without interrupting his message by impertinent questions.

Eddington has remarked, apropos of some little difficulties in the theories of Relativity and the Quantum, that when phenomena seem to be specially artificial and complex it is because they are reaching us through the refracting medium of our own oblique point of view. Similarly the theme of Dr. Strauss Jr. (C F G E C A) has some difficulty in adjusting itself to our harmonic expectations when, being by birth and breeding in F major, it is trying to reach us through the key of F sharp minor.

A tragic and feverish C sharp (with muted horns and trumpets) starts us with reluctant steps (*langsam und schleppend*) in that key, of which it is the dominant.

Ex. 1.

The pianoforte soon intervenes dramatically, evidently as convinced as its own tuner that the offending note will be the better for reiterated emphasis.

A declamatory figure—

Ex. 2.

becomes important later. The main theme develops itself, refracted through many keys, but always ruthlessly brought back to the inexorable C sharp. Finally the struggle is abandoned, and in triumphant F sharp major a new theme bursts out in full swing, with nothing introductory in its manner.

Ex. 3.

Another figure looms large in the bass—

Ex. 4.

and soon a new tune is sailing gracefully over it.

Ex. 5.

The enthusiastic climax of this ends in sudden catastrophe with a plunge into F *natural*.

Dr. Strauss Jr.'s theme shows a deep and worried sense of its responsibilities, and so do the other themes in combination (and sometimes in conflict) with it. The agitation grows as the sequences rise and crowd one on another, until at last the pianoforte, finding C natural (the dominant of F) well established, declaims with more confidence and calm. The fatal C sharp has learnt to explain itself away as D flat—Browning's Abt Vogler would say he had 'blunted it into a ninth' (so that mysterious expression means something at last!).

Then the pianoforte states a happy melody in the most innocent F major.

Ex. 6.

The wood-winds restate it, and the pianoforte, imitated by the orchestra, follows with an adaptation of Ex. 3. Immediately the time changes to a quick 2/4, in which Ex. 6 is transformed in a rapid rhythm. Dr. Strauss Jr. joins the game in semiquavers—

Ex. 7.

and new themes, such as—

Ex. 8.

Ex. 9.

swing gaily in and enter into various combinations. In short, all the previous themes join the dance at full speed, Ex. 4 rising to the surface in as high spirits as the rest. The fatal C sharp reasserts itself and refuses to be Voglerized; but the only result is that Ex. 6 dances back in a still faster 2/4 measure. Ex. 5 also swings along over a double-trot version of Ex. 3. Then, while Ex. 8 is roaming in bass sequences under developments of Ex. 4, it becomes evident that there is no great danger in revisiting F sharp again. Thither we drift, and in that key the following combination intervenes—

Ex. 10.

It returns to F natural without trouble and the work concludes brilliantly in the 2/4 time.

The art of left-hand pianoforte solo writing is of great aesthetic interest, and presents the modern instrument in aspects attractive by contrast with the ordinary tendency to exploit the instrument in voluminous harmony which emulates the orchestra without achieving any character of its own.  The special restrictions are a stimulus to the composer's invention, and there is a wide field of exploration in this medium where the compass of the instrument is practically unlimited, while the hand carries its own compass with it throughout the whole field.

# GLAZOUNOV

## CXXXI. PIANOFORTE CONCERTO IN F MINOR, OP. 92

1 *Allegro moderato (with several changes of tempo).*  2 *Andantino Tranquillo.*  VARIATIONS *and* FINALE.

In this delightful and compendious work Glazounov amuses himself by combining the rules of two games; one, the game of Liszt in his E flat Concerto; the other, the game of Tchaikovsky in the variation-finale of his Trio.  Both these games, as played by their inventors, were meant to be dangerous.  Liszt played his with a more than Byronic ostentation of musical wickedness. Tchaikovsky aims at enshrouding in the blackest tragic atmosphere the spectacle of a ruined gambler dancing a trepak on his mother's grave.  Glazounov is *jenseits des Guten und Bösen* in all the musical possibilities of these moods.  To him the transformation of themes is as easy as his art of orchestration; and is limited only in two ways. He will not make a pedantic transformation, nor will he transform his own themes into other people's.  The opening theme of this Concerto begins gravely and goes through many transformations—

Ex. 1.

It sometimes almost merges into the third theme of Liszt's E flat Concerto—

but the Lisztian perkiness does not after all venture into the precincts of this Russian Olympus; and the first movement works

out its design with noble breadth, associating the transformations
of Ex. 1 with a tragic pianoforte theme—

Ex. 2.

which lends itself to diminution—

Ex. 3.

and a consolatory second group in the remote key of E major—

Ex. 4.

which is also much developed by diminution.

Ex. 5.

As if by way of slow movement, the orchestra propounds a
beautiful theme for variations, beginning as follows—

Ex. 6.

The variations all retain the outline of the melody.  The first three
are simple embroidery, which becomes 'chromatica' in Var. 2,
'eroica' in Var. 3, and 'lyrica' in Var. 4.  The 5th variation is a
lively intermezzo in a mixture of tonic minor and E major.  Var. 6
is a slow fantasia in the minor.  Var. 7 is a mazurka in A major,
which borrows the triangle from the scherzo of Liszt's E flat Concerto; but Var. 8 is a scherzo, also in A major.  At last, on moving
to the key of F, the tonic of the concerto, the theme becomes a
march—

Ex. 7.

and is worked up, with mysterious episodes, into a neatly rounded-
off finale in combination with the themes of the first movement.

# SIBELIUS

## CXXXII. VIOLIN CONCERTO, OP. 47

1 *Allegro moderato.* 2 *Adagio di molto.* 3 *Allegro, ma non tanto.*

Perhaps the Violin Concerto of Sibelius has not yet had time to become popular; but I can see no reason why it should not soon take place with the Violin Concerto of Mendelssohn and the G minor Concerto of Max Bruch as one of the three most attractive concertos ever written. Personally I am impelled to place it above those two famous works, nor do I think that my present enjoyment of it will wear out. Of course the great concerto form of Mozart, Beethoven, and Brahms is another story; instead of being lighter than symphonic form, it is perhaps the most subtle and certainly the most misunderstood art-form in all music. But in the easier and looser concerto forms invented by Mendelssohn and Schumann I have not met with a more original, a more masterly, and a more exhilarating work than the Sibelius Violin Concerto. As with all Sibelius's more important works, its outlines are huge and simple; and if a timely glance at an atlas had not reminded me that Finland is mostly flat and water-logged with lakes, I should doubtless have said that 'his forms are hewn out of the rocks of his native and Nordic mountains'. The composer to whose style the word 'lapidary' (*lapidarisch*) was first applied by the orthodoxy of the 'nineties is Bruckner; and if the best work of Sibelius suggests anything else in music, it suggests a Bruckner gifted with an easy mastery and the spirit of a Polar explorer. Strange to say, the results are of no inordinate length. Sibelius, unlike Bruckner, has an instinct which saves him from misapplying the classical sonata forms to a music that moves at quite a different pace; he does not design motor-cars with a box-seat for the driver, nor does he build reinforced concrete skyscrapers in the style of the Parthenon. There is plenty of sonata form in his works; but it is not a nuisance to him as it was to Bruckner; nor, on the other hand, is he, like Bruckner, at a loss when he diverges from it. The real problems of musical form are always, in the last resort, problems of movement; and Sibelius has his own special sense of movement, which delivers him from the need of Bruckner's desperate and dangerous gesture of 'I pause for a reply'. It gives him complete command of the arts of rousing expectation and of slow gradation to a climax. He does not aim at the time-scale of classical sonata forms, and therefore is not liable to the difficulties of those composers who are not conscious that the time-scale has something to do with the effect of the musical events that are to happen in it. One of Sibelius's most famous and successful devices is that of building up a symphonic finale out of broken figures that come together, like the Vision of Dry Bones, into a broad melody only by way of supreme climax at the end. (Very clever critics have been known to discover that this form lacks the eventful variety of the classical symphonic finale.) But the acid test comes when the inventor of so effective a device has to write a finale where it will not work; as, for instance, in a violin concerto, where it is impossible to ask a solo violin to live upon scraps for three-quarters of the finale, and then to dominate the full orchestra by giving its celebrated imitation (on one string) of the three trombones at the end of the Tannhäuser Overture. Hence there is nothing of the kind in the finale of this violin concerto: the characteristic 'lapidary' vastness is achieved by equally drastic simplicities, accurately to the purpose.

The first theme is a ruminating melody given out by the solo violin.

Ex. 1.

Nothing is more characteristic of Sibelius than the austerely diatonic dissonance of the first note, with its rhythmic position just as far off the main beat as its harmonic position is off the chord. I mark with (a) and (b) two figures that are used in other combinations; but a detailed analysis, though interesting to a student, is unnecessary for the enjoyment on a first hearing of a work which is always lucid, and never more so than in its most original features.

The violin works its melody up to an impassioned climax ending in a cadenza; and, without any transition passage, the orchestra announces the second subject, in B flat and 6/4 time.

Ex. 2.

From this arises an allied figure, to which the solo violin adds an important comment in 4/4 time. We shall find that the style of

Sibelius is nowhere more distinguished than in its novel and yet inevitable cross-rhythms.

Ex. 3.

The violin brings this meditatively to a close in B flat minor, and then the orchestra breaks out grimly with a new theme.

Ex. 4.

This yields to a gentler strain—

Ex. 5.

which, however, is punctuated by fierce accents, and ends in a low-pitched crescendo, which leads to a despairing cadence theme.

Ex. 6.

When this has died slowly away in utter darkness, the violin re-enters and, while the basses continue to hold B flat, changes the key to G minor. An allusion to the main theme (Ex. 1) turns unexpectedly towards A minor, which key is affirmed in an angry gesture from the orchestra. And now the violin plays a highly developed cadenza, modulating widely and working out the main figures of Ex. 1 in an admirable style of extemporization governed by organic life. It returns to G minor, and in that key a recapitulation begins, with the main theme (Ex. 1) in the bassoon. The

violin resumes it with the second phrase. When, at the climax of
this solo, the orchestra intervenes, it is in order to start a new and
impassioned development with rich modulations, the main theme
being welded to a new figure (*x*) which develops a life of its own.

Ex. 7.

At the climax, in B major, trombones thunder out the despairing
notes marked (*f*) in Ex. 6; and then phrases from the middle of the
second subject (Ex. 3) build themselves up, in combination with
the solo violin, reaching a climax of tenderness in the key of D
major, our tonic, which darkens to the minor. The violin solo has
settled into a long trill, beneath which the theme is mournfully
pulsating away. Suddenly there is an uprush of energy, and the
remaining themes (Ex. 4 and 5) enter *in extenso* with a brilliant
counterpoint for the solo violin. The final theme (Ex. 6) gains its
full meaning by the following bold combination with Ex. 1—

Ex. 8.

and thus brings the first movement to an end for which brilliance
is an inadequate term.

The slow movement, after a wistful introduction—

Ex. 9.

settles down to a noble paragraph of melody for the solo violin—

Ex. 10.

When this has come to its close, a dramatic interlude arises from the wistful introductory figure. The following specimen of Eurythmics—

Ex. 11.

shows what Sibelius can make practicable and natural in the way of cross-rhythms. Both the upper parts are played by the solo violin.

Soon the great main melody returns, this time in the orchestra, the solo violin having fine counterpoint until it resumes the melody in its last phrase; after which a single line of coda suffices.

In less than fifty lines of full score the finale achieves gigantic proportions and brilliant high spirits without banality. The form seems elementary, but the spacing is Handelian; that is to say, there is no means of discovering how it has been achieved.

Only two themes need be quoted; the main or rondo theme— evidently a polonaise for polar bears—

Ex. 12.
Strings.

Drums.

and the second subject, in a rhythm known to Couperin, Bach, and Handel as that of triple-time with the 'hemiole' as in a French courante, but taken by Sibelius at a pace and with a swing alto- gether shocking to the eighteenth-century dancers of courantes. It quibbles upon the distinction between twice three and thrice two; and Sibelius used it steadily throughout the middle movement of his third symphony.

Ex. 13.

With this we can safely leave the finale to dance the listener into Finland, or whatever Fairyland Sibelius will have us attain.

# FRANZ SCHMIDT

## CXXXIII. VARIATIONS ON A THEME OF BEETHOVEN FOR PIANOFORTE WITH ORCHESTRA

The high courage which has inspired Paul Wittgenstein's art receives another fitting tribute in this delightful and humorous work. The witty little scherzo of Beethoven's F major Violin Sonata lends itself, with the aid of an orchestra, to the art of left-hand solo 'pianistics' in many ways which reveal the possibilities of that art and shed unexpected new lights on the theme. The most obvious example is furnished by the last note of the whole composition, which avails itself of Beethoven's little joke, sometimes taken by critics of more severity than experience for a defect of ensemble in the performance.

If a set of variations on a humorous theme is to have an introduction, one of the chief functions of the introduction will be to mystify us as to the purport of the theme. The following solemn polyphony might do for a funeral in a certain corner of Kensington Gardens.

Ex. 1.

The horns indicate a later strain of the theme that is to come.

Another more hymn-like aspect—

Ex. 2.

leads to florid developments which, falling into A major (or B double-flat, through D flat), lead to a more animated rhythm.

Ex. 3.

echoed below

The solemn introduction is explained away by the theme—which is *not* buried in Kensington Gardens.

Ex. 4.

We now learn that Ex. 3 foreshadowed the second part.

Ex. 5.

It was a stroke of genius to select this theme. But strokes of genius are tested by the way they are followed up. This is followed by another *genialer Zug*. Franz Schmidt produces a splendid ritornello effect, useful alike to orchestra and pianoforte, by using the trio as well as the scherzo!

Ex. 6.

Then, by way of a first variation, the two themes are combined. This combination of course produces what Pepys or Purcell would have called 'divisions', and Handel, Bach, or the French clavecinistes would have called a 'double'. The next variation is a 'double' in triplets, and the third variation a 'double' in semiquavers.

And now it is time to go farther afield. We have a change to D major 6/8 time, *ruhig fliessend*, and the orchestra waxes erotic, while the pianoforte mocks it in the original tripping measures.

Variation 5 dances a bolero in B minor, which ends in B major, and is followed therein by a slow declamatory variation for pianoforte alone, in common time.

Variation 7, in E major, deals in slow and solemn 3/4 time, primarily with the trio.

Variation 8 (*sehr lebhaft*) in E minor runs away with the scherzo, fugally in 2/4 time.

Variation 9 (*sehr ruhig*, A major 3/4) is a quiet slow waltz with undulating figures.

Variation 10 (*alla-breve* time, *Massig bewegt*) turns the scherzo into a figured chorale in A minor. The pianoforte gradually betrays that *cucullus non facit monachum*, and we are soon rushing along in every conceivable kind of counterpoint to a brilliant and highly developed finale.

Tub-thumping, however, is not its profession. Much butter may have melted in its mouth; but the end is peace, though the hearth-rug be in pieces.

# RESPIGHI

## CXXXIV. CONCERTO GREGORIANO FOR VIOLIN

1 *Andante tranquillo, alternating with Allegro molto moderato and leading to* 2 *Andante espressivo e sostenuto.* 3 FINALE (*Alleluia*).

Ottorino Respighi was born at Bologna on July 9, 1879. He studied at home and at the Liceo Musicale of Bologna until 1899, gaining diplomas as violinist and composer. He then went to Russia to study composition under Rimsky-Korsakov, and afterwards to Berlin to study under Max Bruch.

The Concerto Gregoriano was produced in 1922. It is a subtle and intimate work inspired with the mystic tones of the plain-chants *Victimæ Paschali* and the *Alleluia: Beatus vir qui timet Dominum*, which pervade the second and third movements.

The first movement, though treating the key of A minor in a modal style, is not on Gregorian themes. The orchestra announces a hymn-like Aeolian figure—

Ex. 1.

after which an oboe gives out the main theme, a plaintive pastoral melody taken up by cor anglais and bassoon—

Ex. 2.

The strings resume Ex. 1, upon which the solo violin enters with Ex. 2 (substituting F natural for F sharp). It develops this theme meditatively and soon breaks into an allegro moderato beginning in C major with the following pentatonic theme—

Ex. 3.

Arising out of this a new figure—

Ex. 4.

asserts itself, eventually combining with another as follows—

Ex. 5.

This dies away in F major and the solo violin combines Ex. 1 with it. Then Ex. 2 returns and brings the movement gradually to something that would eventually be a close but for an outburst of energy on the solo violin which gathers up Ex. 4 and Ex. 2 in a spacious slow cadenza leading to the second movement.

## II. *Andante espressivo e sostenuto*

In pure Dorian (D minor without leading note) the violin sings the *Victimæ Paschali.*

Ex. 6.

Arising from this an impassioned free continuation—

Ex. 7.

leads to a Dorian form of F minor, where the *Victimæ Paschali* looms in the bass with profoundly agitated figures and rhythms above. The plainchant having run its course in the bass, its figures are developed more quietly, but with intense emotion and much beautiful and varied colouring. An ominous figure of wordly trouble appears in the bass—

Ex. 8.

and dies away in an extremely low drum.

Then the *Victimæ Paschali* appears in the chords; D sharp minor, solo violin accompanied by high muted strings, celesta, and solemn chords for violoncellos and basses.

Once more Ex. 7 appears, but leads now to another calm setting of the chant, given to low clarinets and developed so as gradually to bring the movement to a close in D major. The bass sustains D while the solo violin in dialogue with horn, oboe, and bass clarinet work out the final paragraph.

### III. *Finale.* Alleluia.

The Alleluia is set like a rousing march, and Respighi does not scruple to add two most secular bangs on the last beat of the accompaniment—

Ex. 9.

Another plainchant forms a second part—

Ex. 10.

As in the slow movement, Respighi builds up a series of settings of this pair of plainchants in various contrasted keys and colours. Towards the middle (after a quiet variation in B flat) the violin, in ethereal mystic tones, gives out another plainchant—

Ex. 11.

Passing from Dorian-Aeolian D minor to D major, this leads to excited development of Ex. 9 on the dominant of E, and thence through F minor to B minor, where the violin has a big cadenza accompanied by the drums. Horns re-enter in B (as dominant of E) with the Alleluia, and then there is a brilliant climax with figure of Ex. 10 on the home dominant. From this there is a slow and solemn decrescendo dying into extreme darkness. Then the solo violin on its sonorous fourth string sings the Alleluia over a conquered world (Ex. 8, from the darkest part of the slow movement, appearing in the bass). It rises to a climax and leads the orchestra on to a dramatic and brilliant end.

# WILLIAM WALTON

## CXXXV.  VIOLA CONCERTO

1 *Andante comodo.* 2 *Vivo, con moto preciso.* 3 *Allegro moderato.*

The style of this work is modern in so far as it could hardly have achieved its present consistency before 1920 (the actual date is 1929); but it does not consist of negatives. Hence it will arouse the anger of many progressive critics and composers in these days of compulsory liberty. Walton's music has tonality, form, melody, themes, and counterpoint. The counterpoint, and hence the harmony, are not always classical. Classical counterpoint is harmony stated in terms of a combination of melodies: classical harmony, when correctly translated from whatever instrumental conditions may have disguised it, is the result of good classical counterpoint where the inner melodic lines are not meant to attract attention. Modern counterpoint tends actually to avoid classical harmony. It prefers that the simultaneous melodies should collide rather than combine; nor does it try to explain away the collisions.

It wishes the simultaneous melodies to be heard; and if they harmonize classically the combination will not assert itself as such. Hence modern counterpoint is no longer a technical matter at all; its new hypothesis has annihilated it as a discipline. But this very fact has thrown new responsibilities on the composer's imagination. A technical discipline becomes a set of habits which, like civilization itself, saves the artist from treating each everyday matter as a new and separate fundamental problem. The rule-of-thumb contrapuntist need not trouble to imagine the sound of his combination; his rules and habits assure him that it cannot sound wrong. The composer who has discarded those rules and habits must use his imagination for every passage that he writes without their guidance. It is by no means true that mere haphazard will suit his purpose. Nor, on the other hand, is it true that any great classical master used rules as a substitute for his imagination. One of the first essentials of creative art is the habit of imagining the most familiar things as vividly as the most surprising. The most revolutionary art and the most conservative will, if they are both to live, have this in common, that the artist's imagination shall have penetrated every part of his work. To an experienced musician every score, primitive, classical, or futurist, will almost at a glance reveal the general question whether the composer can or cannot use his imagination. About details I would not be so sure. To the experienced musician Berlioz has no more business to exist than the giraffe; 'there ain't no such animal'.

Walton is no Berlioz; a glance at his score will suffice to show an art that has been learnt as peacefully as any form of scholarship. And it is possible to read the first twelve bars of this Viola Concerto carefully without finding anything irreconcilable to an academic style in the 'nineties. After the twelfth bar the range of style expands. But let us note that it thereby differs from the many other modern styles which contract. Walton's style is not sentimental; but neither is it anti-romantic.

Similarly, it is neither theatrical nor sensational; and its forms do not at first seem to have more than a slight external resemblance to sonata forms. Yet it has essential qualities of sonata style in its ways of getting from one theme to another and in its capacity to give dramatic meaning to the establishing of a new key. Walton's dramatic power has asserted itself in oratorio; but its unobtrusive presence in this thoughtful piece of purely instrumental music is more significant than any success in an oratorio on the subject of Belshazzar's feast. The sceptical critic can always argue that an oratorio, especially on such a subject, can hardly go wrong unless the librettist's intellect is subnormal. But when a composer can write an effective concerto for viola (an instrument with a notorious inferiority complex) and can move in it at something like the pace of a sonata, it is as obvious that he ought to write an opera as that Bruckner, Wagnerian though he was, ought not, and fortunately did not.

The concerto begins with two bars of orchestral introduction which I do not quote, though I shall have to allude to them later. The viola enters with a broad lyric melody in A minor.

The collision between C sharp in the accompaniment and the C natural in the melody is bold, but it is resolved in the classical way. Nevertheless it is destined to become an unresolved thing in itself and, as such, to be the initial and final motto of the whole work. Accordingly I give this motto here in its tonic position—

though its first appearance (during the counterstatement of Ex. 1) is at a high pitch in the course of a sequence that sweeps round a whole enharmonic circle of keys. But the figure soon detaches itself as an individual actor in the drama, and claims derivation from the first two notes of Ex. 1.

What may conveniently be called the second subject (though as my readers know, I have reasons for deprecating the term) first appears in D minor.

Its essential feature is the coiling of a sequential figure across the rhythm and across the harmony at every sort of angle. Its transformations are shown in every subsequent cantabile that is not derived from Ex. 1. Another new figure—

originates most of the rapid passages in the sequel, and from it, if we wish to use classical terminology, the development may be said to begin. Ex. 1 becomes fierce in an entirely new rhythm—

Ex. 5.

which, sometimes reduced to monotone and ragtime—

Ex. 5 a.

1    2    3    &c.

alternates dramatically with developments of Ex. 3, which steadily grows in beauty and pathos. As the drama unfolds, the motto, Ex. 2, asserts itself. The last phase of the development is introduced when the viola makes its exit with Ex. 4, and the orchestra, entering with Ex. 5 in ominous agitation on the dominant of C sharp minor, rouses itself to tragic passion, and with grand classical breadth works its way round to the home dominant, and so to a pathetic slow decline in which the later figures of the main theme (Ex. 1, the part marked 'N.B.') are heard solemnly augmented.

Over the still reverberating dominant pedal the viola re-enters with a two-part version of the (unquoted) introductory bars, expanded into a short cadenza and leading to the return of Ex. 1. While the viola breaks into a running accompaniment, the melody, softly delivered in a higher octave, makes a single simple statement rounded off with a pathetic cadence, and the viola adds a line of coda alluding to Ex. 3 and ending with the motto, Ex. 2. The whole movement must convince every listener as a masterpiece of form in its freedom and precision, besides showing pathos of a high order.

The middle movement is a lively rondo in E minor with plenty of ragtime rhythms which, unlike those of jazz, are allowed to throw the music out of step, so that the composer has now and then to change the time-signature for one or two bars. The listener need not worry about these changes; an odd bar of 3/4, 3/8, or 5/8 is merely a practical necessity for conductor and players; it happens whenever the composer has found that his groups of 3 or 5 quavers across his 4-quaver bars will land him on a main beat either too soon or too late for his whim. Much has been said in favour of jazz; but jazz, though a composer may be generous in his acknowledge-ment to it, never kept a movement going like this. A list of themes must suffice by way of analysis; letters and figures in the quotations will show a few significant points in the thematic and rhythmic structure. In general scheme the three movements of this concerto agree in the common-sense device of reserving the display of the full orchestra for a penultimate stage in which it can make a big climax, leaving room for a coda in which the solo instrument can deliver its final summary.

Here is the main theme of the scherzo, delivered by the viola, with wood-wind echoes.

From its scale-figure (C) many things result; especially a habit of making accompaniments out of bits of scale marching up or down in obstinate little groups of 3, 4, 5, alone, or in 3rds, and always inclined to collide with beat and harmony. The continuation—

arises out of figure (b) and shows how the ragtime refuses to explain itself away. Jazz has often lulled me to sleep by its underlying monotony; but Walton's rhythms keep me on the alert.

A transition theme, using a figure akin to (b)—

leads to the main theme of the first episode.

The second episode is the beginning of extensive development, starting in F and modulating widely.

Ex. 10.

As the 5-note underlying scale and the semiquaver figures show, it lends itself easily to 'conflation' (as the palaeographist would say) with the other themes; and the transition-theme, Ex. 8, appears conspicuously in the sequel. As in the other movements of this concerto, the orchestra eventually arises in its might, bringing the development to its climax, and leading, at its own leisure, to the final return of the main theme in the tonic. The viola resumes its control in the ensuing compound of recapitulation and coda. The movement ends, according to its nature, with Haydnesque abruptness and Bach-like punctuality.

The lyric qualities of the first movement, and its moderate tempo, have already supplied whatever need this work may have for a slow movement. Yet it is a bold stroke to follow so typical a scherzo by a finale which also begins in a manifestly grotesque style which the bassoon and contrafagotto can do nothing to bowdlerize.

Ex. 11.

But the grotesque is, as Ruskin has defined it, the sublime refracted by terror; and this finale is no joke. In its total effect it is the majestic and pathetic conclusion of a work that is throughout large in all its aspects. The form will explain itself: here is the main figure of the transition theme—

Ex. 12.

and here is the 'second subject'—

Ex. 13.

from which an important figure arises.

Ex. 14.

Later in the movement the viola draws a long line of pathetic cantabile over an ostinato development of the first theme.

Ex. 15.

This cantabile becomes tragically important before the end of the movement.

Another point that may be quoted is the following combination of Ex. 14 with an augmented version of the main figure of Ex. 11.

Ex. 16.

When the orchestra, as in the previous movements, gathers up the threads Ex. 11 reveals itself as a purely majestic subject for a fugal stretto, and the listener will soon become convinced that the total import of the work is that of high tragedy. This is wonderfully realized in the coda. What happens at the end is this: the main theme, Ex. 11, has settled into an ostinato in 9/4 time, and over this the viola brings back the lyric melody of the first movement, Ex. 1, with which the concerto ends, not in the same way as the first movement, but with similar Bach-like punctuality.

There are so few concertos for viola that (even if I happened to know any others) it would be a poor compliment to say this was the finest. Any concerto for viola must be a *tour de force*; but this seems to me to be one of the most important modern concertos for any instrument, and I can see no limits to what may be expected of the tone-poet who could create it.